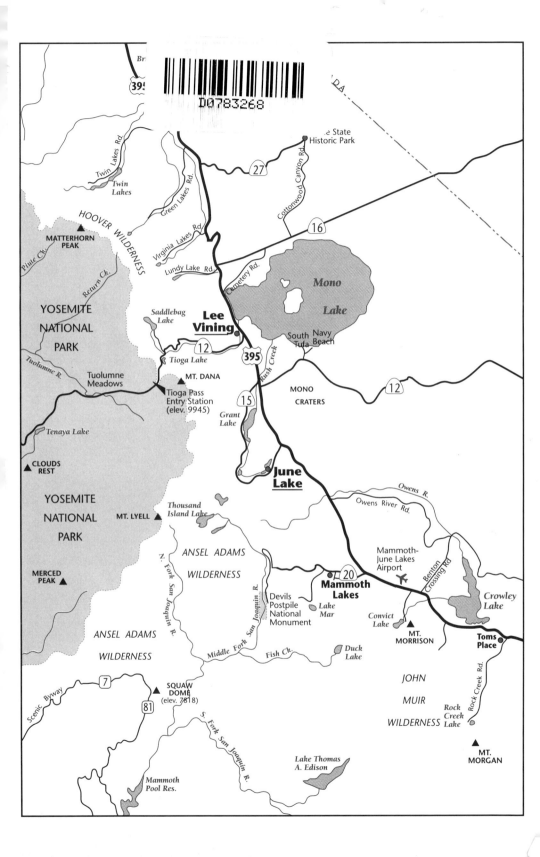

395

27

D0783268

16

Twin Lakes Rd.

Twin Lakes

HOOVER WILDERNESS

MATTERHORN PEAK

Green Lakes Rd.

Virginia Lakes Rd.

Lundy Lake Rd.

Cemetery Rd.

Cottonwood Canyon Rd.

e State Historic Park

Piute Ck.

Return Ck.

YOSEMITE NATIONAL PARK

Saddlebag Lake

Lee Vining

12

Mono Lake

Mono Lake

South Tufa

Navy Beach

Tuolumne R.

Tioga Lake

395

Rush Creek

Tuolumne Meadows

MT. DANA

Tioga Pass Entry Station (elev. 9945)

15

MONO CRATERS

12

Tenaya Lake

Grant Lake

CLOUDS REST

YOSEMITE NATIONAL PARK

Thousand Island Lake

June Lake

Owens R.

Owens River Rd.

MT. LYELL

ANSEL ADAMS WILDERNESS

Mammoth-June Lakes Airport

Benton Crossing Rd.

MERCED PEAK

N. Fork San Joaquin R.

Middle Fork San Joaquin R.

20

Mammoth Lakes

Devils Postpile National Monument

Lake Mar

Convict Lake

MT. MORRISON

Crowley Lake

Toms Place

ANSEL ADAMS WILDERNESS

Fish Ck.

Duck Lake

JOHN

MUIR

WILDERNESS

Rock Creek Lake

Rock Creek Rd.

Scenic Byway

7

81

SQUAW DOME (elev. 7818)

S. Fork San Joaquin R.

Lake Thomas A. Edison

Mammoth Pool Res.

MT. MORGAN

These beautiful days must enrich
all my life. They do not exist
as mere pictures —
maps hung upon the walls of
memory — but they saturate
themselves into every part of the body —
and live always.

John Muir

All Roads Lead To

YOSEMITE

Where to Stay and Play
In and Near the Park

Ellie Huggins

Coldstream Press

Cover Photo: Courtesy of Yosemite Concession Services

Book and Cover Design: Andrea Hendrick
Drawings: Andrea Hendrick
Maps: Sue Irwin
Editor: Dan Wendin
Printing: Malloy Lithographing, Inc.

Publisher's Cataloging-in-Publication

Huggins, Ellie
    All roads lead to Yosemite : where to stay and
    play in and near the park / Ellie Huggins. — 1st
    ed.
        p. cm.
        Includes bibliographical references and index.
        LCCN: 98-73720
        ISBN: 0-9633056-9-7

    1. Yosemite National Park (Calif.)—Guidebooks.
    2. Yosemite Valley (Calif.)—Guidebooks.   I. Title.

F868.Y6H84 1999   917.94'470453
                    QBI99-250

Coldstream Press
Specializing in books about the Sierra Nevada
P.O. Box 9590
Truckee, CA 96162
1-800-916-7450 Fax: 530-587-9081
EMail: dwendin@coldstreampress.com
Website: www.coldstreampress.com

Acknowledgments

A guide of this scope would not have been possible without the assistance of the many who encouraged us and have become friends along the way.

The first and most important was my husband Dan Wendin, who was driver, computer guru, editor, analyst and fact checker, and constant companion on the trail.

We both wish to thank Virginia Chavez and Keith Walklet of the Yosemite Concessions Services for their initial support for the idea of the book and Keith's on-time supply of photographs, many of which were his.

Peggy Kukulus of Yosemite Sierra Visitor Bureau in Oakhurst, Steve Hayes of the Mariposa County Visitors Bureau and Peggy Mosley of the Groveland Hotel put us in touch with many sources in their communities.

Linda Eade of the Yosemite National Park Library helped us find archival photographs and Leroy Radanovich prepared the prints and checked our Mariposa history. When we were first doing research along Highway 140, Ann and Ralph Mendershausen put us up at their lovely home on a hill outside Mariposa and later read the manuscript for accuracy and made several important suggestions. Ralph provided the initial historical research for Mariposa and Oakhurst.

Other innkeepers have graciously acted as hosts and often given us valuable leads: the Kiehlmeiers and Williams of Hounds Tooth Inn, Libby and Norm Murrell of Sierra House Bed and Breakfast, Kathy Lozares of Rancho Bernardo, Ed and Janet Hardy of Bass Lake Lodge, Peggy Mosley of the Groveland Hotel and Denise and Randy Brooks of Brooks Berry Inn.

TABLE OF CONTENTS

TABLE OF CONTENTS

California Road Conditions—1-800-427-ROAD (7623)
VIA Bus Amtrack Connection—1-800-369-7275

United States Forest Service
Campground Reservations—1-877-444-6777
Inyo National Forest, Bishop—760-873-2400
Inyo National Forest, Lee Vining—760-647-3000
Mono Basin Scenic Area Visitor Center—760-647-3044
Sierra National Forest—559-877-2218
Stanislaus National Forest, Groveland District—209-962-7825

Visitor Bureaus
Highway 120 Association—1-800-449-9120
Lee Vining Chamber of Commerce—760-647-6629 www.monolake.org
Mariposa Visitors Bureau—209-966-2456 www.mariposa.yosemite.net/visitor
Mono Lake Committee—760-647-6595 www.monolake.org
Mono Lake Tufa State Reserve—760-647-6331
Tuolumne County Visitors Bureau—1-800-446-1333
    www.mlode.com/~nsierra/visitor
Yosemite Sierra Oakhurst Visitors Bureau—559-683-4636 www.yosemite-sierra.org

Yosemite Association—209-379-2646 www.yosemite.org

Yosemite National Park Numbers www.yosemitepark.com
Ahwahnee Dining Room—209-372-1489
All Room Reservations—559-252-4848
Badger Pass Ski Conditions—209-372-1000
Campground Reservations—1-800-436-7275
  Outside the United States—301-722-1257
High Sierra Camp Reservations—559-454-2002
Information, Weather, Roads—209-372-0200
Tuolumne Meadows Stables—209-372-8427
Valley Stables—209-372-8384
Yosemite Concession Services Switchboard—209-372-1000
Wawona Stables—209-375-6502
Wawona Golf Course—209-375-6572

Yosemite National Park Entrance Fees
Entrance Fee (good for seven days)—$20
Yosemite Annual Pass (good for 12 months)—$40
Golden Eagle Pass (Entrance to any National Park for 12 months)—$50**
Golden Age Pass (Lifetime for citizens or permanent residents 62 or older)—$10**
** Purchase at any National Park entrance or U.S. Forest Service visitor center.

So you are thinking of going to Yosemite. It is far more than the Valley, you know. Yosemite National Park is 1,170 square miles surrounded by three National Forests plus the gateway towns of Oakhurst, Mariposa, Groveland, Lee Vining and June Lake.

This book, one of the *What Shall We Do Tomorrow*® series, describes activities and lodging in the park **and** its gateway communities, including bed and breakfast inns, hotels and motels. Read about the human and natural history of the region and learn about the early roads into the park.

Do you know about the beautiful grove of redwood trees called Nelder Grove near Oakhurst? Or do you know how to book a raft trip on the Merced or Tuolumne Rivers? If you stay in Lee Vining or June Lake, do you know about the beautiful walks, the canoe trips on Mono Lake and horseback tours into special places in the high country? This book will answer all those questions and many more.

How to use this book

The introduction starts with an insider's guide to getting reservations in the park, how to enter the lotteries for the Bracebridge Dinner at the Ahwahnee and the High Sierra Loop trips. A short description of the geology and natural history of the Sierra Nevada is followed by the story of events that led to the discovery and establishment of Yosemite National Park.

The first chapter describes lodging and special activities in the Valley. The next three chapters cover the western gateway communities of Oakhurst on Highway 41, Mariposa on Highway 140 and Groveland on Highway 120 West. The last chapter describes Lee Vining, June Lake and Highway 120 East to Tuolumne Meadows.

The chapters are color-coded on the outside edge. The Valley chapter is green, Highway 41 is blue, Highway 140 is gold, Highway 120 West is purple, and Highway 120 East is red.

Activities are in the second section of each chapter and are identified with the icons shown on the opposite page.

Lodging

 Dining

 Excursions

 Swimming

 Boating

 Fishing

 Rafting

 Hiking

 Bicycling

 Horseback Riding

 Golf

 Ranger Programs

 X-Country Skiing

 Downhill Skiing

 Snowplay

 Snowmobiling

 Museums

 Art Galleries

 Special Events

3

Reservations in the Park

Accommodations in the Valley range from canvas tent cabins at Camp Curry to luxury rooms at the National Historic Landmark Ahwahnee Hotel. In addition, the Wawona Hotel, the Victorian inn on Highway 41, has both tennis courts and a nine-hole golf course.

In the summer, the Tuolumne Meadows Lodge and White Wolf Lodge offer tent cabins close to all the wonders of the high country and with dining rooms offering good food in substantial portions.

Accommodations and other services are all managed by Yosemite Concession Services with a central reservation telephone number (559)252-4848. Call Monday through Saturday 8:00 a.m. to 5:00 p.m. Pacific time. If you are booking for November through March you can get an on-line reservation request form from www.yosemitepark.com, their website. For the peak season our insider's guide to getting what you want in the park follows.

The Insider's Reservation Guide

High season extends from April through October. You will need to plan well ahead to make a reservation. Here are some tips:

All reservations are open to individuals exactly 366 days in advance. If you call the morning of the day exactly 366 days before your intended arrival, you will have the best chance of getting what you want. Call between 8:00 a.m. and 5:00 p.m. seven days a week or from 7:00 a.m. Monday through Friday from May to October. Saturday is the best day to call, as the phone lines are least busy then.

It is especially important to book a year in advance at The Ahwahnee, Yosemite Lodge and Wawona Hotel.

Your best bet to visit the park and enjoy it without the crowds is midweek in November, early December, February and March. During these times hotel rates drop 25% and low-cost ski packages are available. For details call (559)454-0555.

Be flexible and have several dates in mind. Often you can call 30 days, 15 days or seven days in advance of your arrival and get a room. These are common dates when reservations are cancelled.

If Yosemite is a must for you, join a tour with confirmed Yosemite hotel reservations and transportation. Check with your travel agent. You can often combine stops at other scenic locations, and tours often include meals.

Summer High Sierra Loop Trip

You must start early and follow the rules to reserve a spot in the lottery for this famous hiking trip into the high country of John Muir's *Range of Light.*

Official lottery application forms can be obtained from the High Sierra Desk at (559)454-2002. Send your application form in between October 15 and November 30. Forms received before or after these dates are not accepted. You **must** use the official "High Sierra Camp Lottery Application."

Only one application form may be submitted per party. Faxes and photocopies are not accepted. A maximum of eight spaces (six for meals only) may be requested on your application.

Meals only reservations are for hikers who are camping nearby but don't want to carry their food.

You need to list the number of males and females, including children and their ages. Space is usually assigned by gender.

Be flexible, give as many alternate dates as possible.

List daytime and evening/weekend phone numbers and do not send any payment until requested.

The lottery is in mid-December. You will be notified in the spring about your standing.

Do not call to check on the status of your application.

Any cancelled space is filled by pulling lottery applications on file. Notification after May 1st is by phone.

Opening and closing dates for the camps are tentative and change due to weather. Your awarded lottery space is subject to the camp being open for the time you reserved. If you can plan late July or August dates your trip is less likely to be cancelled due to snow. **Good Luck!**

Introduction

The Bracebridge Dinner

With as many as 60,000 requests for only 1,675 guests at five seatings of 335 on December 22, Christmas Eve and Christmas Day, you naturally must enter a lottery. Applications may only be obtained by writing to Yosemite Concession Services at 5410 E. Home Ave., Fresno, CA 93727. Applications are accepted only from December 1 through January 15 for the following year's dinner. That means if you want to attend dinner in the year 2000, your application must be in by January 15, 2000. Each dinner seat costs $215 including tax and gratuity, but excluding wine. You may make your room reservation when you win a lottery place.

Since all roads lead to Yosemite you can use this book to help you find a place to stay just outside and plan your days in the park. Best of all you will discover all the wonderful things to do near your lodging, no matter which road you travel.

The lodging section for the Valley briefly describes the facilities and their price range, as well as the places to dine. The chapter for each highway describes the bed and breakfast inns, motels and resorts in each gateway. The activities for each locale are in the second section of each chapter.

Courtesy of the National Park Service, Yosemite

The squire opens the dinner in 1934.

Courtesy of Yosemite Concession Services

A quiet moment viewing Vernal Fall.

Formation of the Sierra Nevada

The spectacular scenery of the Sierra Nevada was created over millions of years by the opposing forces of mountain building and erosion. Mountain building is the result of tectonic action that pushes the outer skin of the earth upward as heat escapes from deep inside. Wind, water and ice produce erosion, wearing away high places and filling in low spots. The dramatic landscape of the Sierra Nevada and Yosemite Valley in particular is the result of a series of tectonic movements followed by erosion.

While erosion is easily observed and has been understood for a long time, the causes of mountain building have been a mystery until recently. Within the last 40 years a revolutionary theory called plate tectonics has shed new light on the origin of mountain formation.

The earth's skin or crust is broken into pieces that earth scientists call plates. These do not match the continents; most include some ocean floor as well as land masses. Nearly all of Canada, the United States, and the western portion of the Atlantic Ocean make up the North American Plate. A narrow strip of the California coast is on the Pacific Plate.

Tectonic or mountain building activity occurs along plate boundaries. The spectacular scenery of California and the Sierra Nevada is the result of such dynamic interactions, a geologic story still being written by nature and deciphered by geologists. When an ocean plate and a continental plate meet, as along the coast of California, a process

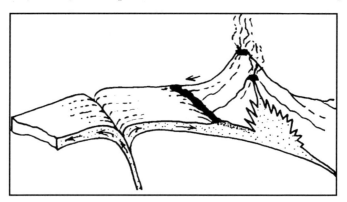

Subduction

called subduction can occur. The thin but heavy plate of the ocean floor slides under the lighter, higher riding continental plate and is remelted in a crustal recycling scheme. The resulting molten rock may rise to the surface in volcanic eruptions. If the subducted material remains underground as it cools, it forms crystalline rocks like granite. Such a massive unit of granite rose slowly from deep within the earth to become the batholith (bedrock) that formed the Sierra Nevada.

About 130 million years ago, after subduction had produced volcanoes and set the batholith in place, earthquakes along lines of weakened rocks called faults jolted the earth in pulses. The fault line along the eastern edge of the ancient Sierra range broke and the 400-mile-long block tilted skyward until the peaks touched the clouds. The resulting Sierra Nevada range rose steeply on its eastern boundary and sloped gently westward toward the Central Valley. This process continued for millions of years.

Then, about three million years ago, the earth's climate changed dramatically. The Ice Age was beginning and for the next two million years a series of glaciers covered the mountain range in sheets of ice. At the height of the last glacial age the floor of Yosemite Valley was beneath 6,000 feet of ice. In the high country of Tuolumne Meadows, a 2,000-foot crushing load of rock-filled ice scraped away the last remains of the ancient Sierra rocks and polished the underlying granite to glass-like smoothness. Glaciers also descended valleys of the steep eastern escarpment of the range, fanning out along the border of the high plain called the Great Basin.

Finally, about 10,000 years ago, the weather warmed and the last ice age slowly ended. The melting ice sent water and rock tumbling down the western canyons of the range carving deep chasms in each river course. At Tuolumne Meadows the landscape would have blinded the eyes of any beholder as the sun's rays bounced off the surface of a marble-like plain dotted with granite domes.

In Yosemite Valley, the receding ice left a lake encircled by precipitous cliffs and spires from which magnificent waterfalls plunged. Eventually the water burst through a rocky dam at the west end and drained the lake, leaving a concave river valley.

To the east of Yosemite, rivers of glacial melt poured into a vast inland sea with no outlet. The uplifted Sierra Nevada created a rain shadow—it's high peaks draining moisture from incoming Pacific Ocean storms. This changed the weather east of the range so that little rain fell. The inland sea shrank until all that was left was Mono Lake.

From that time until the present, the forces of erosion covered rock with layers of soil. Yosemite Valley evolved into a lush meadow and forest land through which the Merced River meandered. Forests began to grow, and the granite plain of Tuolumne Meadows filled with pockets of earth supporting grassy glades encircled by groves of lodgepole pines. The earth was ready for human habitation.

For many years people thought that Half Dome was created by the glaciers as they scraped past on their way from the high country to Yosemite Valley. Actually, the process that created the shape began before the glaciers along a broad vertical fault in the solid piece of granite that forms Half Dome. Over the millennia pieces of the dome broke off along this fault and dropped. The glaciers merely finished the job, while the top of Half Dome was always above the ice.

Yosemite Valley Through the Ages

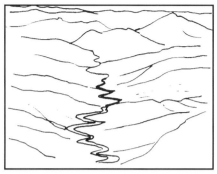

The Merced River valley about 10 million years ago created a precursor to Yosemite Valley.

The last glacier passed through the valley about 30,000 years ago leaving a terminal moraine between El Capitan and Bridalveil Fall.

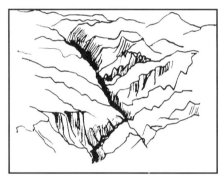

After uplift of the Sierra Nevada the Merced River cut a canyon in the mountain valley.

An ancient lake formed behind the moraine at the end of the glacial age. Today the lake has disappeared leaving meadows and forest through which the meandering Merced River flows.

The first glacier buried almost everything from the high country to the valley about one million years ago.

The Sierra's First Inhabitants

While the glaciers were melting, nomads who had crossed the Bering Strait from Asia on a land bridge began to migrate south along North America's western shores. Many thousand years before Christ was born, the first of them reached the verdant valleys west of the Sierra Nevada. They settled along the water courses of what is now the Central Valley and in the foothills of the range. Summertime found these tribes climbing into the higher mountains to hunt. At some point in time a group found a wondrous valley surrounded by guardian cliffs. A river flowed gently though meadows dotted with oaks that dropped a bountiful crop of acorns every autumn, the staple of their diet. Everything else needed for survival was close at hand: abundant game, fish, plants from which to fashion their carrying and cooking baskets, and cedar, whose bark could secure their huts from the elements. They called their valley Ahwahnee (deep, grassy valley) and called themselves Ahwahneeche.

On the eastern side of the Sierra, other groups had established themselves along the shores of Mono Lake, harvesting the pupae and larvae of the lake's brine flies, which, when dried in the sun, produced a yellow edible kernel about the size of a grain of rice. With salt from evaporated lake water, piñon nuts and obsidian, they wandered to the high country to barter their goods for the acorns and bear skins of the Ahwahneeche.

The two tribes lived in relative peace with one another, while trade and travel over the passes continued for centuries. Their route was called the Mono Trail, going up Bloody Canyon and over Mono Pass into the high country.

California Before the Gold Rush

The Spaniards arrived in California in the 1700s, and by the time colonists on the east coast of the continent were declaring their independence from England, Spanish soldiers and their priests had set up a series of presidios (forts) and missions along the coast of California. Spanish expeditions could see the snow-capped mountains to the east and gave the range its Spanish name, Sierra Nevada, but they were not inclined to explore its wilderness.

The Spanish era of California history drew to a close when Mexico rebelled against Spain in 1821 and secured dominion over the region to the north which they called Alta California. But a weak Mexican government had little control of its California province, and the United States began to think of California as a ripe plum ready for harvest. The U.S. government began supporting expeditions to find easy routes to the west.

Explorers of the Sierra

One early explorer, Joseph Walker, undertook an expedition in 1833 to find a route to California through the Sierra Nevada. Zenas Leonard was appointed clerk of the trip, and his accounts of the journey have helped us determine that Joseph Walker was the first white man to be in the high Sierra above Yosemite Valley. It is still debated whether his crew actually gazed into the Valley, but he may have seen Half Dome and the Tenaya Canyon. He did travel through the giant redwoods of the Tuolumne Grove.

In 1843 an adventurous Army cartographer, Lt. John Charles Frémont, set out on a mapping expedition of the western United States. For more than a year he wandered the West, discovered and named Pyramid Lake in Nevada, and almost perished while trying to cross the Sierra to California. Later, in 1847, Frémont negotiated the purchase of ten square leagues of the Rancho Las Mariposas, about 55,000 acres of unsettled land near what is now the town of Mariposa. Learn more about Frémont in the Highway 140 description starting on page 138.

Gold in the Sierra Foothills

When gold was discovered in 1848, the foothills were invaded by gold-hungry men from all over the globe. Although no wagon trains traversed the Sierra Nevada near Yosemite, rich gold strikes in the southern mines of Sonora and Big Oak Flat brought thousands of miners to the foothills west of Yosemite Valley.

In 1848 miners heading for the southern part of the Mother Lode sailed up the Delta from San Francisco and disembarked at Stockton. Here they packed their canvas tents, pans, shovels and meager food supplies onto their backs or, if lucky, a mule. They headed for the foothills, following former Indian tracks. The long trek could not have been very pleasant. In winter miners trudged through muddy quagmires and were forced to walk across roaring streams. Six months later, they could scarcely breathe in the hot dusty air. The trail out of Stockton became lined with tents, and at night an almost continuous line of campfires lit the way. Mining was mostly centered around Sonora, but a rich strike near Big Oak Flat brought ever-hopeful miners to establish towns beyond present-day Groveland. Early miners were so focused on finding riches that few explored the high mountains.

The arrival of miners in the foothills immediately changed the lives of all native peoples. Their rancherias (villages) were overrun by miners, who had no regard for the tribes' way of life, causing a series of incidents which the miners called Indian depredations.

The Discovery of Yosemite

James D. Savage arrived in California with one of the wagon trains of 1846. He settled among the Indian tribes of the Central Valley. He had several native wives and a facility with their languages. He gained enough respect to be elected a chief and was known as the White Chief. By 1849 he had

established a trading post at the confluence of the South Fork and the Merced River. He hired William Penn Abrams to search for possible mill sites along the river. In October 1849, Abrams left from Savage's to track a grizzly bear. He wrote the following in his diary,

"While at Savage's, Reamer and I saw grizzly bear tracks and went out to hunt him down, getting lost in the mountains and not returning until the following evening. Found our way to camp over an Indian trail that led past a valley enclosed by stupendous cliffs rising perhaps 3,000 feet from their base, and which gave us cause for wonder. Not far off a water fall drops from a cliff, below three jagged peaks into the valley, while farther beyond a round mountain stood, the valley side of which looked as though it had been sliced with a knife as one would slice a loaf of bread, and which Reamer and I calld the Rock of Ages."

Can anyone doubt that Abrams was describing the beautiful Valley of the Yosemite.

By 1850 the location of Savage's trading post threatened the Ahwahneeche living in Yosemite

14

Valley, resulting in an attack on the post. Savage withdrew to locations near Mariposa and Coarsegold, a town on today's Highway 41. A final series of Indian attacks at that location led to the Mariposa Indian War.

Savage was appointed a major and commander of the hastily summoned Mariposa Battalion. They set forth in March 1851 to "smoke out the Grizzly Bears (Yo Semites, Savage's name for the Ahwahneeche Indians) from their holes."

The battalion's first foray into the fortress of the Ahwahneeche found only a 100-year-old woman and a number of dogs. However, the group gave the valley its name Yo Semite and published accounts of the marvels they had seen. On a second invasion by the battalion, the tribe's Chief Tenaya and a few braves were captured in the Valley. The rest of his band was pursued up to the high country where, on the shores of a beautiful lake, they were surprised and captured. The soldiers called the place Tenaya Lake to honor the old chief. The captured Indians were removed to a reservation at Fresno Flats (Oakhurst) but were later allowed to return to their ancestral home.

First Tourists

Although the soldiers had little interest in the beauty of the scenery, the mention of 1,000-foot waterfalls attracted the attention of James Hutchings, a 49er who was also a journalist. In 1855 Hutchings organized a tourist party to explore the wonders of the Yo Semite Valley. The group rode horses on an Indian track over Chowchilla Mountain to the South Fork of the Merced River near present day Wawona and into Yosemite Valley from a spot just above today's Inspiration Point. In 1855 Hutchings wrote in the *Mariposa Gazette* of "five days of luxurious scenic banqueting."

Courtesy of the National Park Service, Yosemite

James Hutchings as a young man.

Starting in 1856 Hutchings published information about the scenic wonders of California in his *California Magazine*. He was so enamored with the splendors of Yosemite that in 1862 he decided to purchase a two-story hotel and took out a claim to 160 acres on the Valley floor. The hotel purchase was finally consummated in April 1864 and Hutchings, with his new and pregnant wife Elvira and his mother-in-law, took up year-round residence in Yosemite Valley and opened their hotel for business.

Hutchings' daughter Florence "Floy" Hutchings was the first white child to be born in Yosemite Valley. Two other children, Gertrude and William, came along soon after. Floy died at age 17 in a terrible accident on the Ledge Trail to Glacier Point and was buried in the Yosemite Pioneer Cemetery. Her father was buried next to her when he died in 1902 at the age of 79 after another tragic accident. His wagon careened off the Big Oak Flat Road and he was thrown from the carriage.

Others followed Hutchings into the wondrous valley. Later in 1855 two other parties including Galen Clark and Milton and Houston

Mann explored the Valley. By 1856 Galen Clark had filed a claim to homestead 160 acres on the banks of the South Fork of the Merced River, the site of the present-day Wawona Hotel.

Clark suffered with consumption and thought his death was imminent. Deciding that life in the mountains, whether it ended in life or death, was preferable to life in the mines, he moved to Wawona, hunted and fished, befriended the Indians and explored the grove of giant sequoias now known as the Mariposa Grove. Clark's cabin became the stopping place for all early tourists to the Valley, so that he soon became a combination hotelier and tour guide. He hosted such notables as Jesse Benton Frémont, Albert Bierstadt,

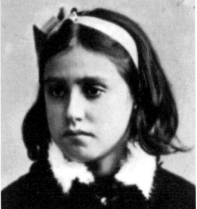

Courtesy of the National Park Service, Yosemite

Floy Hutchings

Courtesy of the National Park Service, Yosemite

Galen Clark relaxing by the South Fork of the Merced River near his cabin at Wawona.

the great landscape painter, and numerous journalists of the day. In 1856 his friends, the Mann brothers, built a 40-mile toll horse trail from Mariposa to Wawona and on into Yosemite Valley.

Yosemite Becomes a Park

By 1860 news of the wondrous waterfalls and the Big Trees had spread far and wide. The numbers of tourists increased, encouraging a citizen effort to create a park. A bill was signed by President Lincoln in 1864, granting to the State of California Yosemite Valley and the Mariposa Grove "to be held for public use, resort, and recreation . . . inalienable for all time." The legislature appointed a Yosemite Board of Commissioners who named Galen Clark to be

Yosemite Guardian, an imposing title with little remuneration.

Horse Trails to Wagon Roads

For the first few years of the new state grant sightseers came to Yosemite Valley and the Big Trees on horseback, enduring long hours in the saddle on steep and sometimes treacherous trails. Trails were added out of Coulterville and Big Oak Flat and by 1871 stage roads had been constructed on these routes as far as Gentry's Station on the north rim of the Valley. At the same time Galen Clark and his new partner, Edwin Moore, headed a group called the Mariposa Big Trees and Yo Semite Turnpike Company. At great expense they built a road from Mariposa over Chowchilla

Mountain to Clark's Station on the South Fork of the Merced (today's Wawona).

Toll Roads and their Boosters

By 1872 hundreds of tourists had come to see the new Yosemite Park and industrious businessmen in nearby foothill towns were busy planning toll roads over the routes of the horse trails into Yosemite Valley.

A group in Coulterville promoting such a road into the Valley formed the Coulterville and Yosemite Turnpike Company. In June 1872, Dr. John McLean purchased controlling shares in the Turnpike Company and applied to the Yosemite Commissioners for exclusive rights to build a toll road into Yosemite Valley. He proceeded to survey his road and in the process discovered a beautiful grove of redwoods (the Merced Grove) near Hazel Green. His road went through the grove and on up to Big Meadow near Foresta, from which it made a precipitous 16% drop to the Merced River canyon near the Cascades. On June 17, 1874, a grand celebration opened the stage route to tourists.

Meanwhile, in Groveland some shrewd businessmen convinced the state legislature to give them the right to bring their wagon road from Big Oak Flat into the Valley via Hodgdon's Meadows and Crane Flat, ending McLean's exclusivity. In fact, his monopoly lasted just 29 days. Thus began a rivalry for tourist dollars, ultimately won by the Big Oak Flat Road boosters because their route had a railroad connection at Chinese Camp. The road was easily converted for automobile use in the mid 1920s.

The completion of the northern roads into the Valley put Clark

Courtesy of the National Park Service, Yosemite

Leaving the Valley on the dusty Big Oak Flat stage road.

and Moore into severe financial difficulty at Wawona. This opened the way for Henry Washburn, who also happened to own a livery stable, to take over the property. He quickly obtained permission from Mariposa County and the Yosemite Commissioners to build a road from Wawona into the Valley over Inspiration Point. In June 1875, his 27-mile road opened for business. By 1877 Washburn had incorporated the Yosemite Stage and Turnpike Company to provide passenger and freight transportation all the way from Madera to Yosemite Valley.

Washburn was a true entrepreneur. Because he owned the stage line and the Wawona Hotel with its nearby attraction of the Mariposa Grove of Big Trees, his operation became an instant success. When he added a road to Glacier Point and acquired the Sentinel Hotel in the Valley and the Mountain House at Glacier point, he was close to having a monopoly of tourist services. He was garnering 60 percent of all the Yosemite tourist traffic.

At the height of Washburn's owner-ship, the Yosemite Stage and Turnpike Company owned 700 horses for 25 top-of-the-line red stages, carriages, freight wagons and other vehicles.

Courtesy of the National Park Service, Yosemite

A stage on the Wawona Road into the Valley with a view of Bridalveil Fall through the trees.

Yosemite National Park is created

In late 1869 a young man by the name of John Muir discovered his "temple of Nature" when he went to work for James Hutchings in the Valley and began to study the landscape and write about its wonders. Visitors from Europe and eastern United States flocked to the mountains to see the place of Muir's writings. In 1889 Muir began to work with the *Century Magazine* and its influential editor, Robert Underwood Johnson. With Muir's writings and the backing of the *Century* and Johnson's powerful friends, Congress in 1890 set aside an area larger than the present-day park as "reserved forest lands," soon to be Yosemite National Park. But the Valley and Mariposa Grove continued under state control.

The Army cavalry was given the job of patrolling the new park lands, at that time overrun by sheep and cattle. The park received no appropriations, forcing the Secretary of the Interior to assign Unites States troops to patrol the park as they were in Yellowstone National Park. Once the sheep and cattle were taken care of, the cavalry went to work collecting tolls, searching for lost campers, planting fish, guiding tourists and fighting forest fires. They also built many trails into the back country, in many cases using centuries-old routes of Native Americans and, more recently, the sheepherders.

In early May 1903, President Theodore Roosevelt, always a lover of wilderness, visited the park. The politically astute Muir took Roosevelt on a little overnight hike to Glacier Point and, with Governor George Pardee, pushed for the United States to take back Yosemite Valley and Mariposa Grove. In 1906 Congress accepted the transfer and the park became as we know it today.

Courtesy of the National Park Service, Yosemite

Muir and Roosevelt at Glacier point.

Railroads and Stage Lines to Yosemite

Henry Washburn was the first to realize that his stage ride needed to be reduced in length. He persuaded the Southern Pacific Railroad to build a line from Madera to the small town of Raymond in 1901. The new mode of travel was an instant success, helping Washburn garner most of the tourist traffic to the park.

Increased tourism spurred others to consider the same. In 1907 the Yosemite Valley Railroad began service between Merced and El Portal, reducing the stage ride to ten miles and dooming the other stage routes—at least until automobiles were common and the roads improved.

Automobiles Arrive in the Park

On Saturday, June 23, 1900, pioneer motorist Oliver Lippincott climbed into his Locomobile with his friend, Edward Russell, a machine shop owner, and left Raymond on a historic journey to Wawona. In a little over five hours he pulled into Wawona, a journey that took stage coaches all day. The next leg of the journey to Yosemite Valley took only three hours. Yosemite had been reached by automobile.

Thirty-three days later Frank and Arthur Holmes drove their modified Stanley Steamer over the same road. More importantly, they had driven all the way from San Jose. During the next two summers other pioneer drivers brought their machines into the

Courtesy of the National Park Service, Yosemite

Arthur Holmes driving his Stanley Steamer in the Valley.

Valley over the Coulterville and Big Oak Flat Roads.

In 1906 Yosemite Valley was administered by the U.S. Cavalry. Major Harry C. Benson, recently named acting superintendent of the park, decided to ban all motor vehicles from Yosemite in June 1907. This incensed automobile owners throughout the state and finally, in 1913, the Secretary of the Interior rescinded Benson's order and automobiles became a part of the Yosemite landscape forever.

On July 31, 1926, hundreds of motorists opened the new all-year highway from Merced to the Valley. A year later, 137,296 cars entered the park and more than a million cars a year were driving through the gates by 1980. This created an environmental problem that forced the park service and others to evaluate how many cars can be in the Valley on any one day. This led to the first General Management Plan to improve the Valley experience. Much discussed and with input from 80,000 letter writers, the 1980 plan sat on the shelf gathering dust. It was the victim of diminishing funds for national parks and, according to some, a lack of will on the part of various administrations and congresses.

Courtesy of the National Park Service, Yosemite

Parking problems at the new Yosemite Village circa 1926.

The Flood of 1997

Like many other locations in California, New Years Day in 1997 found Yosemite Valley in the grips of the worst flood in recorded history. The Merced River overflowed its banks in the Valley to churn through campgrounds picking up picnic tables and throwing them around like bowling balls. It knocked out the sewer system, destroyed employee housing and cabins at Yosemite Lodge and inflicted damage to every road into the park. The park was evacuated except for a few employees and remained closed until mid-March.

The flood became a wake-up call for the park service to assess the locations of campsites in the Valley and of Yosemite Lodge buildings. When Congress funded the reconstruction of park facilities, the Yosemite Valley Implementation Plan (VIP) was prepared to deal not only with rebuilding and relocation but with the reduction of auto traffic sought in the 1980 General Management Plan.

Valley Implementation Plan

The plan was released with proposals for greatly reduced auto traffic in the Valley, including parking structures and bus travel from gateway communities. It also reconfigured the roads in the Valley and reduced lodging. Extensive public comment persuaded Secretary of the Interior Bruce Babbitt to begin a new planning process to include representatives of all groups interested in Yosemite and its future. The revised plan was not yet released when we went to press.

Courtesy of the National Park Service, Yosemite

The plan hopes to avoid this in the future.

Of Trees, Flowers and Animals

Lying between the Central Valley and the snowy High Sierra, the Lower Sierra borrows climate from both neighbors. On summer days hot valley air rises to bake the hills and snuff out the short lives of flowers and grasses. At night cool mountain air descends. Fall air becomes frosty, sparking leaves to color and giving local apples a distinctive crunch. Winter tule fog seldom reaches above the 1,000-foot level and snow falls infrequently.

Innumerable physical conditions exist on the Sierra's western slope, such as differing soil types, exposure, precipitation and temperatures. Soils can be derived from volcanic, granitic, serpentine or sedimentary rocks. Granitic soils are relatively poor while volcanic soils host an array of wildflowers. Rivers have sliced deep canyons westward down the slope resulting in sunny canyon sides facing shady ones.

Rainfall might be fifteen inches on the lower slopes and up to sixty inches at the crest of the range. The gain in elevation provides changeable winter conditions as the temperature lowers about five degrees Fahrenheit for each 1,000 feet of rise; thus, rain at Oakhurst or Groveland will become snow at Badger Pass or Crane Flat.

Called the green wall by some, the western slopes of the Sierra Nevada are banded with five different forest communities. Unfortunately for the observer, the demarcations are not clearly defined. However, the foothill woodland and ponderosa forest communities are the most widespread.

At the edge of the valley, grasslands blend into foothill woodlands, rounded hills are covered with wild oats and dotted with drought-resistant shrubs and trees. The reflective colors of blue oaks and blue-gray digger pines are believed to play a part in the ability of these trees to minimize water loss. The first to bloom in spring is the California buckeye, sending a white candle of blooms above its leaves.

The buckeye loses its leaves in summer leaving bare limbs with fuzzy balls of fruit.

24

Where the foothill woodland community and ponderosa forest overlap is a localized phenomenon; chaparral plants of chamise, manzanita and toyon survive on the hotter, sunny slopes. Across the canyon a forest community thrives in the shade, with evergreen oaks and Douglas fir reaching skyward among the red trunks of shiny-leafed madrone.

Plants of both communities have adapted to fire by being dependent upon the extreme heat for germination of their seeds. Others sprout from the burned root crowns. The ponderosa forest begins where the climate is somewhat cooler and more moist than at lower elevations; it is a living museum of trees that have needles rather than leaves. Its

Ponderosa pine.

predominant plant is, naturally, the ponderosa pine, known throughout the West as yellow pine and a favorite of the lumber industry.

In among the ponderosa you will encounter black oaks, so called because the bark is very dark. It is the largest of the mountain oaks, found between 3,500 and 7,000 feet. At maturity the tree can be 60 to 80 feet tall. It is one of the principal trees in Yosemite Valley, whose acorns were favored by the Native American tribes of the region.

Approaching the snow line, at about 5,000 feet, the stately sugar pine will be a constant companion on roads into the Valley. Towering above the rest of the forest, its sparsely needled, outstretched limbs hold foot-long cones dangling from the topmost branches. It was one of John Muir's favorite trees.

Douglas fir.

Plants and Animals on the Land

The Snow Belt

The 400-mile "snowy range", the Sierra Nevada, is one of the longest single mountain ranges in the world. For that reason it is correct to use the singular *Sierra*. The southern peaks are the highest and include Mount Whitney at over 14,000 feet. The shining, polished granite to which John Muir gave the name the "Range of Light" is beautifully exposed around Yosemite Park in the central Sierra.

The climate of the High Sierra corresponds to that found from the Canadian border north to the Arctic Circle. Plants and animals survive six-month winters. Storms with fierce winds blow across the peaks for several days at a time, dumping many feet of snow.

In heavy winters twenty-foot drifts are not uncommon and snow can remain on north-facing slopes well into the short summer. West of the crest deep snows are released in the spring to fill every river. The Merced, San Joaquin and Tuolumne Rivers rise in high mountain lakes or glaciers within the park and descend across meadows, over granite slabs and down great waterfalls toward the Central Valley. All end in reservoirs that supply water for valley farmers and communities. The Tuolumne is dammed within the park in Hetch Hetchy Reservoir that supplies both water and power to the city of San Francisco.

The snow forest begins about 6,000 feet in the lodgepole pine-red fir forest community. Lodgepoles are tall pines with short needles in bunches of two and cones the size of a baby's fist. The bark flakes off in coin-sized pieces. In and among the lodgepoles where the soil is good grow splendid red firs identified by their dark, furrowed bark and luxuriant clothing of upright single needles along each branch. The canopy of fir branches keeps the forest floor cool and few other plants live in the deep shade.

Near 6,000 feet the ponderosa pine is sometimes replaced by its cousin the Jeffrey pine, which in this part of the Sierra lives on both sides of the crest. The Jeffrey can tolerate higher, colder and drier habitats than ponderosa and often stands proudly on rocky promontories. Near timberline, scattered, gnarled Sierra junipers stand sentinel on rocky, windswept ledges. Low-growing clumps of whitebark pine are joined by the pliant hemlock to make up the forest of the subalpine forest community.

A hike near Tuolumne Meadows or up a peak brings you to the top of the world, where life is in miniature. What plants there are hug the ground, often resembling small, green pincushions. Winter travelers up Highways 120 or 41 will find the forest dressed in snow, while the Tioga Pass Road will be closed to all, impenetrable from early November until June. However, should you come on a summer day, listen to the singing pines and walk among the hemlocks where you will hear the peaceful hymn of the Sierra.

The animals within the park are similar throughout the Sierra

Nevada. Tourists will most often encounter mule deer, chipmunks, ground squirrels and coyotes. In the Valley all these seem tame but they are wild. Regulations and common sense require that you do not feed them. A quick move can scare an animal into charging or biting. The most destructive of all animals are the black bears who are conditioned to human food

Courtesy of the National Park Service, Yosemite

A locked window will not stop a hungry bear.

from many years of garbage and other easy pickings. They are clever and will know when you have left a cooler with food in your car. **NEVER** store food in your car. Use the food lockers available in all campgrounds or rent bear-resistant cannisters for $3 per day for backpacking.

© *Ellie Huggins*

Mule deer in the Merced River.

Plants and Animals on the Land

East of the Crest

As seen from the air, Nevada's mountain ranges resemble immense caterpillars crawling from Mexico to Canada. The ranges are steep and impressive, with some summits reaching over 10,000 feet. They separate mile-high, flat valleys called *basins*. Together they make up the Basin and Range Province, which stretches 500 miles from the Sierra to the Wasatch Mountains in Utah.

In his book *Basin and Range*, John McPhee expresses a feeling common to travelers:

> *"This Nevada topography is what you see during mountain building. There are no foothills. It is all too young. It is live country. This is the tectonic, active, spreading, mountain-building world. To a nongeologist, it's just ranges, ranges, ranges."*

Volcanic action has left its mark. Cone-shaped mountains and mudflow rock are reminders of ancient volcanoes. The area of present-day activity is centered along the California border east of the park near Lee Vining and south to Bishop.

Throughout the area, water heated by underground forces bubbles out as hot springs and has altered some of the rocks, producing rainbow colors. Today water erosion is the dominant sculptor of the desert landscape. It grooves and wrinkles the mountainsides and brings down sediments that form fan-shaped deposits on the flat.

The Sierra Nevada rain shadow dictates the climate of the Great Basin. While the slope west of the park may get over forty inches of moisture per year, the eastern side receives less than ten inches.

The high desert is a land of climatic extremes. Cold winter days of minus-twenty degrees precede blistering summers. Snowcapped mountains loom over cracked soils in the basins. Dry gullies suddenly fill with flash floods after raging thunderstorms. Plants and animals surviving in the desert deserve the utmost respect. It takes special adaptations to withstand heat and desiccating winds. Plants survive extremes of temperature and moisture in a variety of ways. The leaves of perennials are small, furry or scaly and sometimes are coated with a waxy substance. Roots go deep.

Seeds can lie dormant for decades waiting for lifegiving rains; when the rains come, the desert becomes a carpet of colors.

Because of the climate, vegetation is sparse east of the range, which gives erosion a free hand. Much of the basin-and-range terrain is spotted with the dominant shrub that gave Nevada its nickname, the Sagebrush State. Its silvery leaves have a spicy aroma reminiscent of the kitchen herb, but sagebrush is from a different plant family. These shrubs are widely scattered over the desert to allow each plant to obtain sufficient water and nutrients.

Few trees grow in the high desert, not only because of the lack of moisture but also because of intensive lumbering a century ago. Bristlecone pines, the oldest living trees in the world, remain in a few places above 10,000 feet in the White Mountains.

Down the eastern slope of the Sierra Nevada, second-growth Jeffrey pines tower above the sagebrush. Dotted on the hillsides in areas of twelve inches of annual precipitation, groupings of trees in the piñon-juniper woodland community offer shelter to desert animals. Often seen together, neither tree is much more than twenty feet tall. High up in the canyons, the round leaves of quaking aspen turn streamsides to gold in October. Along year-round rivers and streams, willows and stately cottonwood trees predominate, providing shade and security for flycatchers, magpies, orioles, warblers and grosbeaks.

piñon pine.

Introduction to Yosemite Valley

Courtesy of Yosemite Concession Services

Remarkable Yosemite Valley lies in a basin of the Merced River at an elevation of 4,000 feet above sea level. No matter which road you are using to reach the Valley, there is a point during your journey when John Muir's temple of nature bursts upon your senses. His words are only fitting to describe this sublime place.

"It is about seven miles long, half a mile to a mile wide, and nearly a mile deep in the solid granite flank of the range. The walls are made up of rocks, mountains in size, partly separated from each other by side canyons, and they are so sheer in front, and so compactly and harmoniously arranged on a level floor, that the Valley, comprehensively seen, looks like an immense hall or temple lighted from above. ... As if into this one mountain mansion Nature had gathered her choicest treasures, to draw her lovers into close and confiding communion with her."

Like all longtime visitors to the Valley I am renewed each time I arrive. I want to roll down the window of the car and drink in the

Introduction to Yosemite Valley

smells and sounds of the place. Over the last twenty years of visits I have been reminded time and again that nothing in nature is static. And the hand of man has made many changes that have affected the scene that Muir described in the late nineteenth century.

During Hutchings' time the Valley was transformed into a farm, with cattle grazing in the meadows and apple trees planted near hotels. When the National Park Service was created in 1916 with Stephen Mather as its first director, park management changed. Mather strove to make the Valley a place worthy of attracting tourists and taking care of their needs. In 1925 the Curry Company was merged with the Yosemite National Park Company and renamed the Yosemite Park and Curry Company. Under the direction of Donald Tresidder, the company (usually referred to simply as the Curry Company) was encouraged to build the Ahwahnee Hotel. Thus began a long period of efforts to increase visitation. Amenities were added, more hotel accommodations built, the fire fall became a nightly spectacle in the summer again, roads were upgraded and by the late 1930s all were paved.

Camp Curry's 100 years

David and Jennie Curry came to California in the 1890s and fell in love with Yosemite Valley. In 1899 they established a camp to offer reasonable tent accommodations to the ever growing numbers of tourists, and for 81 years the family managed Camp Curry and later the Curry Company. David and Jennie ran a tight ship, attracting devoted employees each summer, many from Stanford University. Their children worked there, advancing to positions of importance. When David died in 1917, Jennie, then affectionately known as Mother Curry, took over. One daughter, Mary, married the dashing Donald Tresidder, a medical student at Stanford. When Mary's brother, Foster Curry, left the company in 1922, Don Tresidder was appointed general manager. The Yosemite Park and Curry Company was created in 1925 putting Tresidder in charge of four hotels, the High Sierra Camps, the stores, garages and transportation divisions. Although he became President of Stanford University in 1943, he stayed involved as president of the Curry Company and his assistant, Hil Oehlmann, took over day to day management. Tresidder died suddenly in 1948, and Mother Curry passed on soon after. Mary was elected President, continuing in that office until her death in 1970, when the company was sold.

Introduction to Yosemite Valley

When the Second World War ended and gas rationing ceased, people began to flock to Muir's "temple of nature and his range of light." The number of campgrounds grew, the Yosemite Lodge was upgraded and motel type rooms were built at Camp Curry.

The Ahwahnee Hotel conscripted

For three years during World War II, the Ahwahnee Hotel was converted to a hospital for use by the U.S. Navy. Even though housed in beautiful surroundings, most of the sailors would much rather have been elsewhere. They found all that nature and their isolation so far from civilization boring. And when they left, the hotel would need complete renovation.

However, by the late 1970s the Department of the Interior and the National Park Service had a change of heart. Environmental awareness had grown to the point where many were demanding changes in the management of the natural resources in the park. Naturalists and others saw the degradation of the meadows and the proliferation of certain tree species to the detriment of the oak trees that had predominated when the Native Americans lived here. In addition, the Valley seemed to have become one big parking lot during high season. By 1980 resource management included regular prescribed burns to reduce the numbers of trees crowded on the valley floor. With money from the Yosemite Fund, restoration of trampled meadows and replanting of oaks are ongoing.

Then several natural events occurred reminding everyone that Mother Nature always would have the upper

Introduction to Yosemite Valley

hand. The rock slide from Glacier Point in 1996, the huge fire of 1989 and the flood of 1997 changed the landscape that longtime visitors knew. The Park Service then seized the initiative to change the way we all may visit Yosemite Valley. Planning began to reduce traffic and move lodging and camping places out of the flood plain. A brief discussion of the Valley Implementation Plan is on page 23 in the Introduction. Exactly how it will be for visitors in the new millennium is still a work in progress.

The Flood of 1997

The flood of 1997 and high water in 1998 took a toll on the Valley's infrastructure. Roads were torn apart, the sewers disintegrated and many buildings suffered enough damage to be condemned. Park reconstruction will take many years. However, the roads are the first to be rebuilt, necessitating road closures on Highways 140 and 120 during 1999 and 2000. The next page describes what we know at press time.

Courtesy of the National Park Service, Yosemite

Flood damage on Highway 140 in January 1997.

Introduction to Yosemite Valley

Highway 140 to Yosemite Valley will be open during the day in the summer. Road reconstruction will occur at night. Next winter travel times will be restricted. The following schedule is current as of March 1, 1999. However, if you want to be sure, we suggest that you call (209)372-0200 for the most up-to-date information. This number is the official recording and is updated regularly.

January to December 1999

From **January 3 to April 30** Highway 140 from El Portal will be open 6:30 a.m. to 8:00 a.m. and 4:30 p.m. to 10:30 p.m.

From **May 1 to October 3** the highway will be open from 6:30 a.m. to 10:30 p.m. every day. The park service warns there may be delays in May and September, 1999.

From **October 3 through December,** except for holiday periods, the road will be open from 6:30 a.m. to 8:00 a.m. and 4:30 p.m. to 10:30 p.m.

January to April 2000

Between the intersection of Highway 140 with Highway 120 and the Pohono Bridge in the Valley the road will be reconstructed and will be open from 6:30 a.m. to 8:00 a.m. and 4:30 p.m. and 10:30 p.m.

VIA Yosemite Connection to Yosemite Valley

Mariposa County sponsors bus service between the Merced Amtrak station and the Valley, with stops at Catheys Valley, Mariposa, Midpines and El Portal.

Call (888)PARK-BUS (727-5287) for the schedule.

Groveland has service as well. Check with(800)449-9120 for the schedule.

Yosemite Valley Bike/Shuttle Bus Routes

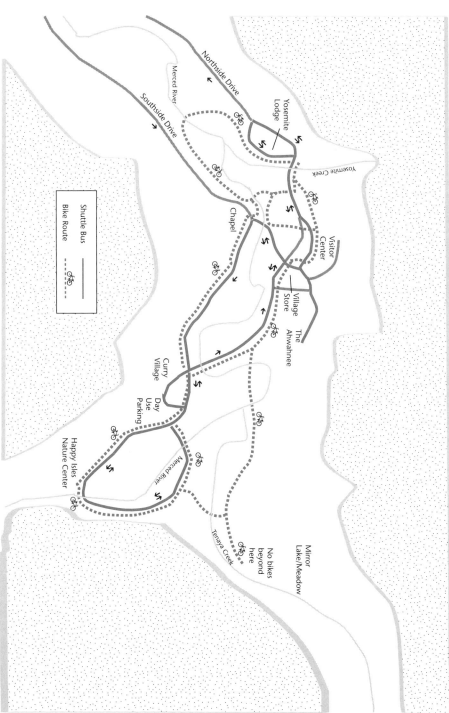

Lodging

The Yosemite Concession Services operates all of the accommodations in the park, while the National Park Service is in charge of the campgrounds. Telephone numbers are listed in the Introduction on page 1, and the Insider's Guide to Reservations in the Park is on pages 4 and 5. A description of the various units in the Valley follows. Prices are for peak season, generally April through October, and are subject to change.

Curry Village
Tent Cabins: from $40
Cabin without bath: from $59.25
Cabin with bath: from $75.25
Standard motel room: from $91.25

Curry Village offers one of the most economical accommodations in the park. There are no phones or TVs in any unit.

Curry Village

All the units have daily maid service. Linens, towels and soap are also provided.

Canvas tent cabins are wood-framed and on raised wooden platforms. Central restroom facilities are nearby. There are electric lights but no heaters or electric outlets.

Cabins without baths are fully furnished with electric lights and a wall heater, and have central restroom facilities.

Cabins with bath are the same as above but have desks, and the bath is in the cabin.

Lodging

Housekeeping Camp

Housekeeping camp units are concrete structures with a double canvas roof and a canvas wall separating the sleeping area from the cooking and dining area. There is a picnic table, and electric lights and outlets.

**Housekeeping Camp
From $43**

Soap and towels are available in the showerhouse. Laundry, restrooms and general store are nearby. There are no phones or TVs. Housekeeping units are very popular so you will need to reserve a year in advance for high season.

Yosemite Lodge

The standard room has beds, a desk, chairs and bathroom. There are in-room phones but no TVs.

A lodge hotel room is larger with a dressing area, table and chairs plus a balcony or patio. Again, there are in-room phones but no TVs.

**Yosemite Lodge
Standard room: $91.75
Lodge Hotel room: $112.00**

Daily maid service is provided but you must carry your own bags. An activity desk can help you make arrangements for tours and other activities.

The Ahwahnee

The Ahwahnee is a luxury hotel offering the finest accommodations in the park. Beautifully decorated rooms feature comfortable beds, upholstered chairs or couches, televisions, refrigerators, bathrobes and hair dryers. Some rooms have king beds. Ahwahnee Parlors are sitting rooms adjoining hotel rooms. These cannot be rented separately. There are duplex cottages with private patios in a forest setting adjoining the hotel.

**The Ahwahnee
Hotel room: $246
Parlors: $229 to $268**

The concierge will help with any of your plans. Room service, bell service and valet parking are all provided. Beds are turned down each night and ice is on each floor. Afternoon tea is served daily in the Great Lounge.

There are dining possibilities of every price range in the Valley.

In the Village, the **Village Grill** serves hamburgers and ice cream. Near the grocery store **Degnan's Deli** sells sandwiches and snacks all day. **Degnan's Fast Food** serves pizza, salads, soup and sandwiches with limited seating inside and picnic tables outside. Upstairs is **Degnan's Pasta Plus**.

At Curry Village the **Cafeteria** serves breakfast, lunch and dinner. The **Hamburger Deck** has sandwiches, ice cream and cocktails. The **Terrace Meadow Deck** serves lunch, pizza and light dinners. There is also the **Coffee Corner** and an ice cream stand.

Yosemite Lodge has a full service cafeteria serving all day. The **Garden Terrace** serves a family buffet for lunch and dinner and the **Mountain Room Restaurant** has fine dining at dinner only. Reservations are a must here in high season. The **Mountain Room Lounge** serves cocktails and snacks are available poolside.

Not all dining facilities are open all year. Check with the front desk or call 209-372-0200 to find out what is open during off season.

Enjoying breakfast on a winter morning.

© Dewitt Jones

YOSEMITE VALLEY DINING

Dining

The Ahwahnee Dining Room

The elegant, vaulted dining room is open for breakfast, lunch and dinner all year. You must make reservations except for Sunday Brunch. Even if you are staying elsewhere you may reserve a table here. If you don't want to pay the full price of a dinner, Sunday Brunch is a great alternative to say that you have dined at the Ahwahnee. It is an experience not to be missed. Sport coats and ties for the men are no longer required, and women may wear nice slacks.

$$$$
Ahwahnee Dinner Reservations:
209-372-1489

Want to enjoy the ambiance of the Great Lounge, especially on a chilly, winter afternoon? Try afternoon tea. It is served between 4:30 and 5:30 p.m. every day.

© Dewitt Jones

The Ahwahnee cloaked in snow.

Yosemite Valley Activities

The Valley Visitor Center

New visitors to Yosemite Valley should start at the Valley Visitor Center. Books and maps are for sale and helpful personnel will be able to answer many of your questions. See the map on page 35.

A word of warning!

The Merced River that cascades so beautifully into the Valley over Nevada and Vernal Falls is to be respected. Its swift waters smooth the granite rock into a glass-like surface. Visitors should obey the barriers near the river; they are there to protect you. People who venture too close to the river's edge have fallen in, and it is a long, deadly ride to the bottom of the fall.

Likewise, on the Mist Trail stay on the trail and use the handrails. Do not try the climb in smooth-soled shoes.

Once you have arrived in the Valley, you are encouraged to use the free shuttle buses, a bicycle or your feet to get to various destinations. If you are only in the Valley for a day, park at Curry Village and begin your explorations there. A visit to Happy Isles and the Nature Center is a must, and if you have time for only one hike, take the trail to the footbridge below Vernal Fall. More ambitious hikers with proper jackets and shoes will want to take the Mist Trail to the top of the fall.

The *Visitor Guide* you received at the entrance station, or the *Yosemite Magazine* from your hotel, have many suggestions. We will not try to cover all the possible hikes. Instead, we will introduce you to two favorites and some little known walks that will take you on the old roads into the park, some with different vistas of the famous walls and waterfalls. Don't forget to take your camera along.

The following section will tell you how to rent bikes, what ranger programs might be of special interest and where you can learn more about the park's natural history.

Excursions

The Yosemite Concession Services operate many bus tours as well as the regular tram tour of the Valley. All of the tours may be reserved at your hotel or the locations below. Tour buses pick up at various locations and free shuttle buses roam the Valley. See the map on page 35.

Valley Floor Tour

On a two-hour 26-mile ride in an open air tram you will learn about the landmarks and have plenty of opportunity to photograph them. Your guide will tell about the geology and history of the park. If you don't want to see the park on a bicycle, this is the best way to be introduced to its wonders. Enclosed buses are used in winter.

Reserving a tour

Tickets may be purchased at the following locations year-round:
    Yosemite Lodge
    The Ahwahnee
Spring to Fall:
    Beside the Village Store
Summer only:
    Curry Village
Reservations are recommended on all but the Big Trees tram tours and shuttle buses.

For Information and reservations:
    209-372-1240

Courtesy of Yosemite Concession Services

Enjoying the view from a Valley tour tram.

41

Excursions

Mariposa Grove of the Big Trees

A six-hour bus tour takes visitors to the Mariposa Grove of Big Trees with a stop at the charming, historic Wawona Hotel where you can enjoy an optional buffet lunch for an extra cost. Of course, you could always bring a picnic and sit out on the grass lawn for lunch. See page 106 for a description of the things to do at the Mariposa Grove.

Courtesy of Yosemite Concession Services

The sublime view of Half Dome and Clouds Rest from Glacier Point.

Glacier Point

This half-day tour goes from the Valley to Glacier Point for vistas of the High Sierra, including the oft-photographed Half Dome and both Vernal and Nevada Falls. An interesting option for hikers is to hike down, or better still, take the Four-Mile Trail up and return on the bus. See page 45 for a description of the hike.

The Grand Tour

If you only have one day to see everything in the southern end of the park, take the all-day grand tour, with stops at Glacier Point and the Mariposa Grove and lunch at the Wawona Hotel. You will enjoy all the sights with a driver who knows the road.

Fishing   Swimming   Rafting

Fishing in the Valley

From the last Saturday in April until November 15 anglers may cast for trout in the Merced River. However, from Happy Isles downstream to Pohono Bridge it is catch and release only using artificial lures or flies with barbless hooks. Bait fishing is prohibited.

Regulations:
A valid California fishing license is required for all persons 16 years and older and must be plainly visible above the waistline.

Swimming

There are swimming pools at Curry Village and the Lodge. The water of the Merced River is cold and, except during late summer and fall, the currents are swift. Use extreme caution and do not swim near waterfalls or rapids.

Rafting on the Merced

Rafting down the Merced River provides a unique view of the Valley. You may rent rafts, life jackets and paddles at Curry Village. The river is swift and cold. For guided trips on the Merced River below El Portal, see page 166 in Activities along Highway 140.

Regulations:
Rafting is prohibited above Yosemite Stables or below the Cathedral Beach Picnic area.

Valley hiking can include casual strolls across the meadows and along the Merced River or serious climbs to the top of Nevada or Yosemite Falls. This guide will not describe all possible hikes. Rather, we have chosen a few favorites and two lesser known hikes along portions of old roads into the Valley.

Courtesy of Yosemite Concession Services

The rewarding view of Lower Yosemite Fall from the bridge across Yosemite Creek.

From the Ahwahnee to Yosemite Falls

A paved path leads toward the Village area from the Ahwahnee gates. At the Church Bowl a trail behind the Medical Clinic climbs above the housing units. Soon you will be on an oak-lined trail that eventually dips down to a bridge across Yosemite Creek below the lower fall. This is a particularly nice early morning walk that brings you to the falls just as the sun is filling the Valley. A paved path heads south to the parking lot, Northside Drive and the Yosemite Lodge buildings. If you wish a longer hike, return to the Village on the paved bike trail, then walk along the north side of the Merced River, crossing the river near Lower Pines Campground and on to Curry Village. At Curry Village you can pick up a shuttle bus.

Hiking

The Four Mile Trail to Glacier Point

This is one of the easier trails to reach the heights above the Valley's south rim. The trail involves a climb of 3,600 feet in 4.8 miles and takes between three and four hours. Pack a lunch and plenty of water.

The trail starts one mile west of the Chapel. A series of switchbacks traverse the oak and pine forest below Sentinel Dome. As you climb there will be glimpses of the Valley below and the meandering Merced River. The switchbacks end as the trail contours below the face of Sentinel Rock in a gentle ascent for about three quarters of a mile to another series of switchbacks that bring you to Union Point at 5,800 feet. Another climb brings you to the last half mile of hiking through a red fir forest to Glacier Point. Here at 7,200 feet is one of the most spectacular vistas in the park. If you walk out to the viewing platform, the entire Valley is visible below. From the new star gazing amphitheater you can see Half Dome, Vernal and Nevada Falls and the Clark Range, a place for memorable photographs.

Courtesy of Yosemite Concession Services

A view of Bridalveil Fall.

Using the Glacier Point Bus

You can take the bus one way to or from Glacier Point between June and November. Since it is hard on your knees and thighs to walk downhill, we suggest hiking up the trail in the morning with lunch at the top and riding the bus back to the Valley.

Hiking

From Bridalveil Creek on the old Wawona Road.

© Ellie Huggins

El Capitan looms to the left with Half Dome and Clouds Rest in the background. This is the view as you descend on the old Wawona Road.

Start hiking across the road from the Bridalveil parking lot on a visible old roadbed below the level of the highway. Walk west about five to ten minutes until the road trace crosses the highway. Carefully cross the highway and start hiking up the old road. The macadam is still intact in many places, but as you climb parts of the road have been washed out by the 1997 flood that ravaged the Valley. Carefully cross one rock slide in about 35 to 40 minutes of walking. Giant sugar pines line the trail as you climb far above the current highway. A trail from Wawona Tunnel intersects and leads upward to Old Inspiration Point. We suggest, however, that the vistas of El Capitan and Clouds Rest are better if you continue on the road for several switchbacks. Just as the road reaches its westernmost turn, a fallen tree will block further hiking. It is not really necessary to go on, for your return trip will reward you with the same beautiful vistas enjoyed by early stage passengers and automobilists. This road was used from 1875 until the Wawona Tunnel was opened in 1934.

Hiking

A walk on the Big Oak Flat Road

Drive west on Northside Drive to the road marker V9 beyond El Capitan Meadow, a little more than three miles from the Lodge. Turn north up a dirt road and continue turning right until the road makes a 180 degree turn. Park here and start your walk going west.

Walk west gently uphill on the old road for less than a mile to a point where you can see through the trees to the south. You will have the prefect framed picture of the 620-foot Bridalveil Fall. Keep walking a bit farther to a major gully enlarged during the 1997 flood. We do not suggest proceeding beyond this point.

Walking around the Valley without climbing out

Trails are shown in the *Visitor Guide* on both sides of the Valley. You can walk on either side of the Merced River as far as you wish. Stop at one of the official picnic grounds or find a spot by the river. If you want a long hike, go as far as Bridalveil Fall, about four miles from the Chapel. Be sure to take your camera as famous vistas will appear around every corner.

Yosemite Mountaineering School for rock climbing in the Valley
209-372-8344

From mid-April until October the Yosemite Mountaineering School conducts classes for budding and experienced rock climbers. Ever since the face of El Capitan was conquered by daring climbers in the 1950s, enthusiasts of the sport have flocked to the mecca of rock climbing. The guides are recognized as some of the finest mountaineers in the country. The school prides itself on taking care that its clients learn good skills in a safe environment.

Classes meet daily at 8:30 a.m. and you may rent any equipment needed. At least three are needed for a class.

Courtesy of Yosemite Concession Services

Students of the climbing school learn the art of belaying.

Horseback Riding

Yosemite Valley Stables

Open April to November.
Reservations can be made at the stable, with the Tour/Information Desk at your hotel or by calling them at 209-372-8348.

Yosemite Valley Stables

A daily two-hour scenic ride takes you to Mirror Lake. The half-day ride climbs out of the Valley to Clark's Point above Vernal and Nevada Falls.

An all-day ride offers you a chance to see some of the best sights in the park, starting at 8:00 a.m. and returning by 5:00 p.m. The tours go to Glacier Point or Half Dome. If you would never hike these long treks, here is your way to get out of the Valley and let the horse do the climbing. Saddlebags are provided for your picnic, water, camera and extra jacket or poncho. Weather can be changeable and you don't want to be cold riding.

Courtesy of Yosemite Concession Services

Helpful staff of the Yosemite Stables make sure that all is well before you start riding.

Bicycling

There is no better way to see the Valley than on a bicycle. With 12 miles of trails, you will get around faster than by walking, and you can use them to get to many trailheads. Bicycles and helmets for all ages and trailers for those too small to ride are available at the Yosemite Lodge and Curry Village from mid-March to November. A map of the Valley roads and bike paths is on page 35.

Valley Tour by Bicycle Path

For safe biking with no cars to worry about, try the bicycle paths. From the Lodge tour the Valley in a counterclockwise direction, crossing the meadows to the south side to Cook's Meadow and Sentinel Bridge where you will be rewarded with views of Yosemite Falls. You might want to stop and look in the Chapel, built in 1879. It has been renovated since the disastrous flood of 1997 and is a cherished place for weddings. If you don't want to return to the Lodge, you will need to ride on the road as far as Curry Village where you can pick up the path again to Happy Isle. It continues north toward the trailhead to Mirror Lake. The path west from the Mirror Lake trailhead will take you back to the Lodge. You may not bicycle to Mirror Lake.

Those renting bikes at Curry Village can follow the tour from that point.

Happy Isles

While at Happy Isles be sure to stop in at the Nature Center. Here you will find family oriented natural history displays and books. A self guided nature trail behind the center explores the site of the 1996 slide.

Across the Merced River trails lead to Vernal Fall, Nevada Fall and points beyond. It is less than a mile on a paved path to the footbridge with its beautiful view of Vernal Fall. The Mist Trail to the top is steep and wet during spring and summer with a climb of 400 feet in about a half mile.

Mirror Lake

Plan to park your bikes and hike the one mile to Mirror Lake where interpretive signs describe the story of Mirror Lake. It was actually dammed in the late nineteenth century and there was a bath house and boats on the lake. The dam was breached to let the area return to its natural state. The flood of 1997 has changed the landscape too.

Ranger Programs

Every visitor receives a copy of the current *Yosemite Guide* at the entrance station. The guide lists all the various ranger-led nature walks, hikes and evening programs. The hikes are listed for each day of the week and children's programs are listed in color. Ranger walks at Glacier Point, Mariposa Grove, Wawona, Tuolumne Meadows and Crane Flat are detailed as well.

YOSEMITE VALLEY ACTIVITIES

Le Conte Memorial Lodge
209-372-4542

Open summer thru September.
Wednesday thru Sunday, 10:00 a.m. to
    4:00 p.m.
Friday, Saturday and Sunday, evening
    programs at 8:00 p.m.

Le Conte Memorial Lodge

The lodge is operated by Sierra Club volunteers and features a children's corner and library. Environmental education programs are specially designed for children. The evening programs are listed at the lodge, campgrounds, the Valley Visitor Center and post office.

Junior Rangers are ages 8-10.
Senior Rangers are 11-12.

Park naturalists lead Junior Rangers weekdays to discover special secret places in the Valley. Programs are listed in the Yosemite Guide and operate only in the summer.

Become a Junior or Senior Ranger

Pick up a Junior/Senior Ranger activity paper at the visitor center and attend one program. Recycle your bottles and cans and pick up trash to deposit in bear proof dumpsters. Have your parents check off that you have done all the activities and turn in the activity paper to redeem a badge.

Ranger Programs

Yosemite Theater

The programs here vary by the season. You may see actor Lee Stetson's stunning portrayal of John Muir, complete with Muir's Scottish brogue. Meet paraplegic, former park ranger Mark Wellman in his one-hour film *No Barriers*. The film depicts his climb back from an accident that left him paralyzed from the waist down to feats of extreme sports including ascents of El Capitan and Half Dome.

Camera Walks

On Saturdays the **Ansel Adams Gallery** presents a 1-1/2 hour photography walk and class to help you discover Yosemite through the lens of your camera.

Yosemite Concession Services offers morning camera walks from the Lodge or The Ahwahnee.

Yosemite Field Seminars

The Yosemite Association gives special seminars from birding to alpine flora from February through October in the Valley, at Crane Flat and Tuolumne Meadows.

Yosemite Theater

The theater is located behind the Visitor Center.

Ansel Adams Gallery

The Ansel Adams Gallery is west of the post office near the Visitor Center.

Yosemite Concession Services

Camera walks are listed in the *Yosemite Guide*.

Yosemite Association
209-379-2646
Fax: 209-379-2486

Call or fax them to receive a full schedule. Classes begin at $100 and range from three to seven days. Members get a discount. You are encouraged to join this organization that supports resource management and interpretive services in the park.

YOSEMITE VALLEY ACTIVITIES

Yosemite Valley Winter Activities

Winter in Yosemite is a magical time. The crowds are gone and the vistas wear a snowy mantel. If you want to downhill or cross country ski at Badger Pass you need not bother with chains or wintery driving if you are staying in the Valley. Buses leave every morning for Badger Pass and return during the afternoon. The programs at Badger Pass are discussed beginning on page 120.

Curry Village Ice Skating

Rental skates are available. There is a small fee for each session.

Enjoying a turn at the Curry Village ice rink with Half Dome in the background.

Ice Skating at Curry Village

Imagine yourself ice skating under the awesome view of Half Dome. The rink is open from October through March. You can skate at any of three sessions between 12 noon and 9:30 p.m. A morning session is added on weekends. A fire pit area near a hot drink and snack stand will keep you warm while you wait to skate.

Snowplay

Snowplay is not allowed at Badger Pass. See page 118 for a description of the snowplay area outside the park at Fish Camp. An official snowplay area is at the Crane Flat Campground off Highway 120. See page 222 for a description.

Courtesy of Yosemite Concession Services

Museums

The Valley Visitor Center

Museums are located next door to the Visitor Center.

The Visitor Center has helpful personnel to answer your questions. Maps and books are for sale as well as a *One Day in Yosemite* multilingual program. An audio visual show entitle *Echoes of Tenaya* is shown regularly in the West Auditorium. It will give you a good introduction to the splendors of Yosemite.

The Yosemite Museum

The museum is west of the Visitor Center. There are books and Native American arts and displays that interpret the cultural history of Yosemite's native tribes, the Miwok and Paiute.

The Indian Village of Ahwahnee

Walk around the village behind the museum to learn about the Ahwahneeche and their way of life. Demonstrations of basket weaving and games take place occasionally. Check at the gift shop for information about times for these special activities.

Courtesy of Yosemite Concession Services

One of the dwellings in the Village of Ahwahnee.

Basket weaving, traditional games or beadwork demonstrations take place at the Museum or in the village. The self-guided trail around the village interprets the life of the Ahwahneeche who lived in the Valley for centuries.

YOSEMITE VALLEY ACTIVITIES

Art Galleries and Programs

The Museum Gallery is not open all the time. The hours are usually posted.

The Museum Gallery

The gallery exhibits historic art from the Yosemite Museum or other exhibits, some selected from juried competitions.

The Ansel Adams Gallery
209-372-4413

Summer, 9:00 a.m. to 6:00 p.m., after November 1, 9:00 a.m. to 5:00 p.m.

The Ansel Adams Gallery

The gallery exhibits the works of Ansel Adams and other photographers. The gallery sponsors regular camera walks on weekends. Be sure to check the *Visitor Guide* for times and meeting places.

Art Activity Center

The center is located at the east end of the Village mall next to the Versatel machine. It is open daily, 9:30 a.m. to 5:00 p.m. Classes are generally from 10:30 a.m. to 2:00 p.m. during spring, summer and fall.

The Art Activity Center

Free art classes are offered to those interested in learning different techniques or just brushing up on your skills. Everything from water color to sketching in black or color or even painting on silk is possible. You can purchase supplies at the center.

Special Events

Special events take place in the fall and winter sponsored by the Yosemite Concession Services. Some are on a lottery and all have package prices including overnight stays. Call 559-252-4848 for reservations.

October

Wawona Autumn Golf Package
Sunday through Thursday enjoy two nights lodging in a room without bath and nine holes of golf each day.

November and December

Vintners' Holidays
California's finest winemakers offer samples of their wines at presentations in The Ahwahnee Great Lounge. The Vintners' Banquet follows in The Ahwahnee Dining Room featuring four wines, each carefully paired with a course of the meal.

The Bracebridge Dinner
A seventeenth century English manor house celebration—one of Yosemite's grandest traditions.

New Year's Eve Dinner
Celebrate the New Year with a swing band at The Ahwahnee by lottery only. See page 6 for information about the lottery for both these events.

January and February

Chefs' Holidays
Great chefs give demonstrations, tastings and a gourmet banquet in The Ahwahnee Dining Room.

March

Yosemite Nordic Holidays
On the first Saturday in March join skiers for a 17-km cross country ski race at Badger Pass.

Yosemite Spring Ski Festival
A winter carnival takes place at Badger Pass on the last weekend in the ski season with a dual slalom plus costume and obstacle course races for all.

Courtesy of Yosemite Concession Services

A wintry view of El Capitan across the Merced River.

Looking west into the Merced Canyon from Highway 41 into the Valley.

Introduction to Highway 41

Springtime alternate route to Bass Lake via North Fork

It will take a bit longer but Road 200 to North Fork with a stop at the Sierra Mono Indian Museum is a flower-filled trip through the rolling countryside of the lower foothills. Cattle graze on the early grasses in oak-studded meadows. If you are on your way to Bass Lake, this could be the shortest and easiest route. When you are in North Fork, you are in the exact center of California.

Sierra Mono Indian Museum
Road 225 at Road 228
North Fork
559-877-2115
Open Tuesday thru
Saturday.

Everyone in the family will like the Mono Indian Museum here. The Tettleton Wildlife collection is one of the finest in the state. Mountain lions, grizzly and black bears, moose, wolves, antelope, plus many smaller creatures and birds are displayed in dioramas of their natural habitats. There are beautiful baskets and arrowheads from nearby archaeological digs as well as gifts and books to buy.

Like an arrow pointing north, Highway 41 leaves Fresno to cross its suburban extensions and nearby rich agricultural lands. In 14 miles, Highway 145 intersects from Madera and Highway 99 to the west. From this point on the landscape takes on the typical rolling typography of the Sierra foothills where cattle ranches abound. Twelve miles from Highway 145, Road 200 heads northeast toward North Fork and thence to Bass Lake.

Climbing toward Coarsegold at 2,000 feet you will notice the first digger pines with their sparse gray-green needles interspersed with blue oak, a deciduous oak whose leaves have a blue tint.

Coarsegold was settled long before other towns in the area. It began life in 1849 as a mining camp, acquiring its name from Texas miners who in 1851 anglicized the Mexican name for the area *Oro Grosso*.

James Savage established a trading post on the creek here, and just as he had done elsewhere, used the local native tribes to pan for gold. He traded the gold for baubles and cloth. The Native Americans here were affected by the actions of local miners, who filed claims on their

Introduction to Highway 41

land and dug it up looking for gold, in the process cutting the natives off from their traditional resources and way of life.

The 1851 Indian attack on miners at Savage's Coarsegold trading post precipitated the Mariposa Indian War and later the discovery of Yosemite Valley. (See page 14 for the full story of James Savage and the Mariposa Battalion.)

However, Coarsegold was not destined to be a major gold country town. In the summer of 1852 miners fled a malaria epidemic that swept through the area. By the 1860s quartz mining had taken over and only the Chinese were left to glean the tailings of placer mining.

Coarsegold had a brief reincarnation when tourism to Yosemite's Wawona picked up in 1876. The town was on the way for travelers heading to Ahwahnee and Wawona. However, when the train to Raymond provided Henry Washburn's stages with a closer connection to Wawona, Coarsegold was cut off from tourist traffic until the current highway from Fresno was built in 1930. Coarsegold is growing again as retirees and valley residents seek homes in the foothills.

**Yosemite Gallery and
  Indian Territory
35463 Hwy. 41
Coarsegold
559-683-8727**

This is a good place to stop and let everyone stretch legs, pan for gold and take part in a demonstration of Indian life and culture. The children may get to play the drums and parents will delight in the vast array of Indian art and jewelry. Gold panning takes place daily between 10:00 a.m. and 4:00 p.m. in the summer and five days a week in the winter.

HWY. 41

Courtesy of Yosemite Gallery Indian Territory

"Gabby" the Coarsegold Prospector invites you to pan for gold. The statue was carved from a single cedar tree by artist Miles Tucker.

Introduction to Highway 41

The Wawona Hotel

The current Wawona Hotel has been welcoming visitors for more than a hundred years. This lovely Victorian inn sits on a grassy knoll overlooking its meadow. Part of the meadow is a nine-hole golf course, one of the most scenic in California. To stay here you will need to make a reservation through the Yosemite Concession Services. Just up the road there are many places to stay at the Redwoods Cottages in Wawona and in Yosemite West, a private development that is one of the best kept secrets in the park. Wawona is also the site of the Yosemite History Center where you can walk across the covered bridge built by Washburn to see buildings from Yosemite's past.

Driving to Mariposa Grove

Off season you can drive to the Mariposa Grove of Big Trees where a tram and trails take you to see the best specimens of the giants of the forest. In summer, you are encouraged to take a free shuttle bus from the entrance or from Wawona.

Highway 41 enters Oakhurst in seven miles where it intersects with the southern-most point of Highway 49. A town grew along both highways when the new road was completed in 1930. However, it is only in the last ten years or so that new businesses and lodging have come to the area. The road begins the ascent to the southern entrance to Yosemite National Park just outside town. Three miles after the Highway 49 intersection, Road 222 heads east five miles to Bass Lake with its many campgrounds and water related activities.

Your journey continues through a forest of black oak, ponderosa pine and occasional sugar pine. In ten miles you come to the entrance to the Yosemite Mountain Sugar Pine Railroad with its steam train rides into the valley where turn-of-the-century loggers worked for the Madera Sugar Pine Lumber Company.

Soon you are in Fish Camp, a small community just minutes from the park. The lodging possibilities here are discussed beginning on page 75. The park entrance is at 5,100 feet where you may turn right to the Mariposa Grove of Big Trees or left to the Wawona Hotel and Yosemite Valley.

Introduction to Highway 41

There are 25 winding miles from Wawona to Inspiration Point. After the turnoff to Badger Pass at Chinquapin, you pass through stark reminders of the 1989 fire. The conflagration swept through Foresta across the Merced River canyon and jumped this section of Highway 41. Hardly a pine or fir was spared but you will notice encouraging sprouts of green from oak and manzanita crowns. You leave the burn area and pass through Wawona tunnel to Inspiration Point, the most dramatic and photographed view of the Yosemite Valley.

The stately sugar pine can be seen above the road in many places along the drive.

A wintery view of Half Dome from Inspiration Point.

Courtesy of Yosemite Concession Services

Off the Beaten Path

Blue oaks are deciduous and are scattered across the hillsides near Raymond. They thrive in poor soil with little summer moisture. You will be able to identify them by the bluish tinge of the leaves that look like small versions of the valley or white oak.

The Raymond General Store

If you chose this off the beaten path trip, the Raymond General Store is well worth a lunch stop. Step back in time here and admire the decorative metal sheets covering the walls inside. The lunch counter serves mammoth burgers with fries and hearty sandwiches. Save room for their homebaked pies.

Alternate Route via Raymond

If you are traveling from the Bay Area via Pacheco Pass, consider taking Highway 152 to Robertson Road that intersects Highway 99 in Chowchilla. Cross Highway 99 to Avenue 26. Follow signs toward Raymond. Jog right on Road 29 to Road 603 that will intersect with Road 600 into Raymond. From there you have a choice of Road 600 to Ahwahnee, the original route of Henry Washburn's stage line to Wawona, or Road 415 into Coarsegold.

Raymond

Raymond sprang from the ground and grew into a major foothill community when, at the behest of Washburn, Southern Pacific Railroad extended its valley line to Raymond in 1886. Instantly a town emerged with the usual array of hotels and saloons, plus the stables for the Yosemite Stage and Turnpike Company's 700 horses. Because of the tourist traffic, the town became a freight depot for the entire mountain region.

The fortunes of the town increased when Frank Ducy's rocky acreage, known as *Ducy's Rock Pile*, was bought by Frederick Knowles for a

Off the Beaten Path

quarry. He founded the Raymond Granite Company in 1892 and started supplying beautiful, white stone for such buildings as the San Francisco Stock Exchange, City Hall and Hall of Justice.

Raymond enjoyed the boom until 1907, when the Yosemite Valley Railroad opened service from Merced to El Portal and took away the tourist business. Only those people bound for Wawona or the Mariposa Grove used Washburn's stages. However, the granite company continued to employ 600 men, whose families still lived in Raymond and nearby Knowles.

The depression dealt a blow to the economies of both towns, forcing the granite company into bankruptcy in 1938. When concrete was introduced, granite production ceased. The railroad pulled out in 1956, signalling the end.

While the town of Knowles has disappeared, Raymond continues as a small rural community. If you stop here, you will join many famous people who have passed this way—President Theodore Roosevelt, the Rockefellers, the Astors and the Mellons.

The Knowles Quarry

Road 606 leaves Raymond south of town and will lead you to the quarry. It is easily visible ahead. The quarry is back in limited operation and can boast of supplying its fine marble for the Mormon Temple in Oakland.

Hills Pride Inn

On Road 606 you will come upon Hills Pride Inn, a watering hole since 1915. It stands on a hill to your left about a mile down the road. Stop in and the owner, Robert Casaurang, who has spent his life here, will gladly dispense tales of the quarry's glory days along with a cold beer. He might even share his photo files of bygone times. Hills Pride Inn sports dollar bills pinned to the ceiling, and if you ask, Robert will take your dollar, recite the rules and give you three tries. Those interested in history will find him a treasure trove of information.

Hills Pride Inn.

© Ellie Huggins

HWY. 41

Courtesy of the National Park Service, Yosemite

Driving through the Tunnel Tree in the 1930s. Unfortunately the tree succumbed in the 1980s. You can no longer drive through this part of Mariposa Grove, but you can take a tram or walk beneath these hallowed trees on our hikes described on page 106.

Lodging along Highway 41

Lodging possibilities are legion in the Oakhurst gateway. You can find a five-star chateau in Oakhurst, a condominium at water's edge in Bass Lake, or rooms at one of the many bed and breakfast inns or motels. Fourteen miles from the park entrance, Oakhurst (2300 feet) is a modest-sized town strung out along Highway 41 near the intersection of Highway 49. Ahwahnee is five miles west on Highway 49. Bass Lake (3,400 feet) has long been a destination for southern Californians and is five miles east of Highway 41 via Road 222. Fish Camp with two resort hotels and a couple of B&B's is less than a mile from the park's south gate. There are also interesting places to stay near Wawona and in Yosemite West, just outside the park boundary near Chinqaupin.

Staying in the Oakhurst area affords the widest possible range of activities in the Sierra National Forest and the southern section of the park. From bicycle trips to horseback rides into the Mariposa Grove, or fishing for the famous bass of Bass Lake, there is something for everyone in the family.

The lodging choices are described on the following pages alphabetically in each community.

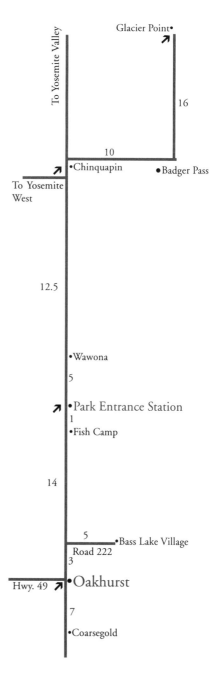

Bed and Breakfast Inns

Apple Blossom Inn
44606 Silver Spur Trail
Ahwahnee, CA 93601
559-642-2001 888-687-4281
www.sierranet.net/web/apple
$80 - $120

Directions:
Drive west on Highway 49 eight miles to Silver Spur Trail. Turn right and follow the road to the end.

Special features:
Six acres surrounding the house feature an organic apple farm. Owner Lance Hays encourages guests to pick apples in season to take home. When his daughter is home from the Culinary Institute of America, she is the sous chef at Erna's Elderberry House. She occasionally helps prepare the breakfasts, a treat for those staying at the inn.

The Homestead
41110 Road 600
Ahwahnee, CA 93601
559-683-0495
www.sierranet.net/homestead
$115 - $149

Special features:
Your kitchen is stocked daily with muffins, fruit, coffee and teas for breakfast. There is an extensive video library, but you are more likely to spend the evening watching the moon come up over the hills from your private porch. You will enjoy a luxury vacation in the quiet beauty of the Sierra foothills here. The Homestead is smoke free.

Apple Blossom Inn

Lance Hays pioneered B&B's in the area. He built Apple Blossom Inn as a charming country house with three rooms with private baths, TVs and computer jacks. The downstairs room has an outside entrance. Upstairs has one room with a queen bed and daybed, and a second with a double bed. These are ideal for families or couples traveling together. The gourmet country breakfasts include special quiches and homebaked breads. Afternoon and evening snacks keep the hunger pangs at bay. The owner lives off the premises, so the entire house is for the guests to enjoy.

The Homestead

The main house plus four uniquely decorated one-bedroom cottages of adobe and stone sit on an oak-studded hillside. Fireplaces warm each cozy cottage furnished with comfortable couches, TV with VCR, kitchen and dining area. A smaller, fifth unit is over the stable. You will enjoy many of the services of a resort, concierge assistance, gas barbeques for your evening cookouts, massages, satellite TV and air conditioning.

Bed and Breakfast Inns

Silver Spur Bed and Breakfast

The small house next door to Apple Blossom Inn is more like a homestay. Two rooms upstairs share a bath, while the room downstairs has an outside entrance and its own bath. There is a barbeque that guests can use. Breakfast is continental-style. There are no special afternoon snacks, but there is a coffee pot for guests in the hall.

Silver Spur Bed and Breakfast
44625 Silver Spur Trail
Ahwahnee, CA 93601
559-683-2896 888-359-9178
www.sierranet.net/web/silver
$50 - $60

Directions:
Follow the directions to Apple Blossom Inn. The Silver Spur is the first driveway on the left.

Special features:
Because you are really staying in someone's home, it is very economical with no frills.

Courtesy of the Homestead

Proprietors Cindy Brooks and Larry Ends sit in front of one of the cottages at the Homestead.

Bed and Breakfast Inns

Chateau du Sureau
48688 Victoria Lane
P.O. Box 577
Oakhurst, CA 93644
559-683-6860
Fax: 559-683-0800
www.relaischateaux.fr/sureau
$335 - $485

Special Features:
Words cannot describe the luxury of this intimate inn. It is truly a world class accommodation. Erna's staff will take special care of you and try to fill your every wish. The entire chateau may be rented for a very special wedding setting, anniversary or family reunion.

Beautiful Chateau du Sureau sits on a hill above the pool.

Courtesy of Chateau du Sureau

Chateau du Sureau

An elegant chateau is connected to Erna's Elderberry House restaurant. From the moment you drive up you are treated as an honored guest. It is the only northern California establishment to receive a five diamond classification from the Automobile Association and is one of only 24 in the United States that is a member of the world-famous Relais & Chateaux hotels. The rooms are spacious, each decorated with beautiful antiques. Erna is famous for her attention to detail, and the rooms and service here reflect this. Aperitifs are served in the Grand Salon furnished with chairs and couches in conversational groupings. A large brick fireplace, exquisite antique tables and a domed music room with a nineteenth century grand piano complete your feeling of having entered another world. Your gourmet breakfast is prepared on the premises and served in the Provencal dining room that features a hand-painted tile fireplace. In warm weather breakfast is served on a patio that is surrounded by colorful gardens. With a swimming pool and Erna's five-star restaurant just steps away, you may just stay put to relax in this lap of luxury and be pampered for a while.

Bed and Breakfast Inns

China Creek Bed and Breakfast

Situated on more than an acre not far from China Creek, a former ranch-style home has been converted into a bed and breakfast. Three rooms are entered off a central atrium, two with a shared bath. One unit has its own entrance. A separate cottage with two bedrooms, livingroom, kitchette, TV, and washer and dryer, is ideal for a family. Breakfast is served in the atrium.

China Creek Bed and Breakfast
49522 Road 426
Oakhurst, CA 93644
559-642-6248   888-246-0720
Fax: 559-683-3216
www.sierranet.net/web/china
$85 - $140

Special Features:
If you are looking for a place with plenty of space for the children to run around, or are planning a family reunion, this might be the spot for you. There is an outdoor unheated pool for cooling off on summer days.

Hound's Tooth Inn

The Kiehlmeier and Williams families built this charming Victorian-style inn in 1997. There are twelve units, each designed with a different decor. Four rooms have king-size beds, two with fireplaces. Five rooms have jacuzzis. All other rooms have queen beds. Bathrooms have either a tub or stall shower with your sink in the room. The units are spacious, with either a couch or two chairs and table. A patio in front of the building invites you to sit outside and meet the other guests. In good weather you can enjoy your breakfast here, which features a quiche of the day and homebaked muffins, plus cereals, juice, fruit and bagels.

Hound's Tooth Inn
42071 Hwy. 41
Oakhurst, CA 93644
559-642-6600   888-642-6610
Fax: 559-658-2946
www.sierranet.net/web/tooth
$85 - $135

Special Features:
Your hosts are happy to help you get reservations for dinner or other activities in the area. Wine and soft drinks are served every afternoon in the breakfast room.

Bed and Breakfast Inns

Norja Bed and Bath Inn
43547 Whispering Pines Dr.
Oakhurst, CA 93644
559-642-6519

Norja Bed and Bath Inn

When we visited this new inn, it was still a work in progress and construction was underway. We suggest that you check it out before booking a room.

Pine Rose Inn Bed and Breakfast
Road 222
P.O. Box 2341
Oakhurst, CA 93644
559-642-2800
$39 - $89

Pine Rose Inn Bed and Breakfast

The inn was being remodelled after the major road construction on Road 222 to Bass Lake. Again, we suggest that you visit before making a reservation.

Sierra Sky Ranch
50552 Road 632
Sky Ranch Rd.
Oakhurst, CA 93644
559-683-8040
Fax: 559-658-7484
www.sierranet.net/skyranch
$75 - $120

Special Features:
If you are looking for an inn with an atmosphere of bygone days, this is a hostelry that will please you. The helpful and courteous staff will make you feel like you are guests of the former ranch family. Lewis Creek and its swimming holes, picnic spots and the trails on the property offer plenty of activities for a family or business group who want something different. The country dining room and bar on the premises means you won't have to drive away for dinner.

Sierra Sky Ranch

In the 1870s it was a cattle ranch, then a dude ranch, and in the 1950s it was transformed into a golf resort that closed in 1980. The current owners are giving the place new life. They have retained the charm of the historical ranch on its 14 acres. The great room has lots of large, comfortable couches, hunting trophies on the walls, a stone fireplace and old family photos on a piano just right for sing-a-longs. With 25 units, including a bunk room for kids, a pool, and Lewis Creek nearby, Sierra Sky Ranch is a wonderful place for a retreat, family reunion or wedding.

Motels

Best Western Yosemite Gateway

The 118 units are situated on a tree-shaded hill with two pools. TVs and phones are in every room with some kitchenettes. Pets are allowed.

Best Western Yosemite Gateway
40530 Hwy. 41
Oakhurst, CA 93644
559-683-2378 800-545-5462
Fax: 559-683-2378
$50 - $90

Comfort Inn

This typical motel has 113 units with TVs and phones, a pool and spa. Pets are allowed in some units.

Comfort Inn
40489 Hwy. 41
Oakhurst, CA 93644
559-658-7030 800-321-5261
Fax: 559-658-7030
www.yosemite-motels.com
$50 - $120

Holiday Inn Express

The Holiday Inn Express has 42 units with TVs and phones and a small pool.

Holiday Inn Express
40662 Hwy. 41
Oakhurst, CA 93644
559-642-2525 800-432-9746
www.sierranet.net/web/holidayinn
$49 - $175

Oakhurst Lodge

This economical lodge with a pool has 60 units with TVs, phones and microwaves.

Oakhurst Lodge
40302 Hwy. 41
Oakhurst, CA 93644
559-683-4417 800-655-6343
Fax: 559-683-4417
www.sierranet.net/oklodge
$40 - $70

Ramada Limited

There are 69 units with pool and spa. TV's and phones and microwaves are in the rooms. Pets are allowed.

Ramada Limited
48800 Royal Oaks Dr.
Oakhurst, CA 93644
559-658-5500 800-658-2888
Fax: 559-683-5500
$55 - $130

Shilo Inn

You'll find 80 units with a pool and spa. Rooms have TVs, phones and microwaves. They serve a continental breakfast.

Shilo Inn
40644 Hwy. 41
Oakhurst, CA 93644
559-683-3386 800-222-2244
Fax: 209-683-3386
www.sierranet.net/web/shilo
$69 - $125

Bed and Breakfast Inns

Bass Lake Lodge
P.O. Box 105
54300 North Shore Rd.
Bass Lake, CA 93604
559-642-2399
Fax: 559-642-6132
E-mail: bllodge@sierratel.com
$125 - $175

Special features:
This is a nonsmoking lodge even outside. Ed has been coming to Yosemite since the 1940s and was former general manager of the MCA concession in Yosemite National Park. He is a student of Yosemite history and can probably answer any question you have. Ed and his wife, Janet, are offering a special behind-the-scenes look at the park called *Yosemite Reflections* . For three days you will enjoy slide shows, lectures and field trips to the park as well as all your meals.

Jonnie's Inn
P.O. Box 717
54323 North Shore Rd.
Bass Lake, CA 93604
559-642-4966
www.sierratel.com/jonnies
$95 - $135

Bass Lake Lodge

Owner Ed Hardy has created a beautiful, stately home on the north shore of Bass Lake, next door to Ducey's and the Pines Resort. He built it using sugar pine cut from his own ranch near the Merced Grove. Each of the four rooms is oriented to the lake with is own outdoor sitting area. A large game room has a wall-sized, computer-controlled TV, a golf putting course set into the carpet and pool table. Guests have use of the dock and free peddle boats, canoe and rowboat. The lodge does not serve breakfast, but the rooms have refrigerators and microwaves, and restaurants are just few steps away.

Jonnie's Inn Bed and Breakfast

Innkeepers Gene and Jonnie Baker invite you to their home that features two individually decorated rooms with bath. The location is ideal, just across from the Pines Village. A third room is being added in the summer of 1999. Jonnie serves a full country breakfast.

Resonts North Shore

Ducey's on the Lake

The funky old former Ducey's burned down in 1988, but it has been revived and rebuilt by the Pines Resort. It now has an upscale restaurant and 20 suites that overlook the lake. All rooms come with in-room spas, refrigerators, microwaves, TVs and sitting area, as well as a deck overlooking the lake. There is a lakeside pool and sunning area reserved for guests of Ducey's and the more modestly priced Pines Resort chalets.

Ducey's on the Lake
P.O. Box 109
Bass Lake, CA 93604
800-350-7463
$105 - $298

Special Features:
All the water related sports for which Bass Lake is famous are in your front yard.

The Pines Resort

The 73 chalets are situated on a tree-covered hill east of Ducey's. Each unit has one bedroom, living room and kitchen. Some have lake views.

The Pines Resort
P.O. Box 109
Bass Lake, CA 93604
559-642-3121 800-350-7463
Fax: 559-642-3902
www.basslake.com
$88 - $173

Courtesy of Ed Hardy

Bass Lake Lodge.

Resorts South Shore

Miller's Landing
37976 Road 222
Wishon, CA 93699
559-642-3633
www.millerslanding.com
$30 - $145

Special Features:
The general store and restaurant can satisfy all your needs. Some units are winterized for use between October 1 and April 30. These can be rented at a 20% discount off summer rates.

Summer only.
The Forks Resort
39150 Road 222
Bass Lake, CA 93604
559-642-3737
$75 - $125

Special Features:
The resort is at the fork of Road 426 from Oakhurst and Road 222 around the lake. You can bring your own boat and reserve a slip at their dock.

Miller's Landing

Rick Miller has owned the landing since 1982. It is a tradition with many families from southern California, so you will need to book early if you want a cabin at this southwest tip of Bass lake, far away from the hubbub of the north shore. Boaters adore this resort, which is close to the free Wishon boat ramp. The least expensive cabins have one bedroom with a refrigerator and stove but outside water faucet. Larger two-bedroom, two-bath units sleep eight and come with all linens provided, a satellite TV and barbeque. The marina provides rentals for all water-related activities.

The Forks Resort

This location has been a favorite of families for generations. Two of the eleven units at the Forks have two bedrooms. The rest are cabins with one-bedroom and decks or patios. One two-bedroom unit has a closed-in porch and a fireplace. Linens are furnished but there is no maid service. All cabins have full kitchens, but you won't want to miss the best-on-the-lake Fork's Burgers at the restaurant, general store and deli. The store personnel can help with all fishing gear and licenses.

Bed and Breakfast Inns

At Fish Camp all of the activities of the southern park are close at hand. You will find golf at Wawona, the Mariposa Grove, horseback riding at Yosemite Trail Pack Station and many hikes, all listed in the Activities section beginning on page 91.

Apple Tree Inn

The 54 units are arranged in chalets on the hill above the main lodge. The configuration is the same in each building—one unit on each floor, with a fireplace, VCR, microwave and coffee maker. The room rate includes a continental breakfast in the main lodge.

Open all year.
Apple Tree Inn
P.O. Box 41
1110 Hwy. 41
Fish Camp CA 93623
559-683-5111 888-683-5111
Fax: 559-642-6280
$80 - $125

Special Features:
The inn has a heated indoor pool and spa, a racquetball court and a conference center.

Karen's Bed and Breakfast

Karen welcomes you to her quaint bed and breakfast located in the forest off Highway 41. Her wooded location assures quiet, cool nights in summer. Two rooms have queen beds and one has twins. A full country breakfast will send you on your way to the many activities nearby. She serves afternoon snacks and is happy to share her library of books about Yosemite.

Open all year.
Karen's Bed and Breakfast
P.O. Box 8
1144 Railroad Ave.
Fish Camp, CA 93623
559-683-4550 800-346-1443
www.sierranet.net/web/karen
$90

Special Features:
Railroad Ave. is west of Hwy 41 just before the Apple Tree Inn. Karen is an ebullient hostess who will help you plan your days in the park. You will have a true B&B experience here.

Bed and Breakfast Inns

Open April thru October.
Owl's Nest Lodging
P.O. Box 33
1237 Hwy. 41
Fish Camp, CA 93623
559-683-3484
Fax: 559-683-3486
$70 - $95

Special Features:
The chalets are spacious with plenty of room for families with children. Babies in diapers are free.

Owl's Nest Lodging

This is not a bed and breakfast, but the four A-Frame chalets offer an economical alternative for families. Each has a barbeque, TV and VCR, and linens are provided. Three chalets have sleeping lofts. All have kitchens, a sitting area and back porches away from the street. The fourth features two separate guest rooms with private baths above a garage.

Open all year
Yosemite Fish Camp B&B
P.O. Box 25
Railroad Avenue
Fish Camp, CA 93623
559-683-7426
$50 - $80

Special Features:
The owners offer discounts on rides at their stable. Winter guests can order a special sleigh ride. They welcome children. A barbeque and swing set are at your disposal.

Yosemite Fish Camp Inn and B&B

This B&B was the first in the area. It is now operated by the owners of Yosemite Trail Pack Station. The decor is definitely western ranch, with three units, two with queens and one with a double bed that share a spacious bath.

Resonts

Tenaya Lodge Resort Hotel

Although the setting is not the Ahwahnee, the entrance hall is reminiscent of the cathedral ceiling and spacious feeling of that famous hotel. This is a full-service resort with a concierge to arrange any number of activities for you. There are two pools, indoor and outdoor, a coffee shop and two restaurants. The grounds still need to recover from the construction, but the rooms are spacious and those on the upper floors have views of nearby Sierra peaks.

Tenaya Lodge Resort Hotel
P.O. Box 159
1122 Hwy. 41
Fish Camp, CA 93623
559-683-6555 800-635-5807
www.tenayalodge.com
$69 - $239

Special Features:
The resort has a conference center. The weight room has all manner of equipment to keep you in shape if you didn't get enough hiking or skiing. You can also book a massage.

© Ellie Huggins

The Tenaya Lodge portal.

Motels/Hotels

Open April 1 to October 31.
White Chief Mountain Lodge
P.O. Box 70
Fish Camp, CA 93623
559-683-5444
Fax: 559-683-2615
$60 - $115

White Chief Mountain Lodge

Here is a truly economical stay. The building is an old style motel with no TVs or phones in the rooms. The location is quiet, about 300 yards off Highway 41, and a trout stream on the property beckons anglers. There is a full-service restaurant and bar on the premises serving breakfast and dinner daily.

Open April thru October.
Narrow Gauge Inn
48571 Hwy. 41
Fish Camp, CA 93623
559-683-7720
$85 - $130

Special Features:
There is a heated swimming pool, hot bubbling pool and a creekside nature trail on the property. Steam train buffs will love being next to the Yosemite Mountain Sugar Pine Railroad.

Narrow Gauge Inn

An old motel was rebuilt in 1972 and transformed into a rustic country inn, complete with large, beautifully decorated rooms, all with views of the forest. Some rooms have creekside locations with balconies. The restaurant and Buffalo Bar on the premises offer excellent dining. (See page 88 for details.) All the rooms have TVs and private baths. Children under three are free and you can obtain cribs for an extra charge. The setting among the pines and oaks is beautiful and the location, just four miles from the south entrance to the park, makes this an ideal spot for a comfortable stay close to all the region's activities.

Hotels

The Wawona Hotel

Yosemite's oldest hotel, a National Historic Landmark, offers rooms with and without bath in a charming Victorian setting. Visitors can step back in time in one of the several buildings on the property. Many rooms are furnished with antiques and some baths have clawfoot tubs. The Annex rooms open onto a verandah where you can relax in wicker chairs before dinner. With a fine dining room on the premises and Tom Bopp playing your favorites on the 1906 Knabe parlor-grand before dinner, you have all the ingredients for a perfect holiday.

The Wawona Hotel
Reservations made through Yosemite Concession Services.
559-252-4848
See page 4 for information about the best way to reserve a room in the park.
$80 - $115

Special Features:
The hotel is closed in January and February until the boiler for heating can be fixed to make a stay here comfortable. The hotel may be open year-round in 2000. The rooms without baths have showers and bathrooms down the hall. There are no TVs or telephones.

Courtesy of Yosemite Concession Services

A room at the Wawona Hotel with its turn-of-the-century furniture.

Bed and Breakfast Inns

Closed January and February.
Yosemite West High Sierra Bed
** and Breakfast**
7460 Henness Ridge Road
Yosemite, CA 95389
209-372-4808
www.sierranet.net/web/sierra
$125 - $190

Yosemite West High Sierra Bed and Breakfast

Three rooms with queen beds, a spacious community room with a dining table and couches await guests of this bed and breakfast inn. Owners Karen and Bob know the park intimately and will be happy to help you plan your days. They will lend you a backpack, guidebook and maps to make your foray most enjoyable. Their spacious decks look west toward magnificent sunsets, and away from suburban lights you will be amazed at the spectacular night sky. They serve a simple breakfast of rolls, fruit, juice and coffee or tea.

Courtesy of Yosemite Concession Services

The lone Jeffrey pine on Sentinel Dome. See page 109 for a description of the family hike here.

Bed and Breakfast Inns

The Yosemite Peregrine B&B

The former judge in Yosemite Valley, Don Pitts, and his artist wife, Kay, welcome you into their home and the newly constructed addition, Falcon's Crest. The rooms in the main house are individually decorated with Kay's murals on the walls. The upstairs living room where wine and appetizers are served each afternoon has unsurpassed views of the region. Two rooms have queen beds and one room with a king-size bed also has a fireplace. Breakfast is served in the dining room, or you can pack a picnic breakfast to enjoy on the lookout less than a mile away. A continental breakfast is served in Falcon's Crest.

**The Yosemite Peregrine B&B and
Falcon's Crest
7509 Henness Circle
Yosemite West, CA 95389
209-372-8517 800-396-3639
Fax: 209-372-4241
www.yosemitewest.com/
         peregrin.htm
$120 - $175**

Special Features:
Hiking and ski trails start from the backyard and a hot tub will soothe tired muscles at the end of your day of mountain activity. Falcon's Crest has three bed and breakfast rooms and an upstairs home with two bedrooms, kitchen and livingroom, perfect for a family group. All the furnishings are tastefully selected for comfort and beauty.

Yosemite Falls Bed and Breakfast

Your hosts, the Ingrams, have 22 years of knowledge about the park. Their inn is in the first house built in Yosemite West. The rooms feature king and queen-sized beds, TV and individual balconies. They serve afternoon wine and appetizers, and a full breakfast which often includes tri-tip steak and eggs.

**Yosemite Falls B&B
P.O. Box 233
Yosemite, CA 95389
209-375-1414
www.yosemitefalls.com
Rooms start at $125.**

Special Features:
You can enjoy a game of pool or enjoy reading from their supply of historical books about Yosemite. You won't go to bed hungry either as special cookies will adorn your pillow at night.

Condominiums and Homes

The Redwoods Cottages
P.O. Box 2085
Wawona Station
Yosemite National Park, CA 95389
209-375-6666
Fax: 209-375-6400
$82 - $414

Special features:
Linens are provided, but no maid service unless you pay extra and the maids don't do dishes.

Yosemite Four Seasons
P.O. Box 2085
Yosemite National Park, CA 95389
800-669-9300
209-372-4691 (on-site phone)
www.yosemitelodging.com
$82 - $125

Special Features:
Propane barbeques are provided and there is a coin operated laundry. However, there are no restaurants nearby. The kitchens are small with no dining area, so the units are cramped for more than two people.

Yosemite West Lodging
P.O. Box 36
Yosemite, CA 95389
209-642-2211 Monday thru Friday
www.yosemitewest.com/
    yoswest.htm
$55 - $345

The Redwoods Guest Cottages

One hundred and twenty-five private homes near Wawona are managed together. The homes vary is size and extras. Some have TV and fireplace or barbeques. The homes can sleep up to 12 people, but most will only accommodate two to four. Only a few homes allow pets.

Yosemite Four Seasons

Forty-seven condominiums located just one-half mile off Highway 41 near Chinquapin have both studio and loft units. The studios have a fold-down queen bed and a queen sofa, bath, kitchen, fireplace and small patio or balcony. The two-story loft units have queen beds upstairs and queen sofa-bed in the living room. Each has kitchen, fireplace and small patio or balcony. Four Seasons also has a few homes to rent.

Yosemite West Lodging

Twenty small cottages have one or two bedrooms with bath, kitchens and satellite TV service. Here is another opportunity to find accommodations near the park and close to skiing at Badger Pass.

Dining

Oakhurst, Fish Camp and Bass Lake offer many dining possibilities, from fast food to Mexican and Oriental cuisine to gourmet dining, as well as pizza and hamburgers for a quick meal or takeout. We cover places that have been reviewed by the author and offer something special.

How we rate restaurants:

$ Inexpensive, including soup or salad—under $15.
$$ Moderate, including soup or salad—under $20.
$$$ Moderately expensive, a la carte—entrées $16 to $22.
$$$$ Expensive, a la carte—entrées over $22.
Tips, wine and tax are not included in our estimates of cost.

Andrade's

J. R. Andrade offers a very solid Italian menu in his little restaurant. There are veal dishes and salmon, interesting pasta offerings, and the meatballs are especially good.

$$
Lunch and dinner, daily.
40291 Junction Drive
Oakhurst
559-658-5929

Crystal Falls Inn

The setting next to Lewis Creek is both elegant and unusual. Decks extending close to the creek are used for cocktails or after-dinner coffee. Each table has a window oriented toward the tree-shaded creek. The menu of California cuisine is limited and the descriptions are often better than the presentation. The food is good, but one would expect better taste for the price. The wine list is fairly extensive, and the desert menu tempting. Certainly the location is one of the most beautiful in the area.

$$$$
Dinner, Wednesday thru Sunday.
Road 222 and Hwy. 41
Oakhurst
559-683-4242

Dining

$$

Lunch and dinner, daily.

41939 Hwy. 41

Oakhurst

559-683-6668

El Cid Mexican Cuisine

El Cid received the Best of the Valley Mexican Restaurant citation in 1991. The restaurant moved to Oakhurst and continues to serve its award-winning Mexican cuisine. Fajitas are offered with beef, chicken or shrimp. There are 92 different combination plates to choose from, including an enchilada vera cruz with succulent shrimp and a special sauce. The Tequila Margaritas are good enough to bring you in just for a cocktail.

$$$$

Brunch, Saturday and Sunday.

Lunch, Tuesday thru Friday.

Dinner, daily.

48688 Victoria Lane

Visible from Hwy. 41
  south of Hwy. 49

Oakhurst

559-683-6800

Special features:

Special events occur throughout the year, and for aspiring chefs, Erna offers a cooking school. So be sure to get on her mailing list. The author highly recommends a journey to Yosemite that includes a stop at this remarkable restaurant.

Erna's Elderberry House

Erna Kubin-Clanin was born in Vienna, Austria. Since coming to this country she has combined her prodigious artistic and culinary talents to produce one of the finest dining establishments in the United States. She quotes Oscar Wilde to explain her philosophy for the restaurant (and of course the Chateau next door), "I have only the simplest of tastes; I want only the best." This desire for the best guides every fine creation that comes from the kitchen. The restaurant, open since 1984, has a decor and ambiance reflecting the French countryside of Provence.

Dining

Erna and her executive chef, James Overbaugh, meet weekly to determine what will be presented in the prix fixe, six course dinners. Often without recipes, their creations use the abundance of fresh products from the Central Valley. Every meal is a discovery of new taste sensations. Wines are selected for each course (also prix fixe) or you may choose from an excellent cellar. Not only will you never be disappointed with a meal here, you will remember it always as one of the finest you have eaten. A less expensive way to partake of Erna's creations is to reserve a lunch table, when you can select from a tantalizing menu.

Courtesy of Erna's Elderberry House

The elegant dining room at Erna's.

Oka Japanese Restaurant

This popular restaurant offers both Tepanaki-style dinners, a sushi bar and a regular full menu of Japanese specialties. The tempura is especially light and tasty, and the sushi menu is as extensive as you will find anywhere. If you have a large group, the Tepanaki table can accommodate you while you watch your knife-wielding cook prepare your dinner. Be sure to make reservations on a busy weekend.

$$
Lunch, Monday thru Friday.
Dinner, daily.
40250 Junction Drive
Oakhurst
559-642-4850

Dining

$$
Lunch and dinner, daily.
Hwy. 41 and Hwy. 49
Oakhurst
559-683-7427

Shari D's Great American Steak House

Shari D's is a steak house offering well-cooked charbroiled burgers, steaks, barbeque ribs, pork, chicken and prawns. For lighter eaters, there is a pasta menu or choice of large salads. With a separate children's menu and moderate prices, this a great place for the family.

$$
Dinner, Wednesday thru Sunday.
Brunch, Sunday.
Sky Ranch Road
Oakhurst
559-658-2646

Sunday brunch features champagne and jazz.

Sierra Sky Ranch Restaurant

The steakhouse and saloon is attached to the newly renovated Sierra Sky Ranch Inn and is full of the same Old West, rustic atmosphere. They offer lots of steaks, plus kabobs, barbeque ribs, chicken and large specialty salads.

$$
Breakfast, lunch and dinner, daily.
Hwy. 222 and Hwy. 41
Oakhurst
559-683-5191

Yosemite Forks Mountain House

In a cheerful, spacious dining room with mountain decor and comfortable chairs, the restaurant serves a large choice of pasta, burgers, charbroiled steaks, chicken and seafood. You may select a half order of many of the dishes. Prime rib is served on weekends and all sandwiches come with a choice of soup, salad, coleslaw or fries. The food is delicious and service friendly.

Dining

Ducey's on the Lake

Both the dining room and upstairs bar and grill have the original Ducey's lake view. Lunch in the bar or on the outside deck offers a full menu of appetizers, great hamburgers and large sandwiches. The dinner menu consists of the usual steaks, pasta and fish plus an interesting rack of lamb. The house specialty is seafood Wellington—salmon, satuéed mushrooms and spinach in a puff pastry with beurre blanc. Be sure to check out the historic photos on the walls of the entry hall. These tell the story of the original Ducey's and the Hollywood films that were filmed here.

$$$
Lunch and dinner, daily.
Below Pines Center
Bass Lake
559-642-3121

The Pines Restaurant

The restaurant features steak, chicken, and even roast turkey, as well as a complete menu of burgers and snacks such as pepperoni pizza cheese sticks or hot wings. Southwestern specialties include steak, enchiladas and chimichangas. The fare is reasonably priced and the servings are generous. Try the New York cheesecake topped with strawberries for dessert.

$$
Lunch and dinner, daily.
The Pines Center
Bass Lake
559-642-3233

Dining

$$$
Open May to October.
Dinner, Thursday thru Monday.
48571 Hwy. 41
Fish Camp
559-683-6446

Narrow Gauge Inn

You'll enjoy old fashioned, California hospitality and romance at this inn with three fireplaces, oil lamps, white linen and attentive service. *Wine Spectator* has given the restaurant the dining guide award of excellence. Two wild specialties are worth considering. The venison steaks and the ostrich, raised on the Mono tribe rancheria, are both succulent and tasty and with half the fat of beef. The candlelight setting may be just right for a Swiss fondue for two. The meals come with salad or soup and hot bread baked on the premises.

$$$$
Sierra Restaurant
Dinner, daily.
$$
Jackalope's
Lunch and dinner, daily.
Tenaya Lodge Resort
Fish Camp
559-683-6555

Special Features:
The Sierra Restaurant holds special winemaker dinners throughout the year.

Tenaya Lodge Sierra Restaurant

Executive chef Fred Clabaugh prepares culinary masterpieces featuring California eclectic cuisine. The appetizers could be an entire dinner with a salad or soup. Entrées range from a seafood pasta to lamb shanks osso bucco or herb encrusted pork loin. The wine list is extensive, featuring many local wineries, and the service is attentive. For more informal dining try the **Jackalope's Bar and Grill** where you can enjoy a microbrew with a burger or pizza and dine under the stars in summer.

Dining

The Wawona Hotel

If you are staying in Yosemite West the Wawona dining room offers the best dining close by. It is only 20 minutes to the hotel. They do not take reservations, but it is not a difficult wait sitting in the parlor with Tom Bopp's piano playing to accompany your pre-dinner libations. The menu offers many possibilities from prime rib, an excellent choice, and steaks to chicken, fish and pasta. The food is delicious and attractively presented and the desserts are very tempting. The atmosphere is congenial with many tables near windows looking out on the lawns and grounds.

$$$
May be closed January and February.
Breakfast, lunch and dinner, daily.
209-375-6556

Directions:
Five miles north of the south entrance to Yosemite National Park on Highway 41.

Courtesy of Yosemite Concession Services

The gracious portico of the Wawona Hotel looks much the same as it did one hundred years ago.

Map of the Scenic Byway

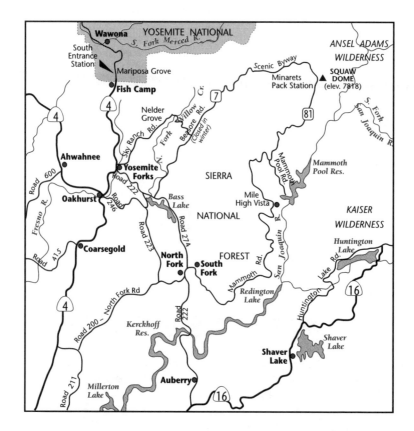

Highway 41 Activities

Winter or summer, the Highway 41 corridor offers a plethora of activities. Not only is the Oakhurst area an easy drive from Highway 99, it is the closest gateway to an area of the park with all kinds of things to do. Nearby Bass Lake offers fishing, boating and swimming, while horseback riding, golf and the high country of the Ansel Adams Wilderness and southern Yosemite National Park can be reached from the Scenic Byway.

Imagine! You can hike in the world-famous Mariposa Grove of Big Trees in the morning, go swimming in Bass Lake in the afternoon, and fish for bass at dusk. The next day you can take a tour that will show you the best of Yosemite Valley while you let someone else do the driving.

Oakhurst and environs are close to all kinds of winter fun. It is a short drive to Badger Pass Ski Area and all the great free cross country skiing and snowshoeing on the Glacier Point Road. You can cross-country ski into the Mariposa Grove, rent snowmobiles at Bass Lake or slide down a hill with the kids near Fish Camp.

Courtesy of Yosemite Concession Services

A skier on the Glacier Point Trail. Imagine skiing with this view for several miles.

Excursions

The Sierra Vista Scenic Byway

Maps and Directions

The Sierra National Forest map marks the byway in red. The starting point is on Sky Ranch Road to the Nelder Grove where the road is dirt for several miles to the intersection with Beasore Road. However, we suggest that you begin at Bass Lake on Beasore Road unless you wish to see the Nelder Grove on the way. See page 105 for a description of this hike.

Hiking to Choquito Pass

If you are looking for a good hike, drive in two miles from Globe Rock on forest road 5S04 to the trailhead. The trail goes to Choquito Lake and the Pass. It is 2.5 miles of steady uphill hiking with 800 feet elevation gain to the pass where you will be looking down into a seldom visited corner of Yosemite National Park. And of course, you can hike farther into the park if you are looking for a longer hike.

Plan a whole day to meander 100 miles through the Sierra Nevada range from Bass Lake to the Mile High Vista where you can see into the San Joaquin River drainage and east to the Minarets. The views are absolutely spectacular, and should you want to stay overnight along the way, there are campgrounds near mountain streams for a secluded car camping experience.

Beasore Road (Road 434) leaves from North Shore Road near Bass Lake Village. The road is paved for 21.5 miles to near Globe Rock. The first winding section climbs through forests of madrone, ponderosa and sugar pine. In 15 miles you are at Jones Store at Beasore Meadows where you can get hamburgers, sandwiches and homemade pie. The area is famous for the great fishing nearby—ask at the store.

The eleven miles after Globe Rock will be on a dirt road. In seven miles you come to the Jackass Lakes trailhead and 0.7 miles farther to the road to the Norris Lake trailhead. The first Jackass Lake is about two miles in with a 1,200-foot elevation gain and the hike to Norris Lake is about the same length and climb.

Excursions

At mile 39 you will come to the turnoff to the Minarets Pack Station. See page 110 for a description of the possible rides here. Shortly the road will begin its descent and be paved again.

The Mile High Vista Point is at mile 67. There is a picnic area and maps describing the unsurpassed views of the faraway peaks of the Minarets which form the backdrop of the Mammoth Lakes area and its famous ski resort and are the headwaters of the San Joaquin River.

The road comes to North Fork at mile 93 where you take Road 274 back to Bass Lake.

Yosemite Sightseeing Tours

Join this group if you want to leave the driving to someone else and see all the best that the Valley has to offer, or have a professional guide show you the Mariposa Grove and Wawona History Center. Tours depart daily from Oakhurst, Bass Lake and Fish Camp. The tour includes in-depth commentary and makes frequent photo stops.

Mammoth Pool Reservoir

At mile 65.2 there is a turnoff to Mammoth Pool on the dammed San Joaquin River. Anglers may wish to explore this, but it is a long way down to the reservoir at 3,500 feet and it is not a particularly special place to picnic.

Yosemite Sightseeing Tours
559-877-8687
www.yosemitetours.com
Reservations required.

Excursions

**Yosemite Mountain Sugar Pine
 Railroad
56001 Hwy. 41
Fish Camp
559-683-7273
Daily, April to October,
 9:00 a.m. to 4:00 p.m.**

The logger steam train runs twice a day in the summer and on weekends the rest of the season. The Jenny cars go every half hour daily, except when the steam train runs.

In summer there are moonlight specials with barbeque dinners, and in July and August a moonlight melodrama by the Golden Chain theater group is part of the evening entertainment.

Yosemite Mountain Sugar Pine Railroad

Bring the camera and the kids young and old to ride behind a real logger steam locomotive or on Jenny cars. Visitors travel a four mile round trip down to the Slab Creek picnic area. With hoots and toots the train makes its journey downhill to the picnic site, where trails lead to an abandoned trestle or to the old sawmill. From 1899 to 1933 the Madera Sugar Pine Lumber Company used a narrow gauge railroad to haul massive logs to the mill at Sugar Pine. From there the lumber traveled a 54-mile flume to Madera. (See page 103 for the Lewis Creek Trail hike that follows the route of the flume.)

This mini railroad trip was the dream of Rudy Stauffer, a Swiss immigrant who owned the Swiss Melody Inn, predecessor of the current Narrow Gauge Inn. Always enamored with the feats of the Shay locomotive, he bought number 10 in 1965 from West Side Lumber Company of Tuolumne, California. He refurbished the engine and on Labor Day 1967 took his first passengers on an a ride on the first 800 feet of track. Along the way he bought a Vulcan gas locomotive and

HWY. 41 ACTIVITIES

Excursions

moved the Thornberry Cabin, residence of a pioneer Madera County homesteader, to the site.

By 1970 the Yosemite Mountain Sugar Pine Railroad was operating daily in the summer on the four-mile round trip you ride today. Rudy sold the Swiss Melody Inn to devote more time to his railroad. Max Stauffer, Rudy's son, now owns and manages the railroad with his mother.

Thornberry Cabin Museum

Be sure to visit the museum and gift shop where pioneer memorabilia and authentic items from railroading are on display. The shop sells all kinds of books and collectibles for train buffs.

Courtesy of the Yosemite Mountain Sugar Pine Railroad

The Shay Locomotive of the Yosemite Mountain Sugar Pine Railroad.

Swimming

Bass Lake is a warm, shallow lake offering some of the best swimming in the Sierra. You can swim from beaches or off the pontoon patio boats. See the next two pages for information about boat rentals.

Bass Lake - South Shore

Each of the U.S. Forest Service picnic areas has access to a beach for swimming.

Miller's Landing and Forks Resort

These two resorts have been around forever and have a loyal clientele. The hamburgers at Forks Resort are considered by many to be the best in the area. See page 74 for descriptions of the accommodations at these resorts.

Miller's Landing

Guests of this resort may swim off the docks. However, anyone can rent a pontoon boat here for the day, find a nice cove and dive in. The water's great!

The Forks Resort

The Forks Resort has a beach that is open to the public.

Bass Lake - North Shore

A beach just east of Willow Creek is open to the public. There is a fee to park.

Wawona Hotel

A swimming pool located at the front of the main building is open to guests. It is unheated, but a great way to cool off after a summer hike.

Boating

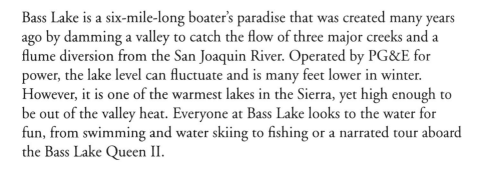

Bass Lake is a six-mile-long boater's paradise that was created many years ago by damming a valley to catch the flow of three major creeks and a flume diversion from the San Joaquin River. Operated by PG&E for power, the lake level can fluctuate and is many feet lower in winter. However, it is one of the warmest lakes in the Sierra, yet high enough to be out of the valley heat. Everyone at Bass Lake looks to the water for fun, from swimming and water skiing to fishing or a narrated tour aboard the Bass Lake Queen II.

HWY. 41 ACTIVITIES

Miller's Landing Marina

Water Skiing

Tige Tournament Ski Boats.

Miller's Landing Marina
Bass Lake - South Shore
559-642-3633

They rent everything for water skiing and also offer professional instruction.

Spending a day on the lake

Patio boats, 24-foot for 12 with a barbeque.
Patio boats, 20-foot for eight, also with a barbeque.
Fishing boats, 6 hp or 9 hp motors.
Waverunners.
Canoes.
Banana boats.

Banana boats are much in demand at Bass Lake. At Miller's the kids can go along with a professional operator.

The Forks Resort

Spending a day on the lake

Fishing boats, 14-foot with 6 hp motor.
Rowboats, 14-foot for four.
Canoes, 15-foot for three.
Patio boats for 10 or 12.

The Forks Resort
Bass Lake - South Shore
559-642-3737

None of their rentals may be used to tow skiers, but you can use your own motor on their rowboats.

Boating

Ducey's
Bass Lake - North Shore
559-642-3200 800-585-9283
8:00 a.m. to 8:00 p.m.

Ducey's rents everything you need for water skiing, including wake and knee boards and wet suits. They also rent fishing poles and gear and will supply an ice chest.

Pontoon boats come with a gas barbeque, table, AM/FM cassette, ice chest, sunshade and swim ladder. They will do your shopping and supply all the ice and other barbeque needs.

The Pines Marina
Bass Lake - North Shore
559-642-3565 559-642-3381
8:00 a.m. to 8:00 p.m.
Fee to use boat ramp.

The Williams family opened their marina in 1930 and have been serving boaters every since.

Ducey's on the Lake

Water Skiing

Tige tournament boats for six.
Professional instruction.
Boat drivers.

Spending a day on the lake

Pontoon boats for eight.
Sun Tracker pontoon boats for 12.
Fishing boats, 14-foot with 6 hp motor.
Banana boats for five.
Jet skis.

The Pines Marina

The Pines boat ramp is the only one on the north shore with gas and a repair shop.

Spending a day on the lake

Ski Boats.
Pontoon boats.
Fishing boats.
Jet skis.
Paddle boats.
Kayaks.
Inner tubes.

Boating

The Bass Lake Queen II

The Bass Lake Queen, a covered stern paddle wheeler, takes passengers on a one-hour narrated tour of the lake. The captain explains the history of the lake when is was created with a dam. You'll learn about the geology of the area, Native American history, and even about the cabin that was built for the movie, *The Great Outdoors,* with Dan Ackroyd and John Candy. With seating for 50, a stereo cassette sound system to play your favorite music, and catering by the Pines Resort, the Queen is just right for a large private party.

Bass Lake Queen
559-642-3121
3:00 p.m., daily.
Memorial Day to Labor Day.
Saturdays only April, May,
**   September, October.**

Bass Lake waterfront on the north shore.

Fishing

Naturally, Bass Lake is famous for its bass, but there are many types of trout to be caught here as well. The lakes and streams on the Scenic Byway offer good trout fishing, some of which are catch and release. Talk to the folks at Jones Store on the Byway for information.

Yosemite Bass Lake Fishing
  Adventures
Ducey's Dock
Bass Lake
559-642-3200 800-585-WAVE
Reservations required.

Yosemite Bass Lake Fishing Adventures

You'll have everything you need for a great three hours of fishing from their patio boats. They know all the best fishing holes. Anyone 16 years or older will need a fishing license, but the kids can fish free and they will take them out without you. So call for a reservation and catch your limit for a fish fry tonight.

Minarets Pack Station
Sierra Vista Scenic Byway
559-868-3405
Reservations required.

Directions:
Take Minarets Road from North Fork 62 miles to the pack station. From Bass Lake drive 32 miles on Beasore Road, with eleven miles of dirt road.

If you've always wanted to fish a high Sierra lake and perhaps hook a golden trout, here's a chance to go with the experts at the pack station and you won't have to carry your gear over the pass.

Minarets Pack Station

You might want to try either a one-day fishing expedition with the pack station, or plan a longer trip. The packers will either drop your party off at one of the lakes in the Ansel Adams Wilderness or give you a full service trip. They pack in everything and even do the cooking. And any non-fishing members of the party can have a great time exploring the wilderness near the lakes.

Fishing

Southern Yosemite Mountain Guides

The professional staff of Yosemite Mountain Guides conduct fly-fishing weekends or full five-day courses at some of the best fishing spots in the Ansel Adams Wilderness and Yosemite National Park. In the summer months they stay in a small rustic lodge in the high country. You will learn how to fish an alpine lake or cast into still or moving water. You can also arrange for a private guide to show you the best fishing in the area.

Southern Yosemite Mountain Guides
P.O. Box 301
Bass Lake, CA 93604
559-658-8735 800-231-4575

Courtesy of Minarets Pack Station

Saddled up and ready to go fishing with Minarets Pack Station.

HWY. 41 ACTIVITIES

Oakhurst River Parkway

The community is constructing a trail along the Fresno River and Oak Creek. If you are staying in Oakhurst, this one-hour hike is a pleasant way to begin your summer morning.

Start at the small shopping center where Road 426 crosses the Fresno River, one block east of Highway 41. If you walk downstream, you will come to the Community Park. You can circle the park and return to proceed upstream following the signs along the eastern shore past the elementary school to a bridge across Oak Creek. The continuation of the trail ends at Indian Springs Road and the Intermediate School. Plans call for two more bridges that will extend the parkway to Yosemite High School. Along the way there is a short detour to the Fresno Flats Historical Park. The many large oaks seen from the trail remind you why Oakhurst is named for that mighty tree.

Valley oak leaves and acorns that you may see along the trail. Notice the deep lobes on each leaf and its relatively large size.

Hiking

Lewis Creek Trail

The National Recreation Trail along Lewis Creek follows the route of the Sugar Pine Lumber Company's wooden flumes that carried lumber from the mill at Sugar Pine 54 miles downstream to Madera. If you walk the entire trail it is eight miles round trip with 400 feet elevation gain to Sugar Pine.

The trail from the upper trailhead makes a gentle climb for 2.4 miles to Sugar Pine.

The upper trail is shaded with ponderosa pine and cedar. In spring white dogwood blooms fill the forest. The trailside is filled with kit kit dizzy, a pungent smelling ground cover that confounded the emigrants who dubbed the plant mountain misery. Some say that it smells like witch hazel. In less than a mile the trail crosses the water on a log bridge. You can start here looking for picnic and wading places along the creek. It will take about an hour of hiking to reach Red Rock Falls. An unofficial trail drops steeply to a spot above the falls.

Diections to the trailheads

There are two trailheads. The first is accessed one mile up Cedar Valley Road off Highway 41 two miles past Road 222. The second trailhead is five miles past Road 222 on Highway 41. This is the midpoint of the trail. The trail ends at the small community of Sugar Pine. You can arrange a car shuttle by leaving one car here and starting at Cedar Flat and hiking the entire four miles, with a picnic stop along the way. Or you can start at the top and hike downhill to Cedar Flat.

Walking from Cedar Valley Road

If you start at the Cedar Valley Road trailhead, you will be hiking on an old roadbed for the first part of the trail. Shortly you start climbing uphill with the creek to your right. In about a half hour you will reach the first possible swimming hole and picnic site, which might be just enough of a hike for small children. Be aware that the creeks run swiftly early in the year and are not suitable for swimming until mid summer. There is poison oak at this elevation so be sure to alert the family about the shiny leaves of three. See the next page for an illustration.

After about 45 minutes to an hour of hiking from the Cedar Flat trailhead you will see Corlieu Falls ahead. There is a lovely flat oak-shaded area here, good for a picnic. The trail climbs steeply around the falls.

HWY. 41 ACTIVITIES

Directions and parking:
The parking area is off Road 274 just west of the bridge across Willow Creek. Turn north and downhill to the parking. Return to the paved road and cross the bridge where a dirt road leads downhill to the trailhead. Do not try to park on this access road.

Watch out for three shiny leaves of poison oak. In the fall they turn brilliant red.

Willow Creek Trail

Willow Creek Trail is a moderate 2.7 mile hike along Willow Creek to McLeod Flat with 1,000 feet of elevation gain.

Heed the warnings on the trail signs. Enjoy this creek from a distance. Every year someone tries to walk out on the granite above the water and slips, resulting in injury or death. The rocks are smooth and very slippery, even when dry, and the swirling pools are dangerous.

The trail climbs up a ridge above the creek. In about a half mile you can see Angel Falls below. Beyond this view the trail follows the contours above the roiling water then flattens out close to the creek again. Here there are quiet pools and some picnic spots. In about a mile, the trail climbs steeply toward McLeod Flat past an overlook of Devil's Slide.

As with all walks below 4,000 feet, watch out for poison oak. In the spring there are mosquitoes and in autumn there are small, pesky flies, so bring bug repellant.

Hiking

Nelder Grove Big Trees

Visit the little known Nelder Grove of giant sequoias in the Sierra National Forest. A one mile nature trail circles through the grove known as Shadow of the Giants.

Start your walk around the grove in a clockwise direction. The trail climbs up through a mixed forest of ponderosa and cedar and an occasional beautiful giant sequoia. This small collection is all that is left after late nineteenth century logging operations. Believe it or not, the wood was used for fence slats and even toothpicks. It is so brittle that often when felled it shattered into thousands of pieces. The entire grove has only about 100 mature trees in an area of 1,540 acres.

This hike offers a rare chance to enjoy the quiet serenity of a giant sequoia grove without trams or tourists. You may be the only people there.

Directions:
Take Sky Ranch Road (Road 632) east for 6.5 miles to a dirt road on the left. Drive two miles on the dirt road to the grove. Signs designate Nelder Grove.

John Muir visited his friend John Nelder here in 1875. He wrote later,

"The name of my hermit friend is John A. Nelder, a man of broad sympathies, and a keen intuitive observer of nature. Birds, squirrels, plants all receive loving attention, and it is delightful to see how sensitively he feels the silent influence of the woods. How his eye brightens as he gazes upon the grand sequoia kings that stand guard over his cabin. How he pets and feeds the wild quails and Douglass squirrels, how tenderly he strokes the sapling sequoias."

After the senseless logging of the area in the 1890s, the grove was acquired by the U.S. Forest Service in 1928 and given the name of the hermit who lived here.

Mariposa Grove Big Trees

Directions and summer shuttles.
The road to the grove leaves from the entrance station at Fish Camp and goes east two miles. During high season, from June to September, parking fills up early. You are encouraged to take the free shuttle from the parking area near the park entrance or from the Wawona store next to the gas station. If you do take the shuttle from Wawona, you can plan an entire day with a hike to the top of the grove then on the Lightning Trail back down to Wawona. The total hike is twelve miles, with three miles uphill and nine miles downhill.

Ranger Programs:

Interpretive hikes of one and a half hours leave from the grove parking lot three times daily in the summer and weekends in the fall. The ranger will lead you to explore the forest and learn about the survival techniques of the giant sequoia. The walk is an easy one through the lower grove. Once a day a ranger led tram ride and walk goes to the upper grove for a 2.5 mile hike down.

There are many ways to enjoy the grove. A tram runs regularly every twenty minutes for a one-hour narrated ride. You may disembark at any point and reboard the tram later or take a trail back down to the parking lot. One lovely easy downhill hike begins at the museum.

The best of the upper grove can be enjoyed by taking the tram to the museum and hiking up to the Telescope Tree. Viewing the heavens through this hollow giant is a must.

The shortest hike follows the self-guided nature trail. Start at the parking area and hike as far as the Grizzly Giant. If you haven't time or inclination to walk farther, this is a must and takes about a half hour. Interpretive signs along the way describe the life cycle and ecosystem of giant sequoia trees.

If you have several hours to enjoy the beauty of these giants of the forest, hike from the parking lot to the museum and then on to the Telescope Tree. Pick up a map at the beginning of the nature trail. On the way up to the museum the trail traverses several prescribed burn

Hiking

sites. In an area with many young cedars look carefully for four to six young sequoias, some as tall as six feet. The burns have helped the seeds to sprout. At the Telescope Tree follow signs to the Galen Clark Tree and continue on the outer loop, about 2.9 miles downhill to the parking lot. The total distance is about six miles with 1,200 feet elevation gain.

About a mile from the Galen Clark Tree signs indicate a trail to Wawona leaving to the right. This is the old Lightning Trail and reaches Wawona in six miles.

Prescribed burning in the Grove

For the past ten years the park service has pursued a program of prescribed burns to decrease the fuel load and burn off the top layers of duff that accumulated during the many years of fire suppression in the twentieth century. It is now recognized that historically in the West forests have burned regularly, keeping the underbrush or fuel load at a minimum and decreasing the chance of large, destructive fires. In the case of the giant sequoia, burning off the duff has an added benefit. Fires expose the mineral soil. This helps the short (about one inch) tap root from a sequoia seed reach nutrients in the soil that will keep a new sprout alive. The bark of a mature, giant sequoia contains a natural fire retardant. You will notice fire scars on many of the oldest and tallest trees, testament to the many conflagrations that have passed this way.

Courtesy of Yosemite Concession Services

Riding the tram in the Mariposa Grove.

Hiking

HWY. 41 ACTIVITIES

The Native Americans called the Wawona area *Pallahchun,* meaning a good place to stop. It was about half way between the foothills and Yosemite Valley, which they called *Ahwahnee* (deep, grassy valley).

Smeaton Chase explored Yosemite on his trusty horse and wrote a beautiful book *Yosemite Trails.* The following is from his visit to the Wawona area.

"All forest places are places of rest, and meadows and valleys are even more so in their nature. Wawona combines them all, and indeed I do not know a more idyllic spot. Seclusion is in the very air, and its beauty is of that gentle and perfect quality that does not so much command one's admiration as it quietly captures one's heart."

Taft Point

Directions:
Take the Glacier Point Road about eight miles and watch for a parking lot on the north side of the road. The trail is marked sloping downhill and heading west. It is 1.1 miles to Taft Point. This is a perfect family outing. The hike to Sentinel Dome also starts here and is marked and heads east. See the description on the next page.

The Jeffrey pine is cousin to the ponderosa and has three needles. The Jeffrey cone is larger than a ponderosa's. Pick one up. It is gentle to the touch, thus the saying "gentle Jeffrey, prickly ponderosa." The lodgepole has two needles and small cones.

Wawona Meadow Walk

If you are looking for a stroll in the forest for an hour or so, take the road across the river that bisects the golf course. Turn left and follow the old roadbed (the former stage road) that circles the south side of the golf course and meadow. At the end of the meadow the road crosses the creek and returns to the hotel on the north side of the golf course.

As with Smeaton Chase (see opposite column), after walking on this pleasant track your heart will be captured and you will want to return again and again.

Taft Point

Taft Point is on the south rim of Yosemite Valley. The hike starts at the Taft Point/Sentinel Dome parking area and heads west and downhill through a forest of Jeffrey and lodgepole pines. You will encounter wildflowers in season along the way, as well as ferns in shady places. After about one mile you come to a clearing and the trail descends on a sandy path. At the end are the fissures, deep crevasses in the rock. Walk carefully to the edge and look at the view of El Capitan and the Valley below.

Hiking

Sentinel Dome

In former times you could drive to Sentinel Dome. Now you must take the trail for a little more than a mile to this famous landmark with 360-degree views of Yosemite National Park. From the parking lot, look for the marked trail heading east. You pass through a stand of trees to a bridge across Sentinel Creek. The dome is visible now most of the way on a gentle uphill stroll to its top, which is at 8,122 feet.

Southern Yosemite Mountain Guides

This company offers all kinds of hiking and adventures. You can elect to be guided six to ten miles a day to learn about the trees, flowers, history and ecology of the high Sierra. On these hikes you stay in a back country lodge and have a bed and hot shower every night. Or, you can hike into their base camp in the Ansel Adams Wilderness. Mules carry in your duffel and guides do the cooking. You will see high alpine lakes in the Merced and Isberg divides country and learn even more about wildflowers.

Sentinel Dome

Directions:
See directions to Taft Point on the previous page. The parking lot is the same.

Special Features:
If you bring a map, you may be able to identify the many granite peaks and domes of the park. The twisted, gnarled form of a dead Jeffrey pine tops the dome. Alive or dead it is a favorite photographic image, especially at sunset.

Southern Yosemite Mountain Guides
P.O. Box 301
Bass Lake, CA 93604
559-658-8735 800-231-4575
www.symg.com

The Mountain Guides also do a strenuous high tour that includes peaks above 10,000 feet, but you must carry your own backpack. If you've always wanted to climb Mt. Whitney or hike the 212 miles of the John Muir Trail, you might want to contact these folks to lead you on one of these trips of a lifetime.

Horseback Riding

Yosemite Trails Pack Station
Fish Camp
559-683-7611
Open May to October.
Reservations recommended for
   longer rides.

Directions:
Take Highway 41 to Fish Camp. Turn east on Jackson Road and drive a mile and a quarter.

Yosemite Trails

These folks have all kinds of activities for riders. Bring your toddlers and lead them around the ring. The stable has lots of gentle horses for that first experience. Five times a day they offer one-hour rides on a scenic loop near the stable. A two-hour ride leaves daily at 4:00 p.m.

The most exciting excursion is an afternoon trip leaving at 12:30 p.m. that climbs to the Mariposa Grove several miles away. There you have an hour to walk around the grove or ride the tram, after which you will return on a different trail to the pack station, arriving at 6:30 p.m. They have special group or family rates and offer Family Pack Trips and a Youth Horsemanship Camp as well.

Minarets Pack Station
Sierra Vista Scenic Byway
559-683-7611
Open when road is clear of snow
   to September.
Reservations required.

Directions:
Take Minarets Road from North Fork 62 miles to the pack station. From Bass Lake drive 32 miles on Beasore Road, with eleven miles of dirt road.

Minarets Pack Station

The pack station is just a few miles from the Ansel Adams Wilderness. If you want to get into the alpine wilderness of the region with its many lakes at 9,000 feet or above and climb a few peaks, this pack outfit can take you anywhere you want to go and they will get the wilderness permit for you.

Horseback Riding

Their day fishing trips involve three to five miles of riding to a fishing spot. And if you want to get the earliest possible start, there are accommodations in the lodge. They serve dinner and a hearty breakfast before taking off on that special fishing expedition. Their favorite lakes are Lillian and Saddle Lakes. Look on a map and see what beautiful country you will be riding through.

The Minarets packers won the world packing title two years in a row at Bishop Mule Days, so you know your duffle will arrive safe and sound at your destination.

Courtesy of Yosemite Concession Services

Views from a ride to the high country.

The Wawona Stables

The stables are operated by the Yosemite Concession Services and offer a two-hour scenic ride on a ridge route above Wawona every day. Other trips include a half-day trip to Chilnualna Fall and an all-day ride to Deer Camp. These two trips do not go every day. Saddlebags are provided for your picnic lunch, cameras, poncho and extra warm jacket. Always bring a water bottle, even on shorter rides.

Wawona Stables
Next door to the Pioneer History
  Center.
209-375-6502
Open May to October.

Reservations can be made at the stable, with the Tour/Information Desk at your hotel, or by calling the stable directly.

Southern Yosemite Adventure Map
RecTech
P.O. Box 669
Oakhurst, CA 93644

The map is available at many retail outlets and the Visitor Information Center on Highway 41 in Oakhurst. Fifty cents from the sale of each map will be donated to the Sierra Forest Foundation and 100% of these funds will be spent on local trail maintenance.

Oakhurst Cycling Center
39993 Hwy. 41
Oakhurst
559-642-4606

The Southern Yosemite Adventure Map

RecTech, working with the U.S. Forest Service, has produced an adventure map for bicyclists. It has details on all the single and double track trails in the Sierra National Forest as well as paved and improved roads. Produced in four-color with topographic information in 100-foot intervals, it is an indispensable guide for all mountain bike enthusiasts. You can plan your ride knowing how much elevation gain and how far, the creeks and lakes to visit and even campsites and special places for a picnic stop. The map can also be used for the Scenic Byway Drive described on page 92.

Oakhurst Cycling Center

You can rent bicycles here as well as use their unique drop-off service. They transport you to one of two sites for great downhill rides. One moderate ride is from one of two spots above Fish Camp. The other is a much longer ride from high up the Scenic Byway that eventually will bring you back to Bass Lake. Experienced cyclists on this route can elect a single track extra loop past Shuteye Peak.

Golf

Ahwahnee Golf Course

The Ahwahnee has an 18-hole championship course laid out across the oak studded foothills. The signature hole is the par-3 14th over the water. The 18th hole is the longest at 551 yards from the back tee. A 12,000-square foot club house features an elegant restaurant and bar, a golf pro shop and a swimming pool.

Ahwahnee Golf Course
46516 Opah Drive
Ahwahnee
559-642-1343
Year-Round.
Reservations recommended.
Course rating 71.1

Directions:
Drive north 2.5 miles on Highway 49 to Harmony Lane. Turn right to Opah and drive two miles downhill to the end.

River Creek Golf Course

River Creek is a charming nine hole course carefully laid out amid pines and oak. It is open all year. The signature hole is the 7th, a 530-yard par-5 that descends to the Fresno River. Loosen up on the practice tee and after your game relax in the spacious club house to enjoy your favorite food and beverage. There is a full line pro shop and a PGA pro to give private or group lessons.

River Creek Golf Course
41709 Road 600
Ahwahnee
559-683-3388
Year-Round.
Reservations required.
Course rating 68.5
Slope rating 122

Directions:
The course is less than a mile south of Highway 49.

Golf

The Wawona Golf Course
209-375-6752
Open April to October.
Reservations recommended.

Wawona Golf Course

Built near the turn of the century, this challenging nine-hole course is in a serenely beautiful location. There is no nicer course for the non-golfer to come along for the walk. The pro shop is located at the end of the Annex and offers snacks and lunch items as well as clothing and equipment.

Courtesy of Yosemite Concession Services

Golfing at Wawona with the Annex in the background.

Winter Activities along Highway 41

Courtesy of Yosemite Concession Services

Touring near Badger Pass with the high country in the background.

The southern entrance to the park leads to all kinds of winter fun, from downhill skiing and boarding at Badger Pass to the miles of cross country trails along the road to Glacier Point. When snow is on the ground at the entrance, you may be able to ski up the road to the Mariposa Grove. Although snowplay is not allowed at Badger Pass, the Goat Meadow area is just 0.8 miles south of the entrance station. See page 118 for a description.

In winter, remember that chains may be required on all vehicles except 4WD with snowtires to reach Badger Pass or Yosemite Valley.

Important winter telephone numbers.

Road conditions (general):
    1-800-477-ROAD (7623)
Park information, weather, roads:
    209-372-0200
Badger Pass ski conditions:
    209-372-1000
Sierra National Forest headquarters:
    559-877-2218
Yosemite Sierra Visitors Bureau:
    559-683-4636

Cross Country Skiing

If you are staying anywhere in Oakhurst, Fish Camp or Yosemite West, some of the best cross country terrain with the grandest views in the Sierra is within easy driving distance. Both groomed and marked back country trails leave from Badger Pass Ski Area.

Yosemite Cross Country Ski Center
Badger Pass Ski Lodge
209-372-8444
Fax: 209-372-8673

Yosemite Cross Country Ski Center

The Yosemite Mountaineering Guides become cross country skiing guides and instructors in the winter. The center offers many classes and courses as well as guided tours to help you get started exploring the area's many trails.

Learn-To-Ski-Package

Classes meet daily and include rental equipment and two consecutive two-hour group lessons.

Introductory Lessons

A two-hour introductory group lesson covers the basis skills of striding.

Intermediate Lessons

Skiers with some experience can take these to improve their kick and glide, master steeper terrain and acquire new skills.

Telemark Lessons

Telemark lessons are taught on the Badger Pass ski slopes. Rental equipment is available. There is a three-person minimum for a class.

Cross Country Skiing

An instructor will guide you for a day of skiing designed to improve off-track skills. Pack a lunch and plenty to drink, and if you don't have a day pack, the center will rent you one.

Guided Day Tours take place on Tuesday, Thursday and Saturday.

Glacier Point Tours

There is a choice of tour packages to the new Glacier Point Winter Lodge where you can enjoy one of the most spectacular winter vistas in the park. All tours take the Glacier Point tracked trail for 17 km to Glacier Point. The lodge has dormitory-style accommodations and your guide cooks the meals. You will need to carry you personal gear.

Glacier Point Tours
209-372-8444
Monday, Wednesday, Friday, Saturday and Sunday nights.
One or two nights.
Midweek Tour Package - Monday Lessons, Tuesday Day Tour, Wednesday overnight.

A full equipment list will be provided with your confirmation. These tours are very popular, so call early in the season to secure a place.

Courtesy of Yosemite Concession Services

Ranger Naturalists lead daily snowshoe tours from Badger Pass. If you don't want to try skiing, this is just like hiking, and the naturalist will instruct you in the basics. It is a great way to enjoy the beauty of a Yosemite winter.

HWY. 41 ACTIVITIES

Cross Country Skiing

A father and daughter on top of the world enjoying vistas of the High Sierra.

Courtesy of Yosemite Concession Services

HWY. 41 ACTIVITIES

Goat Meadow Snowplay

The small hill at Goat Meadow 0.8 miles south of the entrance station is the only designated snowplay area in the region. There is no snowplay allowed at Badger Pass.

Touring on your own.

For a quick easy tour just head out the tracks on the Glacier Point Road. The easiest route follows the road to Summit Meadow and on to Bridalveil Campground. It is three miles with a climb of 200 feet to Summit Meadow and descent of 400 feet to the campground. Here a good intermediate trail (the Ghost Forest Loop) goes through a forest of dead lodgepole and returns to the road via the Bridalveil Creek trail. Experienced back country skiers can buy a trail map at the Center and be off on some of the more difficult marked trails that leave from points along the road or from the top of Badger Pass lifts. The trail to Dewey Point is a black diamond and only for the most experienced skiers.

Goat Meadow Cross Country Ski Trails

The U.S. Forest Service has marked a number of trails out of the Goat Meadow and Long Meadow Trailheads in Fish Camp. Follow the blue diamonds on the trees for trails on a 13-mile loop to Mount Raymond. This trail is not for beginners. However, from the Goat Meadow parking you can find easy trails through the woods.

Cross Country Skiing

Ostrander Hut

The Yosemite Association maintains the Ostrander Hut with 25 sleeping places. It is nine miles from Badger Pass into the wilderness either over Horizon Ridge or Bridalveil Creek. You must bring your own food and gear and be prepared for a long uphill climb that takes about six hours. Since the weather is never sure, you may be skiing in a storm. For those who are able, the terrain near the hut has great views and wonderful slopes nearby for practicing telemark technique.

**Ostrander Hut
Wilderness Office
209-372-0740**

The Hut Reservation System

You can reserve a place in the hut through the Wilderness Office in the Valley. The hut is now so popular that you must request a space in the lottery by mid-November for the upcoming season. Those who must go on a weekend may not get their reservation filled. However, if you can go during a non-holiday midweek, you will probably be able to find space. You can also call after December 1 for a non lottery reservation. Midweeks are seldom full.

Courtesy of the National Park Service, Yosemite

Ostrander Hut has been a favorite destination since the 1940s.

Downhill Skiing and Boarding

Winter sports began in earnest in Yosemite National Park in 1928 with the establishment of the Yosemite Winter Club. Ernest des Baillets was lured here from Switzerland to be director of winter sports. Don Tresidder, the president of the Yosemite Park and Curry Company, pushed the development of all kinds of winter activities to bring tourists to the park. With the opening of the Wawona Tunnel in 1932, ski trails were cut from Monroe Meadows down to Chinquapin.

Badger Pass Ski Area
Ski conditions and snow phone:
209-372-1000

Badger Pass Ski Area

The Badger Pass Lodge opened in 1935. With the Upski to transport skiers up the hill, Badger Pass became the first ski resort in California. A long line of European instructors were hired to teach people how to ski in the best traditions of Austrian ski techniques. Badger Pass was the place to go until World War II. After the war, in 1948, Luggi Foeger invited Nic Fiore, a French Canadian, to come and be an instructor. Ten years later Nic took over as director of the ski school and remains today. He oversaw the addition of T-Bars and chair lifts, but the hill remains much as it was in the beginning.

Courtesy of Yosemite Concession Services

A skier approaches the lodge. Five lifts now serve 85 acres of downhill skiing and riding.

Nic Fiore established the Badger Pups Program more than forty years ago. He and his instructors have probably taught more that 100,000 young skiers and boarders.

Downhill Skiing and Boarding

Nic, on the right, and an assistant help a child get her "ski legs".

Badger Pass offers one of the most affordable ski experiences in the Sierra. If you are staying in the Valley, you pay only $25 per day for two lessons, lift ticket, one free baby-sitting for children ages 3 to 9, ice skating at the ice rink in the Valley and free shuttle to the ski area. What more could you ask to take the chair to the top where a view of the park's high country thrills you before skiing or riding down to the lodge.

Badger Pass pups ready to race.

Yosemite Snowmobile Rentals and Tours
559-642-3200

Yosemite Snowmobile Tours

Yosemite Snowmobile, the only company with a Special Use Permit from the U.S. Forest Service, offers a unique opportunity to experience Yosemite back country with a professional guide. They rent all the necessary clothing for your one-and-a-half to two-hour tour on heated snowmobiles. Bring your camera for some unbelievable photo opportunities.

U.S. Forest Service
Road 225
North Fork
559-877-2218

The U.S. Forest Service Office is open Monday through Friday from 8:00 a.m. to 4:30 p.m. and you can stop by to pick up maps or information about snow conditions.

Whisky Snowmobile Trails

The Sierra National Forest maintains official, marked snowmobile trails off Road 233 and F.S.8509 north of North Fork. The trails lead to Peckinpah Meadow and Whisky Falls or as far as Haskell Meadow. You can also enter the trail system near Hogue Ranch on the Mammoth Pool Road below Fish Creek Campground.

Museums

Children's Museum of the Sierra

If you're looking for a few hours of educational fun for the children, the Children's Museum has it all. In a hands-on environment kids can investigate x-rays in the children's doctor's office, explore a dig as a paleontologist, experiment with gravity and learn about animation, magnetism, light and color. Docent volunteers help kids and their parents use all the wonderful exhibits, with more being added each year.

Children's Museum
49234 Golden Oak Drive
Oakhurst
559-658-5656
Wednesday through Saturday,
**   10:00 a.m. to 4:00 p.m.**
Sunday, 1:00 p.m. to 4:00 p.m.
Fee to use museum.

Fresno Flats Historic Park

Buildings of the turn of the century were brought here so that you can see how the pioneer families lived. The 1869 Taylor Log House, an Ozark design with sugar pine logs, has two rooms separated by a "dog trot." One side was the family and living room where cooking was done, with the bedroom, sewing and work room for the parents on the other side. The Cunningham one-room schoolhouse is next door. It was built in 1874 and served children for 50 years. It was brought over from Nipinnawasee and was Madera County's second school.

Fresno Flats Historic Park
Off Road 427 one half mile east of
**   Hwy. 41.**
Oakhurst
559-683-6570
Guided tours: Saturday, 1:00 p.m.
**   to 3:00 p.m., Sunday, 1:00 p.m. to**
**   4:00 p.m.**
Self-guided tours dawn to dusk
**   every day.**

There are sections of the Sugar Pine-Madera Flume, old farm equipment and exhibits of tools used to build homes in the nineteenth century. The old Raymond Jail is there to see, along with a blacksmith shop and an old barn. The library and historical research center is open only by appointment.

The Pioneer Yosemite History Center
Wawona

The Wawona Hotel and most of the land in the area was privately owned by the Washburn brothers and their heirs, who built the main building of the hotel in 1879. Upon its completion it was called "the grandest hotel in the mountains of California." The Washburns operated the hotel until it was purchased in 1932 by the National Park Service. The Yosemite Park and Curry Company, then directed by Don Tresidder, took over management of the hotel. The last Washburn, Clarence, ran the hotel until 1934, when he left in frustration, as the depression had reduced visitation and the YPCC cut staff to a minimum. He felt that he could no longer carry on the traditions of service that his family had begun. He eventually moved to Indio, California, where he leased the Hotel Potter and was Mayor of the town for 12 years.

The Pioneer Yosemite History Center

When at Wawona, take time to walk across the covered bridge to see the Pioneer History Center where buildings from Yosemite's past have been moved from various places in the park. Docents in costume of the period welcome visitors during the summer months.

Wawona was the largest stage stop in Yosemite in the late 1800s. Inbound stages stopped for the night at the Wawona Hotel before making the eight-hour trip to the Valley. All Yosemite traffic crossed the covered bridge built by the Washburns, who were the proprietors of both the hotel and the stage company. A flood nearly destroyed the bridge in 1955, but it was restored when the center was created. A self-guided tour starts just after the bridge. Each building is described with its history and place in the Yosemite story.

The buildings reflect different periods in Yosemite's past. The cavalry office represents the era before establishment of the National Park Service when the U.S. Cavalry managed Yosemite every summer. Their summer encampment was near today's Wawona campground.

Museums

The Degnans first settled in Yosemite Valley in 1884. Bridget supplemented their income from John's job as a laborer by baking bread. The building here, originally attached to their home, housed her original oven that baked 50 loaves per day until 1900. The family retained ownership of the bakery and delicatessen in the Valley until 1974. However, the Degnan name is still on several eateries there.

Stage Rides

During the summer you can climb aboard a Wawona stage at the history center and experience turn-of-the-century transportation in the park.

Ranger Programs:

During the summer and early fall, ranger led walks are posted at the hotel, the Wawona Campground and the Information Center.

Courtesy of the National Park Service, Yosemite

The stage arrives at the Wawona Hotel when it was "the grandest hotel in the mountains of California."

Art Galleries

There is a lively art scene in the Oakhurst area which has led to the establishment of the Vision Academy of the Arts. The academy offers workshops in all disciplines throughout the year with artists, musicians and actors from the local area. You can call 559-683-1567 or fax 559-683-8338 for information. It may be that there will be a class you might enjoy when you are visiting the area.

Brumley Art Center
Hwy. 41
Coarsegold
559-642-2787

Brumley Art Center

Jean Brumley, a local artist of many years, displays her water colors at the gallery and gives classes. You may sign up when you are in the area or call the Vision Academy of the Arts for her classes offered through that organization.

Yosemite Gallery Indian Territory
Hwy. 41
Coarsegold
559-683-8727
Summer, daily.
Winter, Monday thru Friday.

Yosemite Gallery and Indian Territory

Dick and Lorena Kell have assembled a large collection of Indian art and jewelry. They also sell gold nuggets and jewelry.

Art Galleries

The Silver Spur Center at 40982 Highway 41, Oakhurst, houses several galleries.

Timberline Gallery

Established by the Guild of Mountain Artists the gallery displays art in several media, sculpture, ceramics and hand-crafted items. Mark and Jane Dyer give classes here as well.

Timberline Gallery
559-683-3345
Summer, 10:00 a.m. to 5:00 p.m., daily.
Winter, 10:00 a.m. to 4:00 p.m., daily.

Stavast Studio Gallery

Stephen Stavast not only displays his work of magic realism, but you can see him at work. He writes poetry to accompany his stunning paintings depicting natural scenes. His work is also shown in Palmdale, Scottsdale, St. Helena and Carmel.

Stavast Studio Gallery
559-683-0611
Open 10:00 a.m. to 5:00 p.m., daily.

National Parks Gallery

Mark Gudmundsen shows his work here of those scenes we wish to remember from Yosemite and other park locations. He is also at the Tenaya Lodge.

National Parks Gallery
559-683-3345
Summer, 10:00 a.m. to 5:00 p.m., daily.
Winter, 10:00 a.m. to 4:00 p.m., daily.

Grimmer Gallery

The Grimmers display their own paintings and sculpture.

Grimmer Gallery
559-658-2104
Open 11:00 a.m. to 5:00 p.m., Wednesday thru Saturday.

Special Events

Special Events take place mostly from April through October along the Highway 41 corridor. The *Yosemite Sierra Visitor Guide* has a complete list.

April

Yosemite Film Festival
Oakhurst
559-683-4636

May

Bass Lake Fishing Derby
Over $40,000 in cash and prizes.
559-642-3676

Antique and Classic Wooden Boat Show at Bass Lake
559-642-3676

Bass Lake Jazz, Fireworks
Fifteen weeks of jazz and fireworks, poolside at Ducey's.
559-642-3121

Sugar Pine Railroad Moonlight Series
A 20-week Saturday series until October 9.
559-683-7273

June

Sesquicentennial Wagon Trains and Mule Days Coarsegold.
Celebrating the 150th anniversary of the Gold Rush.
559-673-3444

Bass Lake Arts and Crafts Fair
559-877-3474

July and August

Moonlight Melodrama
Sugar Pine Railroad.
559-683-7273

August

Run Through the Pines
4.5 mile run circling Bass Lake.
559-877-4373

September

Custom and Classic Car Show
Bass Lake.
559-683-2717

Bass Lake Triathalon
559-877-5351

October

Grizzly Century Bike Rally
559-877-2218

Bass Lake Fall Festival and Crafts Fair
559-877-3474

Oakhurst Arts and Crafts Fair
559-877-3474

Introduction to Highway 140

Merced to Yosemite National Park

Highway 140 exits Highway 99 in Merced and heads straight east past peach and pistachio orchards. The tracks of the Sante Fe Railroad are a constant companion until the town of Planada.

When visibility is good, the foothills of Guadalupe Mountain rise above the plain, and travelers will glimpse Chowchilla Mountain backed by the snow-capped Clark Range in the park.

Approaching the foothills, fields on either side of the highway are filled with hummocks called mima mounds. Their other name is buffalo wallows, although this animal had nothing to do with creating them. The current, much favored theory of their formation has both prehistoric and present-day gophers responsible. If you find this hard to believe, remember that a gopher can move up to nine and a half tons of soil in a year. The mounds sit on top of a thick layer of dense clay, impervious to water which collects during the winter. When warm days of spring evaporate the water, magic fairy rings of flowers appear. These are called vernal pools, and those lucky

Yosemite Valley is 80 miles from Merced. It is 36 miles from Merced to Mariposa on a two-lane road with passing lanes. From Mariposa to the park entrance is 34 miles. During 1999, the section of road from El Portal to the park is undergoing major rebuilding to correct serious damage from the floods of 1997 and 1998. The road will be open 8:00 a.m. to 10:30 p.m. from May 1 to October 1. The schedule and phone number to call are on page 34. Drivers from the Bay Area may use Highway 120. Visitors staying on Highway 49 South in Mariposa can also take Highway 49 to Oakhurst and use the southern entrance to the park.

Planada

This community, complete with boulevards and parks, was laid out by a Los Angeles investment company in 1912. By 1914 there were 2000 residents hopefully trying to raise crops, but no irrigation projects came to the valley until the late 1920s, and Planada's population shrank. Dustbowl "Oakies" settled there only to be replaced by Mexican field workers after World War II.

Introduction to Highway 140

Viewing vernal pools

Drive four miles east from Planada to Cunningham Road, then north for a few miles to see some of the best of these beautiful vernal pools. They are most apparent on the left about a mile up the road.

You are crossing lands of several early nineteenth century families who settled here when ranching seemed more profitable than mining. Like all foothill cattle and sheep ranchers, these families drove their cattle to the Yosemite high country every spring.

Catheys Valley

The town was named for Andrew Cathey, who settled here in 1852, having arrived with a wagon train he led from Arkansas. He raised hogs that were allowed to roam free, and it was common in the 1870s to come upon a hog drive on the way to the railhead. At one point there were so many hogs that the California Senate debated a bill to stop the practice in Mariposa County. In 1855 swine cholera did what the legislature couldn't, and cattle replaced the pigs.

enough to pass this way during their brief life will be greeted by a ring of white meadowfoam around a central splash of yellow goldfields and tidytips. Occasionally a centerpiece of blue lobelia completes the colorful array. Vernal pools are found only in California, southern Oregon and South Africa.

Approaching the foothills you will see outcroppings of rock covered with chartreuse and orange lichens. These are ancient volcanic muds that were left in a vertical position after the uplift of the Sierra Nevada. Erosion of the surrounding soils uncovered them. Miners, who were often inclined to be morbid, called them tombstone rocks.

After Catheys Valley you begin the ascent toward a summit from which you may see the snow covered Clark Range in winter. A steep descent takes you to the town of Mariposa that looks much the same as it did a century ago, except that restaurants and motels have replaced the livery stables and saloons.

From Mariposa the road ascends quickly to Midpines Summit at 3,000 feet. The pines of Midpines are yellow or ponderosa pines, favored by lumber companies. Among the stately ponderosa grow

Introduction to Highway 140

incense cedar and the graceful black oak, so named for its dark-colored bark. The understory is mostly ceonothus, California's wild lilac, which in March and April bloom with tiny clusters of white or blue flowers that emit a sweet fragrance. Native Americans crushed the flowers to make a perfumed soapy substance.

After Midpines the highway descends steeply down the Bear Creek canyon toward the Merced River. The hillsides on the far side are covered with hardy chaparral, a community of shrubs well suited to the searing climate of summer. Tiny needlelike or leathery leaves turn vertical to the sun, thus keeping their moisture from transpiring in the heat. The hills have been burned often, but chaparral plants recover quickly, sprouting from their charred crowns. At the bottom of the hill you cross Bear Creek where it joins the Merced River at the location of Briceburg.

The railroad chugged into El Portal until two events signalled the eventual doom of the line. In 1923 the Exchequer Dam was built by the Merced Irrigation District, forcing the YVRR to relocate 17 miles of roadbed along the now flooded river.

The ponderosa pine cone is prickly to the touch when picked up. The needles come in bunches of three and the deeply grooved reddish bark of mature trees sometimes smells like vanilla.

The Yosemite Valley Railroad

Across the river from Briceburg to El Portal is the old roadbed of the Yosemite Valley Railroad (YVRR). The first run left Merced with 12 passengers in 1907. This train ushered in the glory days of pre-automobile Yosemite tourism. A visitor could leave San Francisco on a train bound for Merced, change there to the YVRR for El Portal, where the railroad welcomed passengers to the grand Hotel Del Portal with its 100 rooms, 30 with bath no less. Until 1913 a dusty stagecoach journey still awaited weary travelers. Finally, in that year, the first auto stage was put into service, but the open air ride still left passengers covered from head to toe.

131

Introduction to Highway 140

HWY. 140

Hiking and Biking on the railroad right of way.

Today, the deteriorating roadbed remains, clearly visible across the river. Efforts are under way to created a hiking and bicycle trail between El Portal and Briceburg. However, it is still possible to walk a short way up the river from Briceburg. See page 169 for a description. See page 173 for the bicycle ride on the old YVRR roadbed between Briceburg and Railroad Flat.

Geologic Exhibit

Six miles from Briceburg there is an excellent geological exhibit which explains the origins of the oldest rocks in the Sierra Nevada. These sedimentary rocks that have been uplifted, contorted and metamorphosed are clearly visible on the canyon wall above you. Across the river you can see the geometric design of these mix-mastered rocks on the shiny, water-polished surface.

Yosemite Lumber Company

The principle earnings of the YVRR were from lumber. On the canyon wall north of the highway at El Portal you may be able to spot the scar left by the lumber company's 78% incline, the steepest ever built. Logs were lowered down the track to waiting railroad cars from logging operations above.

No sooner was this completed than the All Weather Highway opened, the same road you are traveling. Americans were becoming wedded to their cars, zooming to the Valley in record time. The railroad suffered such losses that it ceased operation when much of the roadbed was destroyed in a disastrous 1937 flood. In the 1940s the tracks were removed.

Between Briceburg and El Portal the highway is a feast of color in March and April. The hillsides across the river sparkle with golden ribbons of poppies and fiddlenecks. Brilliant magenta redbud shrubs garland the river, which in all but drought years is frothing in its rushing descent to the valley below.

Later in the year, when the river's cascades have subsided, anglers may be tempted to cast a few flies for catch and release, and picnickers may want to stop for swimming or sunning.

One of the best flower shows in the area takes place every spring along the Hite's Cove Trail that leaves from Savage's Trading Post. The trail begins on private property, and those who wish to hike the trail should register at the Trading Post,

Introduction to Highway 140

where the owner will tell you if the time is right. (The trail is closed during fire season.) Flowers or no, the trail itself is a delightful hike above the roaring waters of the South Fork. It leads to the site of John R. Hite's mine, which despite its difficult location and distance from Mariposa, made $3 million for this colorful character. Always take water, for the trail can be steep above the river's edge. See page 170 for a description of the hike.

After following the curving Merced River for several miles, you arrive in El Portal. The town was once the farm of James Hennessey, who got his start with a loan from John Hite. Hennessey raised produce which he sold to early Valley hotels and to Hite's Cove during its heyday. He went bankrupt in 1887 and committed suicide in 1908, a ruined man.

Several miles up a narrow, steep grade above the rushing river, you come to the Arch Rock Entrance Station.

The Story of Lucy Hite

John Hite's common-law wife was a Native American named Lucy, who is said to have shown him the golden treasure buried at the cove. He came under pressure from his family to find a more acceptable wife. Lucy beat him to it, however, and sued him for divorce. Imagine the notoriety of the case as a Native American woman with few rights before the court sued a multimillionaire. She won her case and received some cash. It is rumored that a son drank up the money. Hite died an alcoholic in San Francisco, while she lived out a very long life near Mariposa on land that Hite had given her.

Saving the Merced River.

Between 1983 and 1987 local citizens of the Merced Canyon Committee lobbied Congress to have both the Main Fork and South Fork of the Merced declared a Wild and Scenic River, stopping all plans to dam the river. We are indebted to a large constituency who brought the issue to Congress and to Merced's Congressman Coelho and California Senators Cranston and Wilson, who helped guide the bill to an overwhelming vote in favor of protection. Today both forks are wild and scenic between the park boundary and Lake McClure.

Alternate Route to Mariposa

Superstition Gardens
2536 Old Highway
Catheys Valley, CA 95306
209-966-6277
E-mail
  randcvr@sierratel.com
About two miles from
  Highway 140.
April 1 to mid-May,
  Wednesday thru Sunday,
  10:00 a.m. to 5:00 p.m.

Gardeners who pass this way between April first and mid-May will be greeted by a field of multi-colored iris. This is the home of Superstition Iris Gardens, where iris lovers will find one of the most extensive collections in the West. Hundreds of varieties from dwarf to tall bearded, hybrids and historic plants are arranged in rows for viewing. They will take your order and ship when the iris are ready for planting. Even if you don't wish to buy, wandering among the blooms is a visual delight.

About 21 miles from Merced the Old Highway road exits to the south. This diversion to Mariposa is 16 miles on a two lane road that dips and turns along the contours of the land in the fashion of old wagon roads. In spring (March or April) this leisurely drive is a pastoral delight, with wildflowers of every description carpeting the roadside in hues of blue, yellow and pink. Brodiaeas, both golden and blue, Chinese houses, yellow lupine and shimmering goldfields are a few of the species to be seen. The rock-strewn hillsides support groves of buckeye and blue oak, so named because of the color of its leaves.

Granite outcroppings appear about four miles out and soon you will notice the first digger pine. Their sparse blue-gray needles reflect the sun's rays, an adaptation to survive the intense summer heat.

Blue oak. Although the leaves are similar to the valley oak, they are much smaller and have a distinct blue-gray color.

Alternate Route to Mariposa

In ten miles you cross Agua Fria Creek. The Historical Marker commemorates the town of Bridgeport. The Washburn brothers were once clerks at the stage stop and store here. They moved on to become the prosperous owners of the Wawona Hotel and the Yosemite Stage and Turnpike Company. The town of Bridgeport passed into oblivion after the placer miners left, but the store was kept alive with penny ante poker in the back room. Bridgeport will live again as the Bridgeport Oaks subdivision, a sign of the times, as flatlanders move into the foothills to buy ranchettes and rural homes.

The road descends to its intersection with Highway 49. Here State Historical Marker 393 marks the spot of a former settlement. This was Mormon Bar, so named after the first group to settle here. They did not stay long, but were replaced by other miners and later by thousands of Chinese who reworked the diggings and created Mariposa's Chinatown. The nearby Mariposa County Fairgrounds is on part of their long-gone townsite.

Digger pine. Notice that the needles are very sparse and have a bluish green color.

Off the Beaten Path

Hornitos Loop Trip

Driving to Hornitos

Another Off the Beaten Path can be taken by following Hornitos Road that heads north from Highway 140 two and a half miles east of the Old Highway. A left turn will take you to the once raucous town of Hornitos, named for the round, outdoor bake-ovens that once dotted the countryside.

If you are coming from the north, an interesting route from Highway 99 is J16 that exits eight miles south of Modesto and winds through the foothills via Merced Falls to Hornitos. It is not a shorter route to Mariposa, but it is certainly more scenic and allows a tour of Hornitos.

From Hornitos take the Bear Valley Road (J16) to continue to Mariposa. Two miles north was the Washington Mine, later renamed the Jenny Lind Mine. It was the county's tenth largest, producing $2 million between 1850 and its closure in 1945. For many years the manager was Mose Rogers, an African American who employed many Cornish and Chinese miners. His daughter, Luella, was the postmistress of Hornitos for a period of time.

This trip is especially delightful in March or April when the wildflower show is on. It is about 13 miles to Hornitos through a mostly rural landscape. St. Catherine's Catholic Church with its single steeple sits high on a hill ahead, heralding your arrival in Hornitos. Take the road that circles the town park to the west, ending in a town plaza where flamboyant Mexican festivals once took place.

The ruins of the Ghiardelli store are across the plaza and down the street. Although one lucky Chinese miner reported finding a 34-ounce gold nugget, one suspects that the local merchants, including the Ghiardellis of San Francisco chocolate fame and the Gagliardos, were the prosperous citizens. Once there was a hotel, newspaper and even a bathhouse when the town was an important trading center. Hornitos is the only incorporated town in Mariposa County. Today it is almost a ghost town—you may see more cats than people.

From its earliest days, Hornitos was a multi-cultural mix of Mexican, Chinese, Europeans and black and white Americans working the mines

HWY. 140

Off the Beaten Path

in the area. Its first residents were rowdies who were evicted from nearby Quartzburg in 1850. Joaquin Murietta, a legendary nineteenth century bandit, was often reported in these parts and once escaped capture by using an underground tunnel into the fandango hall. The town of Quartzburg no longer exists, even though it had applied to be the county seat in 1851.

Drive up the hill on St. Catherine Street to visit the lovely, wooden church built in 1865. If you choose to wander around the cemetery you'll find stones dating back to the 1870s.

From Hornitos to Mariposa

J16 climbs steeply through fields dotted with oaks and lined with stone walls to intersect Highway 49 at Bear Valley. Turn right toward Mariposa. Just before you come to Mariposa opposite Airport Road is Mt. Bullion, named for Frémont's father-in-law who championed hard currency in his years as a U.S. Senator. Clarence King once wrote of Mt. Bullion,

"Under the roots of this famous Mt. Bullion have been mined those gold veins whose treasure has enriched so few, whose promise allured so many."

HWY. 140

© Ellie Huggins

St. Catherine's Church in Hornitos.

Mariposa History

How Mariposa got its name.

"In the month of June, 1806 . . . a party of Californians (headed by Gabriel Moraga) pitched their tents on a stream at the foot of the Sierra Nevada, and whilst there, myriads of butterflies, of the most gorgeous and variegated colors, clustered on the surrounding trees, attracted their attention, from which circumstance they gave the stream, the appellation of Mariposa. Hence, Mariposa River, from which the county (also heavily laden with the precious Metal) derives its poetical name."

From a report to the first legislature of California on the derivation and definition of the names of several counties.

From the time of the 1806 Moraga Expedition until the discovery of gold, the land of a future Mariposa County remained the province of native tribes and the beautiful butterflies for which it was named. As with all of the foothills of the Sierra Nevada, the discovery of gold forever changed the landscape and the lives of the Native Americans and animals living there.

John and Jessie Benton Frémont

Colonel John Frémont and his wife, Jessie Benton Frémont, are important figures in the area's gold rush past. In 1847, Frémont bought a 55,000-acre Mexican land grant named Rancho Las Mariposas from Juan Bautista Alvarado for a paltry $3,000. News of California gold reached Frémont in 1849, while he was on an expedition. He quickly dispatched his second in command, Alexis Godey, to accompany Mexican miners and start digging for gold on his Mariposa land near Agua Fria creek.

When California declared statehood, the town of Agua Fria was declared the county seat of a Mariposa County that covered one-fifth of the state. A few miles east of Agua Fria, other miners had assembled in a

Mariposa History

combination of wooden shacks and tents which they called Logtown. When Agua Fria and its courthouse were destroyed by floods, Mariposa, a new settlement near Logtown, became the county seat. Its citizens quickly built a lovely Greek Revival-style courthouse, which is still in use today.

The legality of Frémont's grant soon came into question. Being well connected—his wife's father was a U.S. Senator—his claim was confirmed with new boundaries drawn by his friends that included many mining operations in the area. This did not make Colonel Frémont very popular, but neither did the mine bring him great wealth. He was seldom present to manage his property, spending much of what he made. He was forced to borrow money to run for President in 1856. He lost control of his holdings in 1860 to a shrewd investor who had lent him $250,000. An interesting footnote to this history—the good citizens of Mariposa roundly defeated Frémont, preferring his opponent, James Buchanan.

Discovery of Yosemite Valley

Mariposa is the foothill town most closely connected with the discovery of Yosemite National Park, for it was the Mariposa Battalion headed by James Savage who entered the Valley while chasing the native tribe they knew as Yo Semites. Their discovery was chronicled in the papers of the day, and soon others were following a trail out of Mariposa up the steep grades of Chowchilla Mountain to Galen Clark's lonely cabin on the south fork of the Merced River and on into the Valley.

HWY. 140

Mariposa History

Yosemite attracts winter sports enthusiasts

When the All Weather Highway assured visitors a way into the park in the snow season, the Yosemite Park & Curry Company, headed by its new enthusiastic manager, Donald Tresidder, created opportunities for winter fun in the park. He hired Jules Fritsch, a Swiss mountain guide, to bring his expertise to the park to teach Americans about skiing. Tresidder developed winter carnivals, built an ice skating rink at Camp Curry and formed the Yosemite Winter Club in 1928. He created a small ski hill and ski jump, and soon had a ski school operating. By 1935, when the Wawona Tunnel opened, skiers were driving to the new facility at Badger Pass, with an 800-foot vertical and the West's first mechanical uphill lift, the *Upski*. It is estimated that 30,000 skiers came to Badger Pass in the 1935-36 season, most of them via Mariposa on the new highway. After a hiatus during World War II, skiers began to flock to Badger Pass with its excellent ski school, directed by Nic Fiore. Yosemite National Park had become an all season destination both for its beauty under the mantle of snow and its variety of winter sports activities.

Mariposa from the Gold Rush to the All Weather Highway

Mariposa's heady days of the gold rush ended abruptly in the late 1860s when a disastrous fire destroyed much of the town. Gold mining diminished, and so did the size of Mariposa County until its boundaries today enclose only 1,455 square miles.

Tourists bound for the Mariposa Grove and Wawona, which was still the park headquarters, used stages via Mariposa and Chowchilla Mountain. Those wishing to get to the Valley directly, however, were riding stages from Stockton via the Big Oak Flat Road or from Coulterville through Big Meadow, and later via the train connection at Raymond. Then in 1906 the Yosemite Valley Railroad bypassed Mariposa completely, whisking passengers from Merced directly to El Portal, signalling the death of stagecoach travel. Mariposa was left with little but golden memories.

The town suffered through two decades with nothing more than its position as county seat. This difficult period ended in 1926 when the All Weather Highway (Highway 140) became a reality. Mariposa was back on the tourist map as this new auto

Mariposa History

route brought tourists to the park in all seasons.

Today the town is a key gateway to the park and is known for its many bed and breakfast inns and its historic ambience. Along with the Mariposa Museum and History Center, an active arts community and many nineteenth century buildings, tourists are finding that Mariposa is an interesting destination, not just a stop on the way to Yosemite Valley.

Courtesy of the National Park Service, Yosemite

Opening day of the All Weather Highway 140 on July 31, 1926.

Lodging on Highway 140

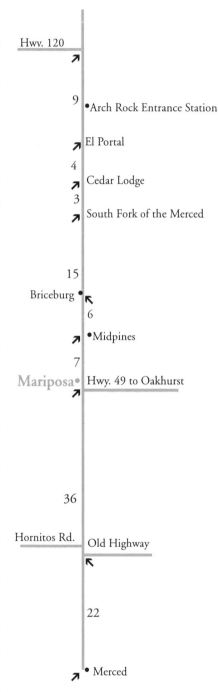

Hwy. 120

9
•Arch Rock Entrance Station

El Portal
4
Cedar Lodge
3
South Fork of the Merced

15
Briceburg •
6
•Midpines
7
Mariposa• Hwy. 49 to Oakhurst

36

Hornitos Rd.
Old Highway

22

• Merced

Mariposa boasts of many bed and breakfast inns. Some are in quiet locations along Highway 49 or off Triangle Road. For those staying along Triangle Road, you need not return to Mariposa to reach the Park, but can continue on the road and intersect Highway 140 above Midpines.

In Midpines there is one bed and breakfast inn, an inexpensive motel and the Yosemite Bug Hostel, a combination hostel, campground and lodge. Here you will find a place to drop your sleeping bag, or a clean, modern hostel room, with reasonably priced dining available at the lodge.

Motels in every price range are in Mariposa proper. In or near El Portal are three motels, two with restaurants, that put you just at the park's edge.

We also describe five B & B's that are out in the countryside surrounding Mariposa that offer a restful retreat complete with spas and pools, gourmet breakfasts and in some cases trails to explore.

Highway 140 lodging is listed alphabetically in each location.

Bed and Breakfast Inns

Rancho Bernardo

Perhaps one of the most unusual overnight experiences is at Rancho Bernardo. Kathy and Barney Lozares invite you to their 120-acre cattle ranch just minutes off Highway 140 on Old Highway. Two unique quarters await you. The studio apartment in the barn offers a queen brass bed, TV, microwave and refrigerator. The guest house has a double lodgepole bed, refrigerator, TV, couches around a fireplace, kitchen and a pool table for those so inclined. A queen bed is in a loft. To start the day off right you will be served a gourmet breakfast that might include fruit, fresh farm eggs or buttermilk pancakes. Staying here is a chance to relax in luxury in the beautiful Sierra foothills that have changed little since the first settlers arrived.

Rancho Bernardo
2617 Old Highway South
Catheys Valley, CA 95306
209-966-4511
mariposa.yosemite.net/lozbnb
$80 - $95

Directions:
Take Old Highway east from Highway 140 in Catheys Valley. Drive three miles. The white fence will herald the gate on the north side of the road.

Special Features:
The ranch cattle, Brahmans and Angus, are really pets according to Kathy. They wander in the fields near the house, separated by a fence of course. In the barn, be sure to meet Barney's quarter horses, whose stalls are across from the room entrance. The barn is so clean and orderly, it is like an extension of the house. Barney is a retired bull rider, and might be willing to tell tales of his rodeos. All the quarters are air conditioned.

Courtesy of Rancho Bernardo

Imagine yourself in this bucolic setting for a stay at Rancho Bernardo.

Passengers in the El Portal Station get ready for the dusty ride to Yosemite Valley. Their trips to Yosemite on the Yosemite Valley Railroad bypassed Mariposa below.

Looking west on Highway 140 in Mariposa during the early 1920s. The road was not yet paved. At this point in time the town's only claim to fame was that it was the county seat. Tourists on their way to Yosemite were taking the train from Merced directly to El Portal. When the All Weather Highway was completed in 1926 tourists came again to Mariposa and the town started its renaissance.

Bed and Breakfast Inns

Boulder Creek Bed and Breakfast

This is a very special B&B with an artist and gourmet chef as your hosts. Owners Nancy and Michael Habermann met in Germany in the mid 1980s, fell in love, married and moved to Mariposa to build their dream inn. Michael designed a European-style inn with his guest's comfort in mind. They opened in 1988 and their guest book reflects the far-flung homes of their visitors over the years. The rooms are tastefully decorated and comfortable. The house is temperature-controlled—no noisy room air conditioners here—and a wood stove warms the living room in winter. A spa and porch for sitting invite you to look out onto their beautiful back yard, where birds come to their feeders and other wildlife may pass by.

Boulder Creek B & B
4572 Ben Hur Road
Mariposa, CA 95338
209-742-7729 800-768 4572
Fax: 209-742-5885
mariposa.yosemite.net/
boulder_creek
$85

Special Features:

Michael has been a chef all his working life, and your breakfast may have breads created from his 200-year-old Kefir culture or some other delicious creation. Nancy is a local water color artist whose paintings decorate the house. Everything is orderly and your hosts are happy to sit and converse with you and help you find attractions to visit or restaurants for dining.

5th Street Inn

Four rooms, two with king beds and one with two doubles have private entrances onto the street. One unit has a kitchenette, another a refrigerator and wet bar. All rooms have TV and are air conditioned. You are just steps from Main Street and all the historical attractions of Mariposa.

5th Street Inn
Corner of 5th and Bullion
P.O. Box 1917
Mariposa, CA 96338
209-966-6048 800-867-8584
$60 - $90

Bed and Breakfast Inns

Ken and Flo's
5022 Mykleoak Rd.
Mariposa, CA 95338
209-966-7677 888-615-5488
mariposa.yosemite.net/kennflo
$55 - $60

Ken and Flo's

Ken and Flo welcome you to their ranch house nestled among oaks off Highway 49 just a couple of miles north of Mariposa. They have two rooms that share a bath.

Little Valley Inn
3483 Brooks Road
Mariposa, CA 95338
209-742-6204 800-889-5444
www.littlevalley.com
$95 - $115

Little Valley Inn

Innkeepers, Kay and Robert Barber, specialize in gold panning. They are happy to help guests learn to pan on their property or take you to some special haunts. The rooms are large, all with separate entrances, private baths and decks looking out on their serene, rural landscape. The sound from two creeks lull you to sleep. One suite that is handicap accessible has a large kitchen and two queen beds. Two other rooms also have queens. All are equipped with VCR's and the inn has free movies. Little Valley Inn is on the original Highway 49. The breakfast is buffet style.

Bed and Breakfast Inns

Mariposa Hotel-Inn

Innkeepers Sal and Sharon Maccarone are third generation operators of the inn, an elegant Victorian style bed and breakfast in a historic building in the heart of downtown. They have totally renovated and redecorated the hotel. Rooms are decorated with a Victorian flavor. All have queen beds and large private bathrooms. There is cable TV with HBO in each room and individually controlled heat and air conditioning. Smoking is only allowed in the garden. There is room coffee and tea. Breakfast is served daily on the verandah.

Mariposa Hotel-Inn
5029 Hwy. 140
P.O. Box 745
Mariposa, CA 95338
209-966-4676 800-317-3244
Fax: 209-742-5963
www.yosemitehotel.com
$84 - $97

Meadow Creek Ranch is described on the next page.

© *Ellie Huggins*

Bed and Breakfast Inns

Meadow Creek Ranch
2669 Triangle Rd. and Hwy. 49 S
Mariposa, CA 95338
209-966-3843
www.sierranet.net/web/meadow
$95

Special Features:
The ranch was formerly a stage stop for Yosemite tourists traveling from Mariposa to Wawona and the Mariposa Grove.

Meadow Creek Ranch

The bed and breakfast inn was established in 1958 in a house that dates back to the 1860s. Recent new owners, Diana and Willy Wilcoxen, continue the long tradition of inn keeping. One room in the main house has a queen bed and private bath. The cottage, an old chicken coop, is furnished with an Austrian queen canopy bed, has a fireplace, clawfoot tub and sitting area. Everything is air conditioned.

Poppy Hill Bed and Breakfast
5218 Crystal Aire Drive
Mariposa, CA 95338
209-742-6273 800-587-6779
$100 - $110

Directions:
Drive 3.5 miles east on Highway 140 to Whitlock, then left 1.2 miles to Crystal Aire Dr. The inn is up the hill at the end of the street.

Special Features:
Mary Ellen is a longtime resident of the area, whose clients return year after year. Peace and quiet is what you will find here.

Poppy Hill

Mary Ellen Kirn welcomes you to her beautiful house that sits on a poppy-covered hill far from the maddening crowd. The three rooms all have private baths and are decorated with antiques that she has collected over many years. The homey livingroom features a grand piano in an alcove with a view of the garden. There is an above-ground pool and a spa for relaxing and the house has central heating and air conditioning. Imagine breakfast or complimentary beverages and hors d'oeuvres served on a deck guarded by an ancient valley oak overlooking a field of golden poppies.

Bed and Breakfast Inns

Courtesy of Poppy Hill

Poppy Hill.

Restful Nest Bed and Breakfast Resort

Visitors at Restful Nest will find a country home just six miles from Mariposa situated on ten acres with a panoramic view of the mountains. Jon Pierre and Lois Moroni have created a quiet retreat. Three rooms in the main house are comfortably furnished with different themes. One room has a king and a trundle bed for two children. All rooms have TVs with VCR and are air conditioned. A separate guest house can sleep four. Lois serves a gourmet breakfast for all guests. Smoking is allowed only on the patio.

**Restful Nest Bed and Breakfast
  Resort**
4274 Buckeye Creek Road
Mariposa, CA 95338
209-742-7127 800-664-7127
Fax: 209-742-6888
mariposa.yosemite.net/restful
$85 - $105

Special Features:
The Moronis are glad to accommodate children and family reunions. There are many attractions on the property, including a catch and release fish pond with blue gill, bass and catfish. Besides swimming in the pool, children can play tether ball or throw sticks to the resident dog who loves to fetch. The innkeepers speak French, German and, of course, English.

Bed and Breakfast Inns

Rockwood Gardens
5155 Tip Top Rd.
Mariposa, CA 95338
209-742-6817 800-859-8862
$65 - $105

Directions:
Take Highway 49 South about 8 miles to Tip Top Road on the left. Drive less than a mile to their driveway on the left.

Special Features:
Gerry is constructing a three-hole pitch and put golf course and you can cool off on warm days in their pool.

Rockwood Gardens

Gerry and Mary Ann Fuller welcome you to their home that sits on a hill surrounded by five acres with lovely gardens and ponderosa pines. Two rooms, each with a queen bed, share a bath. The Manzanita Suite guest house has a king bed, queen sofa bed and kitchen with a microwave and refrigerator. All rooms have an entrance onto secluded gardens. The house has zoned air conditioning. Rooms have TVs with VCR.

Shiloh Bed & Breakfast
3265 Triangle Park Rd.
Mariposa, CA 95338
209-742-7200
www.sierranet.net/web/shiloh
$55 - $85

Special Features:
The Shiloh is within walking distance of the Triangle Pines Restaurant, a new gourmet addition to the dining scene in Mariposa. To get to Yosemite, you can continue on Triangle Road to Midpines and Highway 140.

Shiloh Bed & Breakfast

Here's a bed and breakfast that loves kids. Dick and Gwen Foster have a large yard that features a cable swing that will carry you into trees on a corner of the property, as well as play equipment that will keep the children busy. Nestled among trees, the house has two rooms upstairs that share a downstairs bath. One has a king and one a queen. A separate guest house can sleep five to six persons and has its own kitchen. Breakfast is served in the main house on the sun porch.

Bed and Breakfast Inns

Sierra House Bed and Breakfast

Libby and Norm Murrell welcome you into their beautiful home filled with the collections of their travels while spending 17 years in Saudi Arabia. The rooms are large and comfortable. One room with a king bed is decorated with their middle eastern furniture, while a Southwest theme room has a queen bed. Libby is a fourth generation Californian whose great grandmother's double bed graces the antique room that is filled with pioneer family treasures. Everything about the home is tasteful and you feel like you are staying with gracious friends.

Sierra House Bed and Breakfast
4981 Indian Peak Road
Mariposa, CA 95338
209-966-3515 800-496-3515
mariposa.yosemite.net/sierrabb
$75 - $85

© Ellie Huggins

The Shiloh has plenty of room for kids to roam.

Bed and Breakfast Inns

Yosemite Mariposa Townhouse
  Bed and Breakfast
5174 Campbell Way
Mariposa, CA 95338
209-966-7666 800-624-4858
Fax: 209-966-3150
$55 - $95

Special Features:
The living room invites you to meet the other guests. This is a great place for a group traveling together or for a large family.

Yosemite Mariposa Townhouse Bed and Breakfast

This is a pleasant, clean bed and breakfast in a ranch style house located on a hill in town. The three rooms each have a private bath and a balcony. There is a TV with cable and HBO in each room. The house has central heating and air conditioning. There is a buffet breakfast and refreshments are served in the afternoon.

© Ellie Huggins

The lovely Mariposa County Courthouse is on Bullion Street not far from any of the downtown motels or B and B's.

Bed and Breakfast Inns

The Verandah

Ken and Fran Franken have built a lovely farmhouse on top of a hill surrounded by 14 acres. The wrap-around verandah has views across the Central Valley. On a clear day you may see the Coast Range. Fran is an avid herb and vegetable gardener. Well-behaved dogs, Jessie and Sunny, are loved by the guests and love the guests. Fran has been hiking Yosemite for 30 years and can direct you to the best places off the beaten path. Each room has a queen bed and full bath with claw foot tub. Bubble bath and rubber duckies are included. You may take your full, country style breakfast with fresh baked breads out to the verandah.

The Verandah
5086 Tip Top Road
Mariposa, CA 95338
209-742-6493 800-754-0372
www.bestinns/usa/ca/
**   verandah.html**
$90

Directions:
Drive south on Highway 49 past Bootjack to Tip Top Road. Turn left and drive for one quarter mile to a driveway on the right which curves uphill. The house is at the end of the drive on top.

Special Features:
Karen has a bountiful garden and you are encouraged to take home samples of her herbs and vegetables.

© Ellie Huggins

The Verandah Bed and Breakfast.

Bed and Breakfast Inns in Midpines

HWY. 140 LODGING MARIPOSA

Pimentel's Bed and Breakfast
6484 B Hwy. 140
Midpines, CA 95345
209-966-6847
mariposa.yosemite.net/pimentel
$65 - $85

Special Features:
The owners have 20 years intimate association with the park and will help you find interesting hikes or diversions. If you plan a rafting trip on the Merced or a spring hike at Hite's Cove, this bed and breakfast is close to those activities.

Yosemite Bug Hostel
6979 Hwy. 140
Midpines CA 95345
209-966-6666
Fax: 209-966-6667
www.yosemitebug.com
$12 - $36

Special Features:
The Recovery Cafe on the premises serves wonderful food at reasonable prices, including excellent offerings each evening. The chef makes one vegetarian and one meat dish each day. You may also get deli style lunches or have one packed to go.

Pimentel's Bed and Breakfast

Tom and Nancy Pimentel have created a modern bed and breakfast with a Victorian feel. The front porch invites guests to take breakfast or afternoon snacks there and look out on the oak studded hillside. The farm animals include miniature horses, rabbits, geese, ducks and chickens that lay your fresh breakfast eggs every day. Homemade baked goods and jams along with seasonal fruits complete your breakfast offerings. The three rooms are cheery, each with private bath. One room has twin beds, one a queen and a third a double.

Yosemite Bug Hostel

Here is a hostel with a difference. There are newly constructed lodge rooms for two to eight persons with shared bathroom facilities and a kitchen for hostel guests. They will even rent the linens and blanket. You can reach the hostel without a car on the VIA Adventure bus and take the same bus the next day to Yosemite. There is a laundry facility and you may hang a hammock or put up a tent in their campground. They have bikes to rent and a map. Mariah Wilderness Expeditions rafting starts from here.

154

Motels and Lodges

Best Western Yosemite Way Station

The motel has 78 deluxe rooms, swimming pool and spa. Cable TV and HBO are in every room. A continental breakfast is available.

Best Western Yosemite Way
  Station
Hwy. 140 across from Hwy. 49S
Mariposa, CA 95338
209-966-7545 800-321-5261
Fax: 209-966-6353
www.yosemite-motels.com
$79 - $89

Comfort Inn Mariposa

The Comfort Inn has rooms with one king or one and two queens as well as suites with full kitchens. There is a swimming pool and spa and of course TVs and phones.

Comfort Inn
4994 Bullion St.
Mariposa, CA 95338
209-966-4344 800-321-5261
Fax: 209-966-4655
www.yosemite-motels.com
$80 - $125

E.C. Yosemite Motel

The motel features some of the largest rooms in town with TVs and phones in every room. There is a pool and spa and pets are allowed.

E.C. Yosemite Motel
Hwy. 140 and Jones St.
Mariposa, CA 95338
209-742-6800 800-321-5261
Fax: 209-742-6719
$59 - $82

Holiday Inn Express

Mariposa's newest motel has a pool and conference room. Rooms have TV's with free HBO and phones.

Holiday Inn Express
5059 Hwy. 140
Mariposa, CA 95338
209-966-4288 800-966-9746
Fax: 209-966-4788
www.sierranet.net/web/
   holidayinnmariposa
$89 - $159

Mariposa Lodge

This affordable motel has 45 rooms that have two queen beds. Some are wheelchair accessible. There is a pool and spa and small pets are allowed.

Mariposa Lodge
5052 Hwy. 140
Mariposa, CA 95338
209-966-3607 800-341-8000
Fax: 209-742-7038
mariposa.yosemite.net/marlodge
$65 - $82

Motels and Lodges

Miners Inn
5181 Hwy. 49 N at Hwy. 140
Mariposa, CA 95338
209-742-7777 800-321-5261
Fax: 209-966-2343
www.yosemite-motels.com
$79 - $159

Miners Inn

The rooms are spacious and have a single king bed or two queens, and some deluxe rooms have a spa tub and fireplace. There is a small pool. The Miner's Inn Restaurant and Lounge are on the premises.

Mother Lode Lodge
5051 Hwy. 140
Mariposa, CA 95338
209-966-2521 800-398-9770
$48 - $110

Mother Lode Lodge

The motel has rooms with TVs and phones. Some rooms have kitchens. There is a pool and spa and they will take pets.

Muir Lodge
6833 Hwy. 140
Midpines, CA 95345
209-966-2468
$30 - $70

Muir Lodge

An old but economical motel near Midpines on Bear Creek has 26 units with microwaves and TV and some with queen beds. One unit has a kitchenette. There is a coin laundry and an unheated swimming pool.

Sierra View Motel
4993 Seventh Street
Mariposa, CA 95338
209-966-5793 800-627-8439
Fax: 209-742-5669
$55 - $80

Sierra View Motel

Economically priced rooms have one, two or three beds. There are two suites that have queens and a sitting area. The patio under the trees is the perfect place for your complimentary continental breakfast.

Motels and Lodges

Yosemite Redbud Lodge

A special treat awaits those who stop at Savage's Trading Post at the confluence of the South Fork with the Merced River. Do not be put off by the wooden buildings. Your hostess, Letty Barry, has designed the decor of each large room to reflect her taste for Native American motifs. Each room comes with fresh fruit, muffins and freshly ground coffee and tea, a refrigerator and barbeque. The rooms feature king beds and a sitting area with a balcony that looks out on the river. Suites have kitchenettes and a fireplace.

Yosemite Redbud Lodge
9486 Hwy. 140
El Portal, CA 95318
209-379-2301 800-272-2301
$80 - $120

Directions:
Redbud Lodge is just seven miles west of El Portal. It is two miles from Cedar Lodge where there is dining.

Special Features:
The Hite's Cove Trail leaves from the lodge. This is the perfect place for those who want hiking and fishing nearby or are on their way to ski at Badger Pass or want a winter sojourn below the snow line. See page 170 for a description of the hike.

Cedar Lodge

Several buildings with family suites and rooms of all kinds are just across the highway from the Merced River. Two restaurants, a lounge, and indoor and outdoor swimming pools are in the complex. A gazebo and walk along the river complete the amenities of this fine lodge that is just eight miles from the park entrance.

Cedar Lodge
P.O. Box "C"
9966 Hwy. 140
El Portal, CA 95318
209-379-2612 800-321-5261
Fax: 209-379-2712
www.yosemite-motels.com
$85 - $395

Motels and Lodges

Yosemite Lakeview Lodge
P.O. Box "D"
11156 Hwy. 140
El Portal, CA 95318
209-379-2681 800-321-5261
Fax: 209-379-2704
www.yosemite-motels.com
$82 - $169

Yosemite Lakeview Lodge

Overlooking the rapids of the Merced River just at the border of the park, the lodge has been totally renovated after the devastating floods of January 1997. Many rooms have river views, in-room spas and fireplaces as well as patios and balconies. There are two swimming pools plus a restaurant and lounge.

Courtesy of the National Park Service, Yosemite

The Yosemite Valley Railroad on its way to El Portal before the advent of the All Weather Highway.

Dining

There are many restaurants to choose from in Mariposa and environs. We have listed those that have been reviewed by the author and offer something special. The restaurants are listed alphabetically. Two outside of town are on Triangle Road, so if you are staying off Highway 49 South, you might want to give them a try.

How we rate restaurants:

$ Inexpensive, including soup or salad—under $15.
$$ Moderate, including soup or salad—under $20.
$$$ Moderately expensive, a la carte—entrées $16 to $22.
$$$$ Expensive, a la carte—entrées over $22.
Tips, wine and tax are not included in our estimates of cost.

Castillos Mexican Restaurant

Castillos is a intimate place that offers the best of Mexican food. The menu features an array of house specialties that are very tasty. In pleasant weather you can dine on the patio. The beer list is extensive and they serve some local wines.

$$
Lunch and dinner, daily.
4995 5th Street
Mariposa
209-742-4413

Charles Street Dinner House

The Charles Street Dinner House offers a gourmet menu which can be accompanied with wine from an extensive list that includes local offerings. The restaurant is a favorite of locals looking for good California/American cuisine. You can't go wrong dining here.

$$$
Reservations recommended in high season.
Dinner, Wednesday thru Sunday.
5043 Hwy. 140 at 7th Street
Mariposa
209-966-2366

Dining

$$$
Reservations recommended in
  high season.
Dinner, daily. Sunday brunch.
5109 Hwy. 140
Mariposa
209-742-2100

Gold Rush Grill and Saloon

From appetizers to hearty skillets with cajun spices you'll find much to please your pallet here. Their famous pepper steak is created from a New York cut with mushroom sauce, sautéed green onions and plenty of pepper. Their Sunday brunch will start an active day with everything from salmon and eggs to a three-egg omelet or strawberry crepes and french toast. You won't need to eat until dinner.

$$
Breakfast, lunch and dinner, daily.
5024 Hwy. 140 at 6th Street
Mariposa
209-966-4242

Meadows Ranch Café

Located in one of Mariposa's historic buildings constructed in 1896 for Trabucco's general store, the menu at this large establishment has something for everyone in the family and even a pub menu. There are the usual hamburgers and sandwiches, plus chicken, ribs or steak from the grill, or gourmet pizzas. Their many house dinner specialties include a blackened or grilled fresh fish, Thai curry sauté or stuffed Portabello mushroom. And for dessert lovers and chocaholics there are seven kinds of chocolate desserts to die for. You can also order for takeout.

Dining

Ocean Sierra Restaurant

Ocean Sierra is located outside of town on Triangle Road offering fine dining in a restored 75-year-old country home. The chef and owner, Pam Toney, cooks a special California cuisine featuring seafood, beef or vegetarian dishes. Dinners include soup, salad and your entrée.

$$$
Reservations recommended.
Dinner, Wednesday thru Sunday.
At the corner of East Westfall and
**   Triangle Roads.**
209-742-7050

The Recovery Cafe

You don't have to be staying at the Yosemite Bug Hostel to enjoy the fine food at the cafe. There are only two items on the menu each night, a meat and a rice or pasta dish, all cooked with fresh ingredients and very tasty. The menu is posted each morning, but you can't go wrong by driving here for their great dinners. If you are on your way to a day of activity, stop by and assemble your own trail lunch from their deli.

$
Breakfast, lunch and dinner, daily.
6979 Hwy. 140
Midpines
209-966-6666

Red Fox Restaurant

The dinner menu here offers economical dining with no surprises. Steak, chicken and fish entrées are served with rice, baked potato or fries, vegetable and soup or salad. Hamburgers, chicken nuggets and spaghetti are available for the kids in the group.

$$
Breakfast, lunch and dinner, daily.
Hwy. 140 and 12th Street
Mariposa
209-966-5707

$$
Reservations recommended on weekends.
Dinner, Thursday thru Tuesday.
At the corner of Triangle and Triangle Park Roads.
209-966-7900

Triangle Pines

The Triangle Pines is a new dining place that has become an instant success. The owners decided to leave the pressed board used to create their dining room and decorated it with painted ivy, which makes a cheerful decor. The menu includes several interesting appetizers, including the perennial favorite of deep fried zucchini. The traditional Caesar salad comes with plenty of anchovies and garlic. Entrées come with a tasty selection of well-seasoned vegetables. The chef makes good use of herbs. However, for ice cream fans, you must leave room for the old-fashioned hot fudge sundae topped with real whipped cream and a cherry. The owners have thoughtfully left a corner of the small restaurant as a children's play area with small chairs and tables and plenty of toys.

Highway 140 Activities

The town of Mariposa traces its roots to the gold in the placers and under the various mountains of the region. It is a very historic place with many buildings dating to the 1850s including the 1854 courthouse.

Mariposa sits in a valley at about 1,800 feet and below the summit of Midpines at 2,800 feet. The hills around the town are golden with poppies and other wildflowers in the spring, and fall brings color to the forests in the region.

Highway 140 is the road to Yosemite that is most often free of snow, as it enters the park at El Portal at 1,900 feet. Many of the activities in the area relate to the Merced River.

Mariposa itself has special events throughout the year and, with a large number of bed and breakfast inns, dining and wine tasting in the area, it can be a fine destination.

The activities outlined in the next few pages offer historical walks, museums, exciting rafting trips and a hike along Hite's Cove Trail, one of the best wildflower walks in the entire region.

Wineries of the area

Butterfly Creek Winery and Vineyards
4063 Triangle Rd.
Nine miles off Hwy. 49 S
Mariposa
209-966-2097
Hours: Friday and Saturday, 10:00 a.m. to 4:00 p.m. and by appointment.

Radanovich Winery Tasting Room
Schlageter Hotel
5029 Hwy. 140
Mariposa
209-966-5595
Daily, 11:00 a.m. to 5:30 p.m.

Silver Fox Vineyards
4683 Morningstar Lane
Mariposa
209-966-4800
By appointment.

Mariposa Walking Tour

Mariposa County Courthouse

In 1854 Frémont donated the lot. After an expenditure of $9,300, this lovely white clapboard structure was built with local, hand-planed lumber and joined with square nails. The clock tower was added in 1866. Its bell was shipped around the horn and has chimed on the hour ever since. In the upstairs courtroom many important mining cases were adjudicated. The current presiding judge is only the seventh in the county's history. Pictures of these judges adorn the wall next to the Clerk's office. Be sure to go in and walk upstairs to see the courtroom pictured below.

Mariposa's downtown has changed little since it was first laid out in Frémont's day. Only gas stations and motels instead of livery stables and hotels give this town a modern look.

A Walking Tour

Start your walking tour up the hill on 11th Street one block to Bullion Street. Turn right and walk until you see the graceful lines of the Mariposa County Courthouse encircled by its tree-shaded lawn.

© Ellie Huggins

The courtroom of the Mariposa County Courthouse has not changed since the 1860s. The pot bellied stove still heats the room. The only modern addition is electricity and the computer on the right.

Mariposa Walking Tour

The building housing the Mariposa Gazette is at 9th and Jones Street. Established in 1854, it burned down twice but has never missed an issue.

Keep walking on Bullion Street past 4th Street to the end where St. Joseph's Catholic Church graces the hill above the intersection of Highways 49 and 140. It celebrated 135 years in 1998.

Return on Bullion to 4th Street where the Old Jail sits above the road. It was built in 1858 with two-foot thick granite walls. It burned in 1892, was repaired in 1893 and remodeled in 1949. It was in continuous use until 1963. Turn down hill on 4th Street one block to Main Street.

On Main Street (Highway 140) many of the establishments occupy refurbished buildings of Mariposa's past. The Schlageter Hotel on the north side at the corner of 5th Street was originally built in 1859. It was destroyed in the 1866 fire and rebuilt in 1867, then remodeled in 1902. Across Main Street the Gold Coin is in the Frémont Adobe, reported to have been his assay office in the early 1850s. A little farther up the street the Odd Fellow Hall is still in use since its establishment in 1867.

Mariposa's Victorian Homes

Near the courthouse on the corner of Jones and 8th Streets sits the Trabucco-Campbell home, a lovely Victorian built by Judge Trabucco in 1901. It is now owned by Marguerite Campbell, a third generation native.

On the corner of 7th and Jones Streets is the Jones home, built by a judge in 1858. It has had only three owners.

Rafting

Rafting the Merced

The season, generally April through July, is determined by the depth and melt of the High Sierra snowpack. A late, heavy pack can delay the start for rafting. The Merced River is a solid intermediate run with Class IV and IV+ rapids. Previous experience is recommended by all rafting companies, though an adventurous first-timer in good condition will surely have a great time later in the season.

Most groups listed offer both one and two-day trips. One-day trips put in near Red Bud below El Portal with challenging Class IV rapids along the way. After a lunch stop part way, you take out at Railroad Flat.

Two-day trips end at Bagby on Lake McClure. The section below Briceburg is filled with thrilling Class IV and IV+ rapids that are for intermediate paddlers who are in good condition. The overnight stop is a wilderness camp. A hearty meal is prepared by your guides and a campfire usually precedes bedding down under the stars. The second day has several Class IV rapids and one portage.

The Merced River

This enchanting and challenging river flows out from the Highway 140 entrance to Yosemite National Park. Centuries of glacial and volcanic action and erosion have created a fascinating deep river canyon for raft trips. The river descends from Yosemite Valley in successive leaps, producing stretches of exhilarating wave trains, technical challenges and steep gradient drops. Yet it also offers many opportunities for just laying back in a boat, relaxing and enjoying the forest scenery while the current takes you down. One of the last free-flowing rivers in California, it is rafted in the spring and early summer when the snow, melting in the warm sun, fills the deep river canyon with exhilarating whitewater. At that time of year the surrounding hills are green and the wildflowers abundant.

Rafting

Ahwahnee Whitewater

Ahwahnee offers rides in three kinds of rafts: oar boats paddled by a guide, paddle boats in which you do all the paddling and hybrid boats with oars and paddles.

Ahwahnee Whitewater
P.O. Box 1161
Columbia, CA 95310
800-359-9790
www.ahwahnee.com

All-Outdoors Whitewater Rafting

This company offers one and two-day trips and has been voted one of the best family-run rafting companies in California.

All-Outdoors Whitewater
** Rafting**
1250 Pine Street
Walnut Creek, CA 94596
800-247-2387
www.aorafting.com

American River Recreation

ARR runs one and two-day trips from Red Bud to Railroad Flat and Lake McClure with an option to run the lower quarter mile Class IV or the upper stretch from Red Bud to Briceburg again on the second day.

American River Recreation
P.O. Box 465
Lotus, CA 95651
800-333-7238
www.arrafting.com

American River Touring Association

The first group to offer rivers trips in the West is a nonprofit company, founded in 1963. All profits are donated to conservation groups. Trips on the Merced are for one day only.

ARTA American River Touring
** Association**
24000 Casa Loma Rd.
Groveland, CA 95321
800-323-2782
www.arta.org

Directions:
The meeting place is at a parking area on Highway 140 in El Portal, 25 miles from the Highway 49 North intersection in Mariposa, or 3.4 miles below the El Portal Market.

Rafting

Mariah Expeditions
P.O. Box 248
Point Richmond, CA 94807
800-462-7424
www.mariahwe.com

Mariah Expeditions

Mariah offers one and two-day trips Minimum age is 12 years old. Their meeting place is at the Yosemite Bug Hostel in Midpines, where you can find a campsite or stay at the hostel. See page 154 for a description of the hostel. Mariah meets you at 9:00 a.m. after breakfast (on your own) and drives you to the put-in.

OARS Inc.
P.O. Box 67
Angels Camp, CA 95222
800-346-6277
www.oars.com

OARS Inc.

The company offers both one and two-day trips.

Whitewater Voyages
5225 San Pablo Dam Road
El Sobrante, CA 94803
800-488-7238
www.wwvoyages.com

Whitewater Voyages

One-day trips go from Cranberry Gulch to Briceburg and two-day trips from Cranberry to Bagby on low water days, or Cranberry to Briceburg twice.

Zephyr Whitewater Expeditions
P.O. Box 510
Columbia, CA 95310
800-431-3636
www.zrafting.com

Directions:
The meeting place is Bear Creek Campground on Highway 140 near the Midpines Post Office. You may camp there or stay in local motels.

Zephyr Whitewater Expeditions

Zephyr uses self-bailing boats so that your feet will be out of the water most of the time. They offer both one and two-day trips. If the water level is high, on the second day they repeat part of the run, ending at Briceburg.

Hiking

Briceburg Along the Merced River

During summer months the Bureau of Land Management maintains an information center at Briceburg. The bureau has established three campgrounds along the river between Briceburg and Bagby. The road accessing these campgrounds is actually the route of the former Yosemite Valley Railroad and makes both an excellent biking or hiking trail. In April, when the wildflowers are at their best, the hike is a pleasant walk to McCabe Flat, the first campground. There is a beach, toilets and many nice places to picnic. The next two campgrounds, Willow Placer and Railroad Flat, are farther downriver. Really ambitious hikers can venture beyond the gate at Railroad Flat all the way to Bagby. Be advised that the canyon gets very hot in summer, so these hikes are best done between October and May. Families with small children looking for a picnic site closer to Briceburg can walk about a mile to the first beach access to the river. The river is not for swimming. It runs fast during spring and early summer.

Directions:
Briceburg is 13 miles north of Mariposa on Highway 140. It is located at the confluence of Bear Creek and the Merced River.

Hiking down the river

This is an easy hike of three miles round trip to McCabe Flat on the old railroad bed, or four miles round trip to Willow Placer and five miles to Railroad Flat. There is no piped water at any campground but there are restrooms. This walk is best in spring when the wildflowers are in full bloom. It can be a pleasant hike during the fall or winter, and the river is always fun to watch.

Hiking up the river

It is also very pleasant to hike up the river on the north bank. After crossing the bridge turn right and walk along the same railroad bed as far as you wish. Again, this walk is best in spring when the wildflowers are in full bloom.

Hiking

Hite's Cove Trail

Directions:
The trail starts just east of Savage's Trading Post and the Redbud Lodge.

Stop in at Savage's Trading Post to register. You must traverse private property for the first part of the hike. The trail is maintained by the private landowners and they need to keep track of who is on the trail. You will be walking on an ancient Miwok trail to Yosemite that later served as a route to Hite's Cove Mine. See page 133 for the story of the mine. As you make your way along the trail, imagine those hardy miners and their mules carrying all the machinery along this route. The mine site is four miles from Highway 140, but you may stop at any number of places for a picnic along the river.

You do not need to hike very far to experience the spectacular wildflower display. The flowers begin their show in February and continue blooming in great profusion until April or May depending on the date of the last rains and the temperature. For an amateur botanist, this trail affords closeup looks at a diverse group of California wildflowers, so bring your favorite flower guide to help you determine what species you encounter.

The first quarter mile has the best flower displays of the hike with brodiaeas and poppies being the most common. You may also notice red maids (*Calandrinia cilliata* var. *menziesii*), related to miner's lettuce and garden portulaca. Two kinds of poppies are present. The annual California poppy *Eschscholzia caespitosa* is easily recognized, but see if you can spot cream cup poppies on the first part of the trail. They have slender drooping stems that are very hairy with solitary blooms of six cream colored petals. A partial list of the flowers you might find on your hike is on the following two pages.

Hiking

This list is reprinted by permission from *Wildflowers of the Hite's Cove Trail* by Stephen Botti and Ann Mendershausen, sadly out of print.

Yellow to Orange

Goldfields	*Lasthenia chrysostoma*
Vernal Tarweed	*Madia elegans*
Foothill Pseudobahia	*Pseudobahia heermannii*
Golden Yarrow	*Eriophyllum confertiflorum*
Blazing Star	*Mentzelia lindleyi crocea*
Annual Poppy	*Eschscholzia caespitosa*
Cream Cups	*Platystemon californicus*
Common Monkey Flower	*Mimulus guttatus*
Golden Brodiaea	*Brodiaea lutea scabra*
Fiddleneck	*Amsinckia intermedia*

Pink to Red

Rock Cress	*Arabis sprasiflora*
Indian Pink	*Silene californica*
Live-Forever	*Dudleya cymosa*
Redbud	*Cercis occidentalis*
Harlequin Lupine	*Lupine stiversii*
Farewell to Spring	*Clarkia dudleyana*
Tongue Clarkia	*Clarkia rhomboidea*
Mustang Clover	*Linanthus montanus*
Foothill Shooting Star	*Dodecatheon hendersonii*
Red-Maids	*Calandrinia ciliata var. menziesii*
Indian Paintbrush	*Castilleja applegatei*
Kellogg's Monkey Flower	*Mimulus kelloggii*
Twining Brodiaea	*Brodiaea volubilis*

Purple to Violet or Blue

Fiesta Flower	*Pholistoma auritum*
Mountain Jewel Flower	*Streptanthus tortuosus*
Lindley's Annual Lupine	*Lupinus bicolor microphyllus*
Baby-Blue Eyes	*Nemophila menziesii*
Bird's Eye Gilia	*Gilia tricolor*
Chinese Houses	*Collinsia heterophylla*
Owls-Clover	*Orthocarpus purpurascens*
Harvest Brodiaea	*Brodiaea elegans*
Blue Dicks	*Brodiaea pulchella*

Wildflowers of Hite's Cove

White

Fringe-Pod	*Thysanocarpus curvipes*
Buckeye	*Aesculus californica*
Varied-Leaf Nemophila	*Nemophila heterophylla*
Caterpillar Plant	*Phacelia cicutaria*
Woodland Star	*Lithophragma affinis*
Fairy Lantern	*Calochortus albus*
Popcorn Flower	*Plagiobothrys nothofulvus*
Western Rue-Anemone	*Isopyrum occidentale*

Courtesy of Leroy Radanovich

Hite's Cove Mine in 1881. The structures are no longer there, having been destroyed by fire in 1925.

Bicycling

There are many back roads in the area that are great for cycling. At the time of printing the Yosemite Bug Hostel in Midpines offered the only map for cyclists. However, Will Riskit Mountain Cyclists is also planning a booklet about good rides.

Will Riskit Mountain Cyclists

The shop is off Highway 49 South on Ashworth. They rent, repair and sell bikes and give advice about the best riding in the area.

**Will Riskit Mountain Cyclists
4949 Ashworth Road
Mariposa
209-742-5239**

Yosemite Bug Hostel

Not only can cyclists find very economical accommodations or a campsite here, but the hostel rents bikes, has a map and shares their expertise about the best rides in the area.

**Yosemite Bug Hostel
6979 Hwy. 140
Midpines
209-966-6667
www.yosemitebug.com**

Briceburg to Railroad Flat

This is the best easy ride in the area. Since the road follows the canyon of the Merced River on the old railroad bed, it is a perfect family ride with great picnic spots, campgrounds with facilities and beaches along the way. It should be avoided during a hot summer day, but is very enjoyable the rest of the year. Naturally, like all springtime activities in this region, your ride will be accompanied by a splendid wildflower show.

Directions:
Briceburg is at the confluence of Bear Creek and the Merced River, 13 miles north of Mariposa on Highway 140.

Page 169 in "Hiking" has a complete description of the road to Railroad Flat. There is no water available. Be sure to have several water bottles.

**Mariposa Museum and
History Center
209-966-2924**

The museum is found behind an old stamp mill and wooden-wheeled freight wagon on Jessie Street just north of 12th Street.

Mariposa Museum and History Center

Friendly volunteer docents will be glad to tell you stories about the historic old town. Colonel John Frémont and his wife, Jessie Benton Frémont, are prominently featured among the imaginative and authentic exhibits of Mariposa's gold days. Of particular interest are the "Dear Charlie" letters. The originals, owned by the Society, were written by Horace Snow to his boyhood friend in Cambridge, Massachusetts. Excerpts appear on blue paper affixed throughout the exhibits and are accurate and fascinating descriptions of life in the mines more than a century ago. The shop sells books, souvenirs, postcards and gold.

**California State Mining and Mineral
Museum
Mariposa County Fairgrounds on
Hwy. 49 South just outside town.
209-742-7625**

May 1 to September 30, daily except
Tuesday, 10:00 a.m. to 6:00 p.m.
October 1 to April 30, Wednesday thru
Sunday, 10:00 a.m. to 4:00 p.m.

**At press time funding for the
museum was uncertain. Check at
the Visitors Bureau in town.**

California State Mining and Mineral Museum

If open, rock hounds will want to visit this museum where California's mining heritage is on display along with minerals, meteorites and nuggets of California gold and diamonds. The shop sells minerals and other related items and books.

Art Galleries

The Mariposa County Arts Council

A lively arts scene is promoted and assisted by the arts council. They hold juried exhibits and host an annual Young Masters Youth Art Exhibit every February. There are shows of quilt making and photo club winners as well as workshops.

You can obtain information from the council at the number listed opposite or join the organization and get their regular newsletter. They operate the gallery listed below.

The Mariposa County Arts Council
P.O. Box 2134
Mariposa, CA 95338
209-966-3155 800-903-9936
mariposa.yosemite.net/arts/

5th Street Gallery

The gallery and gift shop has changing exhibits of works by local artists. These may include oils, watercolors, prints, jewelry or sculpture.

5th Street Gallery
5009 5th Street
Mariposa
209-966-3155
Monday thru Saturday, 9:00 a.m.
** to 5:00 p.m.**

Mariposa hosts storytellers, Indian pow-wows and more from March through December. See the Mariposa County Visitor Bureau's guide for a complete list.

March

Storytelling Festival
Tales by storytellers from around the country.
209-966-3155

April

Annual Civil War Reenactment
Parade through downtown, authentic Civil War reenactment and craft fair.
209-966-2456

May

Mariposa County Indian Council Pow-Wow
209-966-5229

Bluegrass Festival
209-966-3155

June

Mariposa Junior Rodeo
209-966-5779

Mariposa County Pioneer Wagon Train
Thirty-two mile trek from Fish Camp to Mariposa.
209-742-6596

July, August, September

Mariposa Evenings
Entertainment by both amateur and professional performers.
209-966-3155

October

Mountain Bike Race
2,500 feet elevation gain over varied terrain from 12 to 32 miles.
209-966-6666

November

Sequel Storytelling Festival
Local amateur storytellers.
209-966-3155

December

Mariposa Crafters Holiday Festival
Handmade crafts and jewelry.
209-966-3555

Year-Round

Mariposa Film Club
Quality movies shown Friday and Saturday nights at the Old Masonic Hall. Nonmembers pay $5 at the door.

Courtesy of the National Park Service, Yosemite

In 1901 the first automobiles were photographed leaving Crocker's Station on the old Big Oak Flat Road. It would have been a very dusty ride. Crocker's Hotel is no longer, and the Big Oak Flat Road is now a realigned and paved Highway 120 into Yosemite National Park. However, you can drive a portion of the old road that is now Hardin Flat Road.

Introduction to Highway 120 West

The Tong Wars of Chinese Camp

It is hard to believe that 5,000 souls, mostly orientals, inhabited Chinese Camp in the heady days of the early Gold Rush. They made a good living harvesting the gold left in the tailings by the rough and hasty methods of early miners. There were enough Chinese here to engage in an authentic Tong War. The Sam Yap and Yan Woo societies engaged in a mostly mock battle described by Captain Ayres of Tuolumne County.

> "Everybody marched as he pleased or ran about hooting and shouting. Chinamen on horseback hovered around the flock and it looked like a band of cattle being driven. One man was killed, one wounded, who was bayonetted. He was carried from the field as they carry a hog. His (pig)tail and heels tied to a pole."

If you detour to drive through town, notice the trees of heaven with fernlike leaves that were planted everywhere the Chinese settled.

From Manteca to Oakdale Highway 120 traverses the bountiful farmland of the San Joaquin Valley. At Oakdale you join with Highway 108 and enter the Stanislaus River valley passing oak-studded pasture lands, rising through hills with strange geologic shapes. Vertical black rocks rising out of meadows adjacent to the road are called tombstone rocks. Mary Hill in her book, *California Landscape,* describes these as "outcroppings or fingers of slate eroded from nearly vertical layers. A group of tombstone rocks has the aspect of a deserted graveyard."

At Yosemite Junction Highway 120 turns south to Chinese Camp, while Highway 108 continues east to the famous gold rush towns of Sonora, Jamestown and Columbia. Trips to these towns are described in the "Off the Beaten Path" section on page 188. From Chinese Camp you skirt the edge of Don Pedro Reservoir to Moccasin where the steep Priest Grade begins. While not suitable for campers or trailers, the cutoff saves time for cars and is 2.5 miles shorter than the main road. As you drive this narrow, twisting road think what it would have been like in a stagecoach a century ago!

Introduction to Highway 120 West

From Priest Station you follow much of the original Big Oak Flat wagon route. You'll pass through Big Oak Flat and Groveland, towns with colorful gold rush histories.

The gateway communities of Groveland and Pine Mountain Lake provide interesting opportunities for overnight lodging and dining. It is a jumping off place for hikes, fishing, horseback riding, rafting on the Tuolumne River and golf.

Just before crossing a bridge over the South Fork of the Tuolumne River two miles east of Buck Meadows, a road to the right leads down to Rainbow Pool, a favorite swimming hole of the area. See "Swimming" on page 209 for a description.

You enter the park at the Big Oak Flat Entrance Station, then climb to Crane Flat (6192 feet) through a mixed forest of sugar pine and white fir. The stately sugar pine is easily identified with its sparsely needled branches held straight out, and 20-inch cones dangling from the ends of the topmost branches. In the spring the dogwood blooms create clouds of white in the nearby forest, while summer garlands of blue lupine fill the roadside's granite soil.

The driving time from Manteca to the Yosemite National Park Big Oak Flat Entrance Station is about two hours (87 miles). From the entrance station to the Valley Visitor Center is another 25 miles and takes about an hour, especially with stops to admire the views.

The big fire of 1987

At Buck Meadows you enter the Stanislaus National Forest, where charred timbers all around are grim reminders of the 1987 forest fire. It raged from August 29 to September 5. At the height of the conflagration there were 5,000 fire fighters on the lines. One team barely escaped death huddled underneath aluminum protectors as the fire rushed past them. It was the worst fire ever to ignite the Stanislaus National Forest, destroying more than 147,000 acres. As you drive through Buck Meadows, threatened three times by flames, you will marvel at the courage of those who worked the fire line to save this community.

Introduction to Highway 120 West

At Crane Flat the Tioga Pass Road (Highway 120) turns left, heading for Tuolumne Meadows and over Tioga Pass to Highway 395.

Continuing straight you begin your descent into Yosemite Valley. Several turnouts offer tantalizing previews of the grandeur ahead. Between April and July your journey will be accompanied by the music of melting snow, as every crevice and creek runs with cascading torrents. You join Highway 140 at the bottom of the grade for the last few miles into the Valley.

It took tons of dynamite and hundreds of holes to blast the granite for the Highway 120 construction from Crane Flat into the Valley in 1936. Here a worker drills the first of many holes before packing the dynamite and blasting the section of rock apart. There were no hard hats for construction workers in those days.

Courtesy of the National Park Service, Yosemite

History of the Big Oak Flat Road

The Big Oak Flat Road to Yosemite National Park is very historic. Tales abound of newcomers streaming to the southern mines around Sonora and of early visitors to the park who were jostled and rocked as top-heavy stagecoaches negotiated hairpin curves.

The discovery of Yosemite Valley and publicity about its wonders sparked much competition among foothill towns to build toll roads into the Valley. With the transfer of the Yosemite Grant to California by Congress in 1864, a race began to lure tourists onto toll roads on stages instead of horseback.

The battle of the toll roads

In 1868 influential Tuolumne County businessmen organized the Yosemite Turnpike Road Company to create a stage route from Chinese Camp through Big Oak Flat to Hodgdon's Station and Crane Flat, and on through to Gentry's Station above the Merced River canyon. This road was completed by July 1871.

The Coulterville and Yosemite Turnpike Company incorporated in 1870 to build a toll road via Bower Cave to Crane Flat and into the Valley through Big Meadow.

The Yosemite Turnpike Road Company loses rights then gets them back.

In 1869 the Big Oak Flat toll road company received exclusive rights from the Yosemite Board of Commissioners to build their wagon road within the grant from the north side of the Valley. However, this right was contingent upon completion of the road by July, 1871. When it was apparent that the road from Gentry's into the Valley could not be completed in the allotted time, the company was granted an extension to January, 1872. By this time the company was out of money and time and did not ask for another extension, thus forfeiting its exclusive rights. The Coulterville group was quick to act and petitioned the Board of Commissioners in favor of their toll road.

The Tuolumne County group realized by 1873 that they still needed rights for a road into the Valley. Even though the Yosemite Board refused their petition twice, the influential businessmen persuaded the California legislature to override the Board. By early 1874 the race was on to see which road would reach the Valley first and garner the most tourist traffic through their towns.

History of the Big Oak Flat Road

Priest's Station

News of Yosemite Valley's wonders spread fast, and soon tourists were coming in ever-increasing numbers. The Big Oak Flat Road sprouted stage stops placed strategically along the way, and hotels were built to accommodate tourists during their two to three day journey to the park. Priest's Station, still there at the top of the grade of the same name, was one of those. It served tourists from 1855 until it burned in 1980 and was rebuilt as a motel. It was founded by Alexander Kirkwood, whose wife was the proprietress and renowned for her hospitality and excellent kitchen. The name Priest's was given to the hotel after Mr. Kirkwood died and his wife married William Priest, who gladly left the hotel management to her. He became active in Groveland affairs and later was construction superintendent for the Tioga Road.

In 1872 the company received the exclusive rights abandoned by the Big Oak Flat boosters, but not for long (see sidebar on previous page). Coulterville completed its toll road into the Valley in 1874 just 29 days before its rival completed the road from Groveland. Having lost his exclusivity, Dr. John McLean, principal investor in the Coulterville company, sued the state to recover his investment. The suit was not settled until the early twentieth century after McLean had died.

Both roads dropped steeply into the Valley. Imagine sitting next to the stage driver as he began the precipitous 2,000-foot descent. On hairpin turns wagon wheels were at the very edge of the cliff and granite boulders as big as houses perched next to the road.

With billowing dust choking all on board and thoughts of broken harnesses and missteps by the horses filling passengers' minds, the stage would stop when the Valley came into view. Fear would vanish in the face of such beauty.

Historic Groveland and Big Oak Flat

After climbing the Priest grade, Highway 120 passes through Big Oak Flat. Before settlement by miners, it was a Miwok rancheria. The natives' grinding rocks can still be found, but the flat meadows upon which their village stood and the oaks they harvested for their excellent acorns disappeared in the miners' zeal to find golden riches beneath the soil.

Mining claims in Big Oak Flat and Garrote (now Groveland) started small. However, by the 1860s flume mining companies controlled up to a half mile of creekside each. Over $25 million was extracted from the earth between 1849 and the 1870s. In 1895 a hard rock mining boom began, with two active stamp mills and several deep shaft mines plus numerous quartz mines. As with all hard rock mining in California, the fixing of gold prices and World War II sounded the death knell for the mines.

Groveland and Big Oak Flat, however, experienced a building boom and prosperity during the construction of the Hetch Hetchy Dam between 1916 and 1925. A railroad was built to supply men and materials and Groveland became the construction headquarters.

The story of the big oak

The giant oak for which Big Oak Flat was named was about 12 feet in diameter. Its roots entwined rich deposits of golden nuggets. Miners worked the soil around the tree until it was greatly weakened. A fire stripped it to a charred trunk. In 1869 the top fell off in a storm and lay on the ground for 30 years. In 1900 a camper accidentally set fire to it. Only a few charred pieces can be seen in the decrepit historic marker on the south side of the road just as you enter the town.

How Groveland got its name

Groveland was formerly known as "First Garrote." The dictionary defines garrote as a Spanish form of capital punishment in which a metal collar is tightened around the condemned until he dies. That name was perhaps in keeping with the settlement's lawless past and its "Hangman's Tree." A second hanging took place down the road a piece, and the site was dubbed Second Garrote and immortalized in Bret Harte's story about two faithful comrades, *Tennessee's Partner*. As far as anyone knows no further hangings took place. First Garrote became sedate and big enough to have its name changed to Groveland, after the hometown of an early settler from Massachusetts.

HWY. 120 W

183

Historic Groveland and Big Oak Flat

When Hetch Hetchy activity stopped, the town went into a sleepy decline until it was revived by growing travel to Yosemite National Park.

Groveland's many historic buildings date back to 1849. The most famous, the Groveland Hotel, is a registered historic landmark. The adobe structure in the Monterey style was built by George Reed, a prominent Gold Rush sawmill operator. It has been a hotel since the 1860s, enjoying several decades of increased activity. When the Hetch Hetchy construction frenzy was underway, Tim Carlon erected a large annex to the east in the Queen Anne style. The hotel closed its doors briefly in the 1970s until it was bought by its present owners, Peggy and Grover Mosley. They have lovingly restored and upgraded the building, added air conditioning and found a good chef for the restaurant.

Hotel Charlotte

Hotel Charlotte began life in 1918 when Charlotte DeFerreri opened a hostelry for the Hetch Hetchy workers. She had a policy of good food and comfortable rooms. The current owners keep up the tradition, continuing to operate a restaurant on the premises.

Both the Groveland Hotel and the Charlotte Hotel are listed in the section on lodging which begins on page 192.

Historic Groveland and Big Oak Flat

© Ellie Huggins

The graceful Monterey adobe building of the Groveland Hotel, the only one of its kind in the foothills, graces the main street at the eastern end of town.

© Ellie Huggins

The Iron Door saloon is just west of the Groveland Hotel in a stone building that was established as Watts and Company sometime before 1852. When James Tannahill became sole proprietor in 1868, he named the enterprise the Granite Store. It is believed that Giacomo DeFerreri started a saloon in the building in the 1890s.

Off the Beaten Path

Knight's Ferry

Directions:
Twelve miles east of Oakdale on Highway 108 take the turnoff to Knight's Ferry. Drive north about a mile until you cross the Stanislaus River. A right turn will bring you to the Corps of Engineers Interpretive Center and Park.

The Center features excellent exhibits telling the story of the Stanislaus River ecology and the New Melones Dam.

Knight's Ferry

The interpretive center and park here is a mitigation project. Because the New Melones Dam to the east destroyed many miles of wild river, the Corps of Engineers agreed to establish camping and water related activities for all the river below the dam. Knight's Ferry park is part of a chain of camping spots developed along the river.

Take a walk on the trail that leads you past the brick building, once a flour mill and later a power house for the town of Knight's Ferry. Walk across the covered bridge. Notice the sturdy construction methods brought by the builder from his native New England. Although destroyed in the great flood of 1862, its owner rebuilt it, using special timbers he selected high in the mountains. It could not have been an easy task to float those timbers down the river during the drought of 1863.

The town of Knight's Ferry hasn't changed much since it was the river crossing point for the road to the mines. It's gold rush history is a fine example of American entrepreneurial spirit. Its founder, William Knight, first passed this

Off the Beaten Path

way in 1841. He had grown up in Baltimore and was educated as a doctor. However, he decided to go west, first to Sante Fe, where he married the daughter of a former governor of the Mexican province, and then to California. He settled on the Sacramento River, served as a guide with Frémont in 1844, and finally returned to Knight's Ferry in 1849 when the gold rush was in full swing. He set up a trading post and a skiff that could ferry five or six miners across the Stanislaus River. He was apparently a quick tempered man and was killed in a gun fight in November 1849. Two former lawyers from Missouri, John and Lewis Dent, and their partner Mr. Vantine, took over the business, constructing a proper barge to ferry wagons and freight across the river. In one day in 1850 they ferried more than a hundred freight wagons. Like others in the Gold Rush towns they made a sizable fortune providing a service to miners.

Later David Locke arrived, dammed the river upstream to power his lumber and flour mills, and finally built a bridge across the river. With the bridge came prosperity to the small town of Knight's Ferry.

You can have a fine lunch next to the river at the **Knight's Ferry Resort** in town. Or you can get ice cream at **Shenanigan's Ice Cream Parlor.**

HWY. 120 W

Self Guided Canoe Trips
Knight's Ferry to Oakdale

You can rent canoes or rafts from two companies to take a leisurely river trip down the Stanislaus River between Knight's Ferry and Oakdale. Three parks along the way offer stopping places for picnics.

River Tour
209-847-4671

Sunshine Outdoor Center/
  River Adventures
209-847-8908

Call ahead to make reservations. You'll need to arrange a car shuttle.

Off the Beaten Path

In Jamestown

If you're hankering for a great hamburger and milk shake in a 1950s style diner, try **Boomer's Diner.**

If you are looking for a place to picnic, try the city park, with playground equipment, tables and restroom facilities.

Railtown 1897 State Park

The park is open daily from 9:30 a.m. to 4:30 p.m. except on Thanksgiving, Christmas and New Years Day. There is a fee to enter the park.

Mother Lode Cannon Ball Trail

Train excursions and tours are on weekends from April through October, and on special holidays. Adults can even ride in the cab. The train goes to Chinese Camp and back.

Jamestown

Instead of taking Highway 120 at Yosemite Junction, continue on Highway 108 for 10 miles to Jamestown and Railtown 1897 State Park. Take the right fork into the original old town. Park your car and spend an hour or so wandering along Main Street with its many shops and restaurants.

Railtown 1897 State Park.

Train enthusiasts and children of all ages should not pass up a visit to Railtown 1897. In this age of autos zooming to destinations on freeways, you can experience travel on the rails as your grandparents did.

Riding the Mother Lode Cannon Ball train.

Special events take place at the park throughout the year, so be sure to pick up a calendar. On Memorial Day, for instance, you can ride the steam train at 11:00 a.m. and 3:00 p.m. and enjoy an old fashioned ice cream social.

In the depot you can view a free video about the history of the Sierra Railroad and many photos of the railroad's glory days.

Off the Beaten Path

The depot store is open daily with all kinds of items to please railroad buffs and a few you wouldn't expect. Many Hollywood westerns were filmed in Jamestown or on the railroad. Videos of movies filmed here are for sale. Gary Cooper and Grace Kelly fans can buy *High Noon*.

Columbia State Historic Park

There is much to do and see in Columbia, the best preserved gold rush town in California's Mother Lode, especially in 1999, the 150th anniversary year of the Gold Rush. Allow at least a half day.

At the park you can ride a 100-year-old stagecoach, enjoy live theater in the Fallon House or listen to toe-tapping music in one of the saloons. The museum is staffed by knowledgeable docents who would be glad to answer your gold rush era questions. Docent-led walking tours leave from the museum at 11:00 a.m. and 1:30 p.m. daily.

The kids in the family will enjoy the blacksmith shop, where you might even take home a sample horseshoe hammered out over a fire kept hot with bellows just the way it was done in 1849.

Columbia State Park

Directions:
Take Highway 108 into Sonora. Drive four miles north of Sonora on Highway 49 to the road into Columbia which is clearly marked.

For shoppers there is the **Cheap Cash Store** with antiques and collectibles and the **New York Dry Goods** store where you'll find old fashioned yard goods or clothing of pioneer days.

Lodging in Columbia

Blue Nile Inn B&B
Spacious rooms with private baths.
209-588-9309

City Hotel and Fallon Hotel
Bed and breakfast inns with Victorian comfort.
800-532-1479

Harlan House B&B
Turn of the century Victorian overlooking Columbia. All rooms have private baths.
209-533-4862

Off the Beaten Path

Hardin Flat Road

Hardin Flat Road is part of the original Big Oak Flat Toll Road, constructed by Tuolumne County businessmen to attract tourists on their way to Yosemite Valley in the 1870s. This section of the narrow twisting wagon route was still used by motorists until the 1960s. A widened modern highway 17.5 miles east of Groveland has left us with seven miles of untouched old road to explore on the present day Hardin Flat Road. If you divert here you can experience pre-1960 travel to the park and pass by remnants of the stagecoach days.

Exit Highway 120 at Hardin Flat Road. Soon you will pass the Berkeley Tuolumne Camp, one of many summer camps established locally for residents of various Bay Area communities. You can inquire for an overnight accommodation here for they sometimes have vacancies. The road will twist and turn up through deep forest. Near the top a road to the south marked 33569 Hardin Flat Rd. is the entrance to the Sunset Inn. See page 199 for a description of the cabins here.

Nineteenth century travelers had to endure many days of bone jarring, dusty travel to get to Yosemite. The stage drivers needed to make many changes of teams and travelers needed overnight accommodations. Hostelries sprang up quickly to meet these needs. If you drove the Priest grade, you can imagine that horses and tourists were ready to stop at Priest's Hotel. Other stopping places appeared along the way at Hamilton Station, now Buck Meadows, and at the Rainbow Pool toll station.

The Sunset Inn sits on the site of Franklin Babcock's homestead. He was known as a master shake maker. He split them from local sugar pine and cedar. It was a fine art. His were so good that local cabins still had his shake roofs in the 1950s.

Off the Beaten Path

Just up the road you will notice a large meadow to the north. You may see some fruit trees and a fence. This is all that is left of Crocker's Station, an important hotel that Henry Crocker built here in 1880. He and his wife were famous for their food and hospitality and their register listed such notables as John Muir, James Hutchings, Stewart Edward White and Herbert Hoover.

Crockers Station was sold in 1904 after Henry died. Subsequent owners tried to keep it going until 1920. After that the buildings succumbed to neglect, snow loads and finally a lumber camp. Their trucks obliterated the original entrance road and the buildings disintegrated.

Courtesy of the National Park Service, Yosemite

The Crocker's daughter Celia is shown on her skis in 1899. Although few tourists stopped here in winter, Berkeley professors and other friends often made it this far to enjoy skiing and snowshoeing.

Lodging along Highway 120

Highway 140

10

Tioga Pass Rd.

9

Evergreen Rd.
to Hetch Hetchy

Big Oak Flat
Entrance Station

Hardin Flat Rd. East

14

Hardin Flat Rd. West

Cherry Lake Rd.

3

Buck Meadows

Moore Park Rd.

Smith Station Rd.
to Coulterville

11.4

Groveland

3

Top of Priest Grade

Groveland and nearby Buck Meadows have the greatest number of lodging possibilities in all price ranges. After the historic Groveland Hotel was successfully renovated and turned into a destination in itself, bed and breakfast inns seem to be sprouting like flowers in the spring. A brand new one was built in 1998 and another is being created out of a long vacant Victorian that will open in 1999.

In Buck Meadows, where ten years ago there was only a small motel, the Yosemite Westgate Motel has been adding rooms and facilities every year. This year it will take over the old Buck Meadows Lodge, renovate the motel and keep the restaurant in operation.

Perhaps one of the most interesting overnight options is the Yosemite Lakes, a membership resort that has space open to the public in all categories, from tent sites to yurts to lodge rooms.

If you want to explore the trails and fishing at Hetch Hetchy, you can't get closer than Camp Mather, where a reasonably-priced lodge has cabin accommodations.

The lodging choices are listed alphabetically.

Bed and Breakfast Inns

All Seasons Groveland Inn

Jack Jenkins left his job as manager of all restaurants in the Mark Hopkins Hotel in San Francisco to bring his knowledge of hospitality to Groveland. He is turning an 1897 Victorian into a stunning new bed and breakfast that will open in the spring of 1999. His theme is "quality will be enriched by service." Five rooms will be decorated with antiques and murals, each reflecting a different theme. One room will even have a waterfall. All rooms will have full baths, some with jacuzzis and one with a steam room, and some will have fireplaces. Breakfast will be served and later the owner hopes to add dinners.

All Seasons Groveland Inn
18656 Hwy. 120
P.O. Box 244
Groveland, CA 95321
209-962-0232 Fax: 209-962-0250
www.allseasonsgrovelandinn.com
$110 - $175

The Berkshire Inn

The inn is listed as a bed and breakfast, but it is not currently being run that way. The rooms and common room are nice, but the breakfast is self service from a bar and the management seems indifferent. The property is showing signs of neglect.

The Berkshire Inn
P.O. Box 207
19950 Hwy. 120
Groveland, CA 95321
209-962-6744
$59 - $180

Bed and Breakfast Inns

Brooks Berry Inn
7567 Hamilton Station Loop at
  Buck Meadows
Groveland, CA 95321
209-962-4663 888-867-5001
Fax: 209-962-7889
www.brooksberryinn.com
$105 - $125

Directions:
Across from the Shell Station in Buck Meadows take Moore Creek Rd. south off Highway 120 to Hamilton Loop.

Special Features:
Denise will also pack a lunch basket complete with silverware and glasses for your trip to the park.

Brooks Berry Inn

The Brooks built a charming new bed and breakfast on a knoll in a quiet location off the highway. Two beautifully decorated rooms await you, one with a queen and the other with a king. Each bed has featherbeds both under and over you. Randy and Denise are natives of the area and are happy to share their knowledge of the area. The library in the sitting room is full of books about Yosemite. Denise cooks a gourmet two-course breakfast every day. There is a 24-hour cookie jar and fruit basket that is always full of treats.

© Ellie Huggins

Brooks Berry Inn where you can relax in luxury.

Bed and Breakfast Inns

Chalet de Fontenay

Ralph and Janet McDonald have set up a three bedroom two-bath house as a fly-in bed and breakfast at the Pine Mountain Airport. A tie down for you plane is on the property. There are two bedrooms upstairs that share a bath and one downstairs with its own bath, plus kitchen and livingroom.

The Groveland Hotel

Peggy Mosley left the Bay Area and a successful career as a manager at Lockheed and owner of a flying business to transform this 1850s National Historic Building into a first-class modern hotel. The beautiful rooms are furnished with antiques, all with private baths. Rooms are upstairs in the original building that also houses the restaurant, and on both floors of the Queen Ann style addition. There are 17 rooms, including two suites with spa tubs and fireplaces. Every room has a name and is decorated accordingly. The Lola Montez room is comfortable and romantic with mauve tulip wall coverings. The honeymoon suite, named appropriately for Lilly Langtry, has a spa tub and fireplace.

Chalet de Fontenay
209-962-5629 800-495-9619 x201
www.chaletdefontenay.com
$90

Directions:
On Hemlock Road near the airport.

Special Features:
Room rates include a voucher for breakfast or lunch at the Corsair Coffee Shop.

Groveland Hotel
18767 Hwy. 120
P.O. Box 481
Groveland, CA 95321
209-962-4000 800-273-3314
www.groveland.com
$125 - $195

Special Features:
All rooms come with luxurious terry bathrobes. Be sure to ask the story of the resident ghost Lyle, whose room features a French bed. The hotel serves a continental breakfast of baked goods, cereal and fruit downstairs. In the summer you can repair to the patio in the back while you drink your coffee and read the newspaper.

The hotel has a modern conference room. With dining on the premises Peggy offers many special activities, such as murder mystery weekends or Mark Twain dinner shows. Peggy likes her work so much that she offers seminars in the art of innkeeping and will gladly help brides plan a beautiful wedding.

Bed and Breakfast Inns

Hotel Charlotte
P.O. Box 787
Hwy. 120
Groveland, CA 95321
209-962-6455 800-961-7799
$31 - $56

Hotel Charlotte

The hotel began life in 1918 when Charlotte DeFerreri created her hostel for the men building the Hetch Hetchy dam. Today Ruth and Jim Kraenzel continue Charlotte's good food and good beds policy and offer a hostelry that is a true step back in time. There are two suites for four with connecting baths that are great for families, as one room has a queen bed and the other twins. Four rooms have private baths. Three less expensive rooms share a bath at the end of the hall. A continental breakfast is served downstairs and the restaurant on the premises serves dinner most nights from May through October.

Inn at Sugar Pine Ranch
21250 Hwy. 120
Groveland, CA 95321
209-962-7823 888-800-7823
www.bizware.com/sugarpine
$110 - $150

Special Features:
This is a nonsmoking inn. Elaine serves a full breakfast every morning and offers afternoon tea. A real plus on those hot summer days is a large pool that sits on a bluff with lounge chairs under a gazebo. There is plenty of walking on the property, too.

The Inn at Sugar Pine Ranch

Craig and Elaine Maxwell are the new owners of this longtime establishment. They have totally remodelled and refurbished the old house and painted and redecorated the cabins to create an inviting bed and breakfast. Situated on 60 acres under groves of pines, there are three rooms with private baths in the original ranch house plus several spacious cottages. Most units are for two people, although there is one family unit.

Bed and Breakfast Inns

Manzanita Hill

Bill and Elaine Corcoran have built a new bed and breakfast inn high on a hill above Highway 120 with 360-degree views. On a clear day you can see the peaks of the high country. The house is spacious and elegantly furnished. Two sitting areas and an east facing porch are for guests. Two bedrooms have queen beds and one has twins. Each bedroom has its own private bath across a hall. Terry robes are supplied. Each room has a sliding glass door out to the patio. Wine and cheese are served in the afternoon.

Manzanita Hill
19210 Hwy. 120
Groveland, CA 95321
209-9625-4541
Fax: 209-962-5575
www.manzanitahill.com

Directions:
The driveway up to Manzanita Hill is just east of the Yosemite School on the north side of Highway 120.

Special Features:
This is a totally nonsmoking inn and they cannot accommodate children under 16.

Courtesy of Manzanita Hill

The elegant livingroom at Manzanita Hill.

Motels and Lodges

May to November.
Evergreen Lodge
33160 Evergreen Rd.
Camp Mather, CA
209-379-2606 800-935-6343
$75 - $102.

Special Features:
The Mather Corral nearby offers all kinds of horseback riding, and there is plenty of fishing and hiking nearby. And of course you are not far from the Hetch Hetchy park entrance.

The Groveland Motel
P.O. Box 175
18933 Hwy. 120
Groveland, CA 95321
209-962-7865
Fax: 209-962-0664
$27 - $95

Year-round.
Lee's Middle Fork Resort Motel
11399 Cherry Lake Road
Groveland, CA 95321
209-962-7408 800-626-7408
Fax: 209-962-7400
www.sonnet.com/usr/yosemite
$50 - $150

Special Features:
Good fishing is nearby in the Middle Fork of the Tuolumne River.

Evergreen Lodge

The lodge on the road to Hetch Hetchy has 20 cozy, old-style cabins situated under towering trees. There is a restaurant, bar and general store as well. Cabins are for two to four persons and are perfect for families. Although modestly furnished they are clean and the lodge is well run. A covered patio is used for picnics and barbeques and has pool and ping pong tables.

The Groveland Motel

This older motel has economical motel rooms in cabins, or one and two-bedroom mobile homes. To really save money, try their teepees with one and two beds and shared bath facilities with hot showers.

Lee's Middle Fork Resort Motel

Large, comfortable one and two-bedroom cabins are situated in trees next to the Middle Fork of the Tuolumne. The motel is just one half mile from Highway 120. A continental breakfast is available in the lodge. The location is restful and quiet.

Hostel, Cabins

Sunset Inn

Bill and Lauren Nickell have renovated two cabins that sit under trees near their home. Each cabin has a queen bed, woodburning stove, full kitchen and a bath with stall shower. The porch on each unit looks out across meadows and forest. Their 22 acres are surrounded by U.S. Forest Service roads that are ideal for hiking and biking.

Sunset Inn
33569 Hardin Flat Rd.
209-962-4360
From $75

Directions:
Drive east on Highway 120 for 17.5 miles to the second Hardin Flat Road. Turn south for one mile. Turn east up the gravel driveway to the cabins.

Special Features:
The owners have lived here for 25 years and can surely direct you to all kinds of special places to hike or bike.

© Ellie Huggins

A cozy cabin at Sunset Inn.

Yosemite Lakes

This is a membership camping resort, but nonmembers may rent at slightly higher rates. You can rent a tent or RV site, cabin, hostel or inn room or a yurt. Yurts are wonderful circular, canvas structures with windows, doors and skylights. They feature two queen futons, kitchen, full bathroom, air conditioning, stoves, microwaves, TV and outdoor barbeque.

May to November.
Yosemite Lakes
31191 Hardin Flat Road
Groveland, CA 95321
209-962-0121 800-533-1001
$16 - $89 for nonmembers

Directions:
The entrance to the lodge is 7.5 miles east of Buck Meadows on Highway 120.

Special Features:
The resort has a spa and offers horseback riding. The location is superb, just minutes from the entrance to the park.

Motels and Lodges

© Ellie Huggins

A Yosemite Lakes yurt described on the previous page.

Yosemite Gatehouse Lodge

May to October.
Yosemite Gatehouse Lodge
34001 Hwy. 120
Groveland, CA 95321
209-379-2260
$86 - $106

Three double cabins above the lodge sit under a canopy of pine and oak on the original Big Oak Flat Road. Each cabin comes with two queen beds, microwave, refrigerator and TV. There is a small store in the main lodge that has two motel units. These modest and very affordable accommodations are just one mile from the entrance station.

Yosemite Westgate Motel

Open all year.
Yosemite Westgate Motel
7633 Hwy. 120 at Buck Meadows
Groveland, CA 95321
209-962-5281 800-341-8000
Fax: 209-962-5285
From $89

Special Features:
There is a swimming pool on the property.

Family owned and run, the Yosemite Westgate offer 44 rooms, all with queen beds, in room coffee, TV and air conditioning. Some suites have kitchenettes. The units are spanking clean and the management helpful. They recently bought the Buck Meadows Lodge and Restaurant.

Dining

Dining is limited during the off season. However, in the height of the summer we recommend that you make reservations at the two hotels and the country club. In winter we suggest that you check what dining is open before you venture out at night.

Restaurants are listed alphabetically.

How we rate restaurants:

$ Inexpensive, including soup or salad—under $15.
$$ Moderate, including soup or salad—under $20.
$$$ Moderately expensive, a la carte—entrées $16 to $22.
$$$$ Expensive, a la carte— entrées over $22.
Tips, wine and tax are not included in our estimates of cost.

Buck Meadows Lodge

The restaurant will continue to serve its menu of sandwiches and hamburgers plus dinners under the new management of the Yosemite Westgate Motel. The menu has beef, chicken and pasta dishes plus a salad bar; nothing fancy, just solid American food. If you have kids along, they will be very happy.

$
Lunch and dinner, daily.
7647 Hwy. 120
Buck Meadows
209-962-5281

Cocina Michoacana

The Gonzales family operates this excellent Mexican restaurant on Highway 120 in downtown. In a small, cheerful room they cook up some very tasty treats from south of the border. You can't go wrong here for a moderately priced lunch or dinner. This is one of the few restaurants that is open daily all year.

$
Summer, 11:00 am. to 9:30 p.m., daily.
Winter, closed from 2:00 p.m. to 4:00 p.m.
18730 Hwy. 120
Groveland
209-962-6651

Dining

Evergreen Lodge

$$
Summer, lunch and dinner, daily,
  weekends in off season.
33160 Evergreen Rd.
Camp Mather
209-379-2244 800-935-6343

This funky old lodge with a fireplace and full bar serves family style. The good American food is reasonably priced. Groveland residents often drive up here for a dinner among the towering pines. If you are staying or camping near the park, this is a great choice for dinner out. During high season they even show movies.
The deli in the store makes great sandwiches for your day on the trail.

The Groveland Hotel

$$$
Open all year.
Reservations recommended in
  high season.
Dinner, daily.
18767 Hwy. 120
Groveland
209-962-4000 800-273-3314

Dining in the Groveland Hotel is an elegant affair in the Victorian dining room with quiet harp or chamber music in the background. The menu is varied and the wine list extensive. Each night one appetizer is a "chef's inspiration." Entrées include steak oscar (an unusual menu item these days), poached seafood or rack of lamb. All come with soup or salad. No matter where you are staying in Groveland, this is the place for a romantic dinner.

Dining

Hotel Charlotte

The Hotel Charlotte dining room is best known for prime rib dinners. However, there is a full menu of pasta, meat and fish as well. The food is good with hearty servings. The atmosphere is nostalgic, reminiscent of its Victorian origins. There is a good selection of California and French wines on their list.

$$$
Reservations recommended on weekends.
Dinner, Thursday thru Monday, May thru October.
Hwy. 120
Groveland
209-962-6455 800-961-7799

Iron Door Saloon and Grill

At the saloon, surrounded by historic photos of the town and Yosemite, you can mix with the locals who may be watching the sport of the evening on the TV. You can order most things from the grill menu and eat there or move to the dining room for dinner. The menu offers hearty portions of beef, chicken or pasta, and the appetizer list is full of all those high cholesterol items that taste so good. If you are hankering for a hamburger, this is the only place to be. Naturally the bar will mix anything you wish and has some microbrews on tap.

$
Open year-round.
Lunch and dinner, daily.
Reduced hours in winter.
18761 Hwy. 120
Groveland
209-962-8904

$
Open year-round.
Breakfast, lunch and dinner, daily.
18986 Hwy. 120
Groveland
209-962-7501

PJ's Cafe

Parker and Nan Johnson have been serving up three meals daily since 1986. Aside from hamburgers, salads and homemade soups, there are daily specials to please every palate. Pizza is available there or for take and bake after 4:00 p.m. every day.

$$
Reservations recommended.
Open all year.
Breakfast, lunch, dinner,
  Wednesday thru Sunday.
12765 Mueller Dr.
Groveland
209-962-8638

Directions:
Drive north on Ferretti Rd. past the entrance to Pine Mountain Lake to Mueller Dr. Drive east up the hill past the condominiums to the country club on the right.

Pine Mountain Lake Country Club

Pine Mountain Lake is a year-round resort community with a golf course. The clubhouse restaurant serves some of the best food in the area. The 16,000-square foot restaurant and lounge overlooks the golf course and has views of Yosemite peaks in good weather. There is an outside deck for those warm days. The menu has several signature items, among them the Angus prime rib served the way many like it with au jus and a house horseradish sauce. An Asian grilled duck breast using locally raised ducks is prepared with a cherry sauce. You really should try this restaurant when you are in town.

Highway 120 West Activities

Highway 120 leads to the Big Oak Flat entrance to the park and to Hetch Hetchy Reservoir. From this gateway you can access the wild and scenic Tuolumne River with its world-class rafting and fishing. The South Fork of the Tuolumne is close to the road for a cool dip in a beautiful pool during summer and there are two giant sequoia groves that you can visit on foot, skis or snowshoes in grand solitude most of the year. The following pages describe hikes, excursions, horseback riding and golf, all close to the highway.

Courtesy of the National Park Service, Yosemite

This photo of Hetch Hetchy shows a beautiful valley with a miniature El Capitan and cascading waterfalls, surrounding a marshy meadow that John Muir considered a rival to Yosemite Valley. Before the dam was built as many as 400 people a year visited this lovely place named by the Miwok for a species of grass that grew here. Their name, *Hatchatchie,* was corrupted to its present form. The excursion to the dam is described on the next three pages. A hike across the dam is described on page 216.

Excursions

HWY. 120 W ACTIVITIES

Directions:

Drive 25 miles west from Groveland on Highway 120 to Evergreen Road. Turn left toward Hetch Hetchy. It is 18 miles to the dam.

The narrow, two-lane road from Highway 120 winds down to Aspen Valley Junction where it crosses the original Tioga Pass Road. The town of Camp Mather was named for the first Director of the Park Service, Stephen T. Mather. Although it is now a recreation camp for residents of San Francisco, it was the home for the hundreds of workers who toiled to build the dam. It took until 1920 to finish the work and begin to fill the reservoir.

The road follows the same route Michael O'Shaughnessy traveled on horseback on his first trip to Hetch Hetchy Valley in 1912. It was widened for the railroad bed by 1917, converted to an automobile road in 1927 and paved in 1931.

After climbing over Poopenaut Pass at 5,064 feet, the Canyon of the Tuolumne and the dam come into view for the last few miles of the drive to the dam overlook and parking lot.

Hetch Hetchy Dam

This interesting side trip takes you to the O'Shaughnessy Dam, built by the City and County of San Francisco between 1914 and 1920 to provide power and water for that city 150 miles away. However, it would take another 14 years before the aqueduct and pipes would be completed to bring water to the city.

Prior to the turn of the century, San Francisco was at the mercy of private water companies. Officials had tried unsuccessfully to find dependable sources for city water. The great fire following the 1906 earthquake destroyed much of the city and the situation was so acute that the city fathers began to look to the Sierra for their water.

The city had to reckon with John Muir, however, who was vehemently opposed to the scheme. His allies were the Sierra Club, the cities of Turlock and Modesto, who had prior water rights on the Tuolumne River, and Pacific Gas and Electric Company.

However, after several years of maneuvering San Francisco and its lobbyists succeeded in getting the Raker Act passed in Congress. This permitted the city to dam the

Excursions

© Ellie Huggins

Hetch Hetchy Reservoir in 1998, taken from the dam.

© Ellie Huggins

From the dam you will be able to see the water release into the canyon below.

Tuolumne River inside Yosemite National Park. John Muir and shocked members of his fledgling Sierra Club fought the proposal, but public sentiment at the beginning of the twentieth century could not conceive of a park being more important than development and progress. Congress authorized the project in 1913, and shortly thereafter Muir died, some say of a broken heart.

Take time to walk across the dam. It took twenty years to finish the system. The original dam was raised 85 feet in 1938, and 150 miles of pipe and tunnels was constructed to carry the water to the Bay Area.

The Hetch Hetchy valley was known by Muir and his friends as Little Yosemite Valley. Like its big sister to the south, it was carved by glaciers. When they receded they left a lake that over the last eight to ten thousand years filled with soil. That was how Muir knew it. The photograph on page 203 shows the valley before the dam was built.

Excursions

On October 24, 1934, the first release of water headed to San Francisco was made with the President's wife, Eleanor Roosevelt, in attendance.

The lake stores 360,000 acre feet of water from 459 square miles of watershed, most of which is above 6,000 feet, providing the purest water of any California system. As you take in the watery scene the ghost of John Muir may stand beside you. Look up the lake at the Wapama Waterfall dropping from its hanging valley and imagine a valley 350 feet deep below the water level. You can easily hike to these falls. The moderate hike is described on page 216 in "Hiking."

Look below the dam, where the spray of water from the lower gates marks the release made to keep the fish habitat downstream healthy. In the summer, these releases fill the Tuolumne, keeping rafters busy. The river below this point has Class IV and Class V rapids. If you are ready for the thrills this represents, see "Rafting" beginning on page 211 for the companies leading trips.

The Tuolumne River Preservation Trust

In 1981 the Trust began efforts to protect the Lower Tuolumne River downstream from the dam. In 1984 they finally were able to have the main Tuolumne River declared Wild and Scenic for 83 miles between the dam and the Don Pedro Reservoir.

In 1995 they defeated an effort by the Turlock Irrigation District to build a dam on the Clavey River, the most pristine and wildest tributary of the Tuolumne. Today, the only way to see the Clavey is on a raft trip that has the most difficult rating.

Chinook salmon historically had spawned in the lower Tuolumne River, but the Don Pedro Dam severely restricted flows. This threatened the Chinook spawn. In 1996, through the efforts of the Trust, an agreement was reached to increase flows from Don Pedro and provide funding to bring back the habitat for these native fish.

You can learn more about the Trust and its work at their visitor center in Groveland.

Swimming

A stop along the route to the park offers one of the few opportunities on any road into Yosemite for a dip in an official swimming hole in one of Yosemite's rivers.

Rainbow Pool and Falls

A lovely pair of falls drop a few feet into a cold, deep pool, just right for cooling off on a hot summer day. There are picnic benches and restrooms. You are swimming in the South Fork of the Tuolumne, which you will meet again when it is but a stream on Highway 120 to Tioga Pass.

Directions:
Drive 14 miles east of Groveland on Highway 120. Just before the bridge over the South Fork turn south on the road down to the pool and its parking.

Until 1915 this was the site of the toll station along the old Big Oak Flat Road. Later the Cliff House welcomed guests until it burned in 1939. For a hike along the South Fork of the Tuolumne up the highway, see page 215.

© *Ellie Huggins*

Imagine yourself swimming under these falls on a hot summer day.

Rafting

Eight companies are currently licensed to take rafters on the river. There are a limited number of permits for individuals.

The Tuolumne River

The river is a rare combination of one of the greatest, most challenging rivers in California and a beautiful canyon that few can visit, except on a raft. Trips on this river are a complete wilderness experience. Camping along the way is at campsites near streams and canyons to explore on foot. This is a wild and scenic river where eagles and hawks may be spotted overhead and perhaps bobcats or raccoons on shore, to say nothing of the many birds that visit the canyon. Only two rafting companies per day may put in, assuring the solitude you wish for such an experience.

The river drops steeply in many locations, including the awesome Clavey Falls section that is a Class V rapid. You may walk around this one if you wish. The rest of the rapids, particularly in early season, are Class IV or IV+ and most raft companies say that you should have previous paddling experience and be in good condition.

Stanislaus National Forest
Groveland District
24545 Hwy. 120
Groveland, CA 95321
209-962-7825

All groups put in at Meral's Pool near the Lumsden Campground and take out 18 miles later at Ward's Ferry in Lake Don Pedro.

One day trips are early in the season and for experienced paddlers only. They run the entire 18 miles with its 26 rapids. This is a first-class whitewater trip, with the emphasis on white. Minimum age is 16.

Midsummer and fall trips are two or three days, with time to explore canyons at your campsite, find side creeks with warm pools for a dip. The river is dam controlled from Hetch Hetchy, which means that paddling begins after the water has risen. Most groups run these trips from June to October.

Raft permits for individuals

Information for non-commercial permits may be obtained from the Groveland District of the Stanislaus National Forest. Twelve campsites are available for non-commercial rafters on a first-come, first-serve basis between May and September. This river is only for experienced paddlers.

Rafting

Rafting companies on the Tuolumne

All Outdoors

The company uses both oar/paddle assist and all-paddle rafts. Those choosing all-paddle rafts must have good skills. Minimum age is 16 and you must be able to swim.

All-Outdoors Whitewater Rafting
1250 Pine Street
Walnut Creek, CA 94596
800-247-2387
www.aorafting.com

Ahwahnee Whitewater

Ahwahnee is a small company with one, two and three-day trips from late March to September. Their food continually earns superlatives and many of their clients are returnees. The minimum age is 12 for the two and three day trips.

Ahwahnee Whitewater
P.O. Box 1161
Columbia, CA 95310
800-359-9790
www.ahwahnee.com

ARTA River Trips

ARTA is a nonprofit organization that was founded in 1963 by Bill and Robin Center. Their motto is, "a rafting company for those who seek inspiration from our natural world." They are committed to the environment, so much so that surplus revenues are donated to conservation organizations.

They run one, two and three-day trips with oar/paddle assist rafts.

ARTA American River Touring Association
24000 Casa Loma Rd.
Groveland, CA 95321
800-323-2782
www.arta.org

Rafting

ECHO
6529 Telegraph Avenue
Oakland, CA 94609-1113
800-652-3246
www.echotrips.com

Echo: The Wilderness Company

Echo is a large company whose only California offering is the Tuolumne. You can choose to be in a paddle, paddle/oar or oar boat, where you just sit back and let the guide do all the work. They call the Tuolumne the "Dom Perignon" of whitewater and wilderness rafting. The one-day trip has a minimum age of 16, while 12-year-olds may join you on two or three-day trips.

Mariah Expeditions
P.O. Box 248
Point Richmond, CA 94807
800-462-7424
www.mariahwe.com

Mariah Expeditions

Mariah uses paddle boats with six paddlers and a guide plus an oar boat for food and gear. Their minimum age for the Tuolumne is 14. On two-day trips they raft the upper section of the main Tuolumne, scout and run Clavey Falls, and make camp below the falls for a well deserved evening on the river. There is plenty of time to rest or play while guides prepare a wonderful dinner and campfire. On three-day trips you get to stay in camp the whole day or go exploring, fishing or birding. There is no wilder place to engage in these activities, and the fishing is great in this wild trout river.

Rafting

Sierra Mac River Trips

Sierra Mac River Trips have been providing fine whitewater experiences since 1965. Your guides are experienced and on two and three-day trips will take you on short hikes to Gold Rush and Miwok Indian sites. They use oar paddle boats and trips include a donation to a river conservation group.

Sierra Mac River Trips
P.O. Box 366
Sonora, CA 95370
800-457-2580
www.sierramac.com

Whitewater Voyages

This large company operates trips, team building expeditions, whitewater schools and summer camps for kids in California and Oregon. The use mainly paddle boats, although you may request oar boats. Their minimum age is 14. Trips are one, two, two and a half and three days.

Whitewater Voyages
5225 San Pablo Dam Road
El Sobrante, CA 94803
800-488-7238
www.wwvoyages.com

Zephyr Whitewater Expeditions

Zephyr has specialized in California rivers for 24 years. One-day trips on the Tuolumne are in April and May, while two and three-day trips are available from June to October with a minimum age of 12. Three-day trips have two different campsites on side creeks that are well worth exploring. They offer free use of wet suits.

Zephyr Whitewater Expeditions
P.O. Box 510
Columbia, CA 95310
800-431-3636
www.zrafting.com

Fishing

The Tuolumne River is renowned for wild trout that seldom see anglers. For a rare fishing experience, try a three-day rafting trip that allows plenty of time for casting your flies. The Groveland District office of the Stanislaus National Forest can help you find camping near the river. However, all campgrounds are reached on dirt roads that descend steeply into the Tuolumne Canyon. The South Fork of the Tuolumne can be approached near Lee's Middle Fork Motel and easily along the hike on the next page. The company described below offers classes and trips.

Yosemite Creek Outfitters
P.O. Box 762
Groveland, CA 95321
209-588-1306
www.sierraflyfishing.com

Check out their website for other classes and trips not mentioned here.

Yosemite Creek Outfitters

Yosemite Creek Outfitters is the leading guide service in the Central Sierra Nevada. Located in Groveland, they concentrate on the Tuolumne River. Their trips include full-day wade and walk or float trips from January 1 to November 15. Three-day flyfishing adventures access 20 miles of wild trout water on the Tuolumne. They provide all the meals, guides, shuttles and gear. They also offer a Sierra Sampler of two or three days of flyfishing on one or more of their home waters, with accommodations in local inns, gourmet meals and guides plus any gear you need.

A special Lake Eleanor canoe trip will introduce anglers to trophy stillwater fishing from float tubes.

Hiking

Hiking near Groveland is best done during the spring and early summer before the lower elevations become hot. There are two books of interest that will lead you to numerous walks in the area, *Wildflower Walks and Roads of the Sierra Gold Country* by Toni Fauver and *Hiking between Groveland and Yosemite* by Hap Barhydt. Details of these are in the Bibliography on page 299. We have chosen two local hikes that are easy to find, plus a favorite at Hetch Hetchy and hikes to the less visited Tuolumne and Merced Groves of Big Trees.

Groveland Ranger District Little Golden Forest Trail

The U.S. Forest Service has created a self-guided nature trail near the district office with eight interpretive posts explaining the effects of the 1987 forest fire that swept through the area. You will have a chance to discover how certain tree species survived the fire, see how the forest is returning and find grinding rocks of the Native Americans in the area.

Groveland Ranger District
24545 Hwy. 120
Groveland, CA 95321
209-962-7825

The trail leaves from the office on a half-mile interpretive loop and a two mile general trail. A brochure about the trail is available in the office. It was produced in partnership with the National Arbor Day Foundation, the Little Golden Children's Books and the U.S. Department of Agriculture Stanislaus National Forest.

Along the South Fork of the Tuolumne

The hike is a most pleasant stroll on an abandoned road for 1.5 miles with the river on your right. There is little elevation change. Walk to a primitive campground and continue to a fork in the trail. The right fork leads to the river. The left fork comes to a creek where across the way are fine rocks for a picnic.

Directions:
Drive 8.5 miles east of Buck Meadows. One mile after the Yosemite Mini Mart and just before a bridge over the South Fork, there is a green gate on the north side of the highway. The hike starts here.

The trail crosses creeks with nice displays of shade-loving wildflowers. In spring the black oaks' first leaves present a shimmering pink backdrop to the evergreen forest around you. To identify the flowers, we suggest you get a copy of *Wildflower Walks and Roads of the Sierra Gold Country* listed in the Bibliography on page 299.

Hetch Hetchy Dam

Directions:
Drive 25 miles west from Groveland to Evergreen Road. Turn left toward Hetch Hetchy. It is 18 miles to the dam. Pick up a map and the information packet at the entrance station.

The hike to Wapama Falls is 2.5 miles and takes about 2 hours each way. It is very hot in summer and you will need to carry water.

Courtesy Yosemite Concession Services

Giant sequoias loom overhead on your walks into the Tuolumne and Merced Groves. Descriptions are on the next page.

Hetch Hetchy to Wapama Falls

The trail leaves from the parking lot at the dam. Walk across the dam and through the tunnel to the far side, where the trail begins a climb up onto the ridge above the lake. For the first part of your hike you are on a road that will bear left in about a mile and switchback up the canyon to Lake Eleanor.

In about 30 minutes of walking you will pass a lovely fern grotto. The trees around you are predominantly black oak and digger pine with an occasional ponderosa. Evidence is everywhere above you of the fire in the summer of 1996 that burned 87,000 acres in the area.

In 40 minutes of walking there is an overlook of the Canyon of the Tuolumne and the upper reaches of the lake. This is an excellent place to stop with children, have a picnic and return to your car. The total hike to Wapama Falls, which usually runs year-round, takes about two hours.

As with all hikes at this elevation, watch out for poison oak and be aware that this is rattlesnake country. However, rattlesnakes are usually inactive when it is cold.

Hiking

Merced Grove of Big Trees

Just west of Crane Flat is an easy hike to a small grove of giant sequoias called the Merced Grove. The trail is really a road that descends about a mile to the first group of giants of the forest. Unlike its more famous counterpart on the southern end of the park, your walk will probably be alone and you can see the trees without trams or other tourists. There are three small groups of trees on down the road. The last is a pair next to a cabin. Sitting on the porch for a snack or picnic, you will notice dogwoods, sugar pine and alders. A spring trip here is particularly rewarding.

The Tuolumne Grove

The Tuolumne Grove lies on the former Big Oak Flat Road from Hodgdon Meadow. Today you may not drive into it. The trail (a paved road) curves down for about a mile where a half-mile interpretive loop in the grove awaits you. Were you to continue downhill, you would eventually come to the Hodgdon Meadow Campground. Hardy hikers might wish to arrange a car shuttle, leaving one car at the campground.

Merced Grove

Directions:
Drive 4.7 miles west on Highway 120 from Crane Flat. The parking lot for the hike is on the south side of the road.

When Mr. McLean built the Coulterville road to the park, he envisioned turning the Merced Grove into another tourist attraction, similar to the Mariposa Grove. His toll road made a special detour of several miles from Hazel Green to be sure that his passengers would see this group of trees.

The Tuolumne Grove

Directions:
The road to the grove leaves from a parking area on Highway 120 (Tioga Pass Rd.) just east of Crane Flat. There are restrooms.

Joseph Walker, who crossed the Sierra on the Mono Trail in 1833, is believed to have passed through the Tuolumne Grove and perhaps the Merced Grove on his way down to the Central Valley. The chronicler for his trip, Zenas Leanoard, wrote of specimens "16 to 18 fathom round the trunk."

Horseback Riding

Three stables offer trail rides in the area. The Pine Mountain Equestrian Center near Groveland has a full-service operation where you may board you own horse. One stable near Hetch Hetchy offers rides into the high country above the reservoir.

June to October.
Mather Corral
Camp Mather
209-379-2334

Directions:
Drive seven miles from Highway 120 on Evergreen Road. This is on the way to Hetch Hetchy.

Mather Corral

Jay Barnes corrals his horses at Camp Mather near the Evergreen Lodge. He offers hourly rides as well as a half-day ride that includes swimming or fishing. The all-day trip climbs up to 8,000 feet offering wonderful vistas of the high country.

Year-round, 9:00 a.m. to 5:00 p.m.
Pine Mountain Equestrian Center
13309 Clifton Way
Groveland
209-962-8666
www.pinemountainlake.com

Directions:
Take Ferretti Road north out of Groveland for five miles to Clements. Drive one mile on Clements to Clifton, turn right. You can board your horse with them.

Pine Mountain Equestrian Center

On Tuesday through Sunday year-round, you can take guided rides for one or two hours. They also offer a three-hour Tuolumne River outing that includes fishing. Special breakfast, full moon and barbeque campfire rides fill out the schedule.

Tuolumne Trails
20843 Hwy. 120
Groveland
209-962-7745

Tammy also offers private western riding instruction, has pony rides and gives private pony birthday parties.

Tuolumne Trails

Tammy Dunn is a professional guide and instructor. She offers one and two-hour rides with spectacular vistas of the Sierra. You can also plan an outing with your own personal itinerary.

HWY. 120 W ACTIVITIES

Golf

Pine Mountain Lake Country Club

Golfers who have vacation homes at Pine Mountain Lake write extolling the beauty and challenge of this course. With vistas of Sierra peaks in Yosemite from many holes, it is no wonder that people like to golf here. The course is open to nonmembers, although the pro suggests that you reserve a tee time several days in advance of your arrival. Eighteen holes snake through groves of oak and pine. The longest hole is 489 yards.

Pine Mountain Lake Country Club
19228 Pine Mt. Drive
Groveland
209-962-8620
The course rating is 70.6 from the back tees, slope rating: 125

Directions:
Drive north on Ferretti Rd. past the entrance to Pine Mountain Lake to Mueller Dr. Drive east and turn right up the hill past the condominiums to the country club on the right.

The course is open year-round. Twilight rates start at 3:00 p.m.

Courtesy of Pine Mountain Lake Country Club

Looking down the fairway at Pine Mountain Lake Country Club.

Ranger Programs

Groveland District, Stanislaus National Forest
24545 Hwy. 120
Groveland, CA 95321
209-962-7825

Groveland District of the Stanislaus National Forest

In June, July and August the district offers interesting day long hikes and interpretive programs. The walks are with wildlife biologists, archeologists and even fire fighters to discover special sites in the area.

Some hikes may include a trip to Pilot Peak, a historic fire lookout, or a study of the rich prehistory of the area on a hike to Preston Falls along the Tuolumne River. The list of hikes is available at the district office.

Crane Flat Ranger Programs

Directions:
The parking area for the Tuolumne Grove walk is just east of Crane Flat on the Tioga Pass Road. Crane Flat Campground is on Highway 120 just west of the intersection with Tioga Pass Road.

Crane Flat

Rangers lead walks to the Tuolumne Grove daily in the summer and on weekends in the fall. Walks meet at the Tuolumne Grove parking area near Crane Flat. The Crane Flat Campground has one-hour evening campfire programs of stories, legends and fun.

Directions:
The Big Oak Flat Information Station is at the entrance to the park eight miles west of Crane Flat.

Big Oak Flat Information Station

On Saturdays in the summer, a ranger walk goes to the Merced Grove for four to six hours leaving from the entrance station.

Cross Country Skiing

You can cross country ski in three locations from Highway 120. Since the Tioga Pass Road is closed a little above Crane Flat, you can make your own trips up the road as far as you wish, and both groves of big trees offer opportunities for skiers. All these trails are perfect for snowshoes as well. In winter, remember that chains may be required on all vehicles except 4WD with snowtires to reach Crane Flat or Yosemite Valley. For road conditions call (209)372-0200.

Tioga Pass Road

The gentle grade of the Tioga Pass Road out of Crane Flat as far as Tamarack Flat is an ideal outing for skiers of all abilities. Since the road is closed as soon as the snow is too deep to plow, you can start the season here before many other places are open. Just follow the road as far as you want, pack a lunch and water, take a pad to sit on for your picnic and head out.

Tioga Pass Road Parking

Directions:
There is parking at the end of the plowed road. You can also venture out from the Yosemite Institute buildings into the meadows in the area.

Merced Grove

Again, the unplowed road down to the grove offers an opportunity for skiers with good downhill skills. The first mile is only gently downhill, then the last mile or so is curving with a fairly steep gradient. However, the reward is there at the end—to see the giants of the forest under a mantle of snow. If the snow is not very deep, this trip may best be done on snowshoes.

Merced Grove

Directions:
Drive 4.7 miles west on Highway 120 from Crane Flat. The parking lot is on the south side of the road.

Cross Country Skiing and Snowplay

Tuolumne Grove Parking

Directions:
Parking is just east of Crane Flat on Tioga Pass Road. There are restrooms.

When the snow is not deep at Crane Flat or it is icy, this trip would be better on snowshoes.

Crane Flat Campground

Directions:
The campground is on Highway 120 just west of the intersection with Tioga Pass Road. This is the only official snowplay area in the park. The road is plowed back to a parking area with restrooms.

Tuolumne Grove

The same road you use for hiking is an official cross-country skiing excursion. The trail to the grove is marked with a number "1" high on trees along the way. There are some steep hills. The very best time for skiers of all abilities is just after a fresh snowfall when the descent is easiest. The first part of the trail is through a deep forest with fir and magnificent sugar pines towering above you. It is only a little over a mile until you come to the first eight-foot diameter giant that will dwarf all other trees around it. You can turn right up a short way to the Tunnel Tree here. Farther down the main trail are more giants of the grove, but always remember that you must climb back out.

Crane Flat Snowplay Area

There is no open hill here for sledding, but you can find places between trees to use your sleds. For the most part snowplay here means just that, playing in the snow. About 0.7 miles west of Crane Flat on Highway 120 there is parking on the north side of the road. This area is not official but is often used for sledding.

© Ellie Huggins

A skier is dwarfed by the first sequoia you see in the grove. The marked trail to the Tunnel Tree is across from this tree.

Special Events

Special events in Groveland are small town community affairs from a safe Halloween festival to craft fairs and melodramas on a summer evening. The Groveland Hotel also hosts an array of weekend events. To check on exact dates call the hotel at 209-962-4000.

January

Groveland Hotel - Elvis Nights, Murder Mystery Weekend.

February

Groveland Hotel - Romantic Valentines Dinner, Murder Mystery Weekend.

March

Groveland Hotel - Murder Mystery Weekend.

April

Groveland Hotel - Victorian Tea, Progressive Dinner About Town.

May

Strawberry Festival at Camp Mather, Memorial Day weekend. Blue grass, jazz, music workshops and special children's programs. 209-553-0191

June

Forty-Niner Gold Rush Days the first weekend after Father's Day. 800-449-9120

July and August

Pine Cone Performers Two shows of old-fashioned melodramas. 209-962-6892

September

Strawberry Festival at Camp Mather, Labor Day weekend. 209-553-0191

Chili Cookoff on the weekend after Labor Day. 800-449-9120

October

Safe Halloween bonfire in the Community Park with hot chocolate and cider. Main Street merchants dress up to receive trick or treaters.

Groveland Hotel - Art sale and jazz, Murder Mystery Weekend, Oktoberfest, Mark Twain History Dinner Show.

November

Thanksgiving Craft Fair.

Looking east across Tuolumne Meadows where Mt. Dana and Mt. Gibbs stand guard.

INTRODUCTION TO HIGHWAY 120 EAST

The eastern gateway to Yosemite National Park is a place of scenic alpine wonders. The escarpment of the Sierra Nevada rises dramatically four to six thousand feet out of the Mono Basin. In every other direction are stark reminders of the volcanic convulsions that have shaped the land—barren cones of the Mono Craters and the cliffs of Black Point behind the dark mound of Mono Lake's Negit Island.

Highway 120 heads west from Highway 395 less than a mile south of Lee Vining. This is the famous Tioga Pass Road which takes you up to the High Sierra that John Muir described as "The Range of Light." It is the most dramatic of all the roads into the park. It snakes up the beautiful, glacier-carved canyon of Lee Vining Creek. In the fall the canyon is ablaze with the gold and orange hues of aspens lining the creek. Mountains of ancient red metamorphic rock are visible next to peaks of shining granite. A few miles before reaching the pass the highway clings to a cliff far above the cascades of Lee Vining Creek. Just below the park entrance station you pass Tioga Lake. Try a walk around the lake's western shore, where any day during the fishing season anglers will be casting for rainbow.

Driving south from Reno

Your trip south along Highway 395 will take you along the beautiful Walker River where reminders of the January 1997 flood are everywhere. Hardly a tree is left standing, and the root crowns of 100-year-old pines lie scattered along the banks where they fell. Barren hillsides are carved out on either side of the river showing the power of water to reshape the landscape.

After climbing up to Hell's Gate, the road dips down to the green pastures of Bridgeport with the often snow-covered peaks of the Sawtooth Range and Matterhorn Peak to the west. Notice the white clapboard elegance of the Mono County Courthouse on your left about the middle of town. The climb to Conway summit begins after Bridgeport. About six miles south of town is Highway 270 to Bodie State Park, the best preserved ghost mining town in the West. Six miles from the turnoff to Bodie you reach the summit at 8,138 feet, and a half mile farther is the overlook for Mono Lake and its dramatic vista. The highway then winds down to the lake and Lee Vining.

INTRODUCTION TO HIGHWAY 120 EAST

The first vistas of Yosemite's alpine scenery appear after passing Tioga Lake. Look south after the entrance station where Dana Meadows is dotted with small lakes called tarns, left by the retreating glaciers. For a few miles the road descends through a forest of lodgepole pine to the wide open spaces of Tuolumne Meadows. The distinctive shapes of Cathedral and Unicorn Peaks are to the southwest, while the broad expanse of the 12-mile-long meadow stretches to the horizon.

Driving north from Mammoth Lakes

Highway 395 north from Mammoth Lakes crosses the 8,000-foot Deadman Summit to Highway 158, the June Lake Loop. This road passes June, Gull, Silver and Grant Lakes, considered by many to offer some of the finest fishing in the Eastern Sierra. The very economical accommodations and dining here are described later in this chapter, along with the many summer and winter activities, including downhill skiing at June Mountain.

> Tuolumne Meadows is 67 miles from Yosemite Valley via Crane Flat . Tioga Pass Road closes with the first snows in November and reopens in the late spring.

HWY. 120 E

Courtesy of the National Park Service, Yosemite

Driving through Tioga Pass Entrance Station in the 1920s.

HISTORY OF THE TIOGA PASS ROAD

The Great Sierra Consolidated Silver Company and its wagon road

Mining fever even struck high in the mountains above Tioga Pass. Miners hauled machinery up Lundy Canyon to May Lundy and other mines. Men and mules carried thousands of pounds of engines, boilers, compressors and drills up a vertical rise of 2,160 feet.

The Great Sierra Consolidated Silver Company was incorporated in 1883 to drill for silver in the mountains near Bennettville, a mile east of Tioga Pass. The company sold thousands of dollars of stock to eastern investors and hired hundreds of workers, including many Chinese, to build the Great Sierra Wagon Road east from Crocker's Station on the Big Oak Flat Road. In one summer they felled trees, and hacked and blasted through granite to complete the road all the way to Bennettville. But in 1885, before the road could begin to supply the mine or take the silver to market, the company went bankrupt. Bennettville was abandoned and all that was left from the investment was a wagon road across the Sierra to Tioga Pass. There is an easy one-mile walk to see the abandoned tunnel and remaining buildings in Bennettville. See page 271 in "Hiking."

Building the Tioga Pass to Lee Vining connection

The California legislature authorized construction of an east side link to Tioga Pass and the Great Sierra Wagon Road in 1899. In 1902 construction began and by 1905 all but the last few miles to the summit were finished. The road was finally completed in the summer of 1908. The route up from Lee Vining made it possible for adventurous automobilists to reach Mono Lake on a dirt road all the way from the Big Oak Flat Road at Crocker's Station. However, it would not be until 1915 that Stephen Mather, the newly appointed Director of the Park Service, would find a way to purchase the Great Sierra Wagon Road and begin to maintain it.

HISTORY OF THE TIOGA PASS ROAD

Stephen Mather buys the Great Sierra Wagon Road

When the newly appointed first director of the National Park Service realized that an improved road would bring visitors to Yosemite National Park up to the high country, he arranged for gifts of $15,500 to the government to buy the Great Sierra Wagon Road.

The road was then maintained but unpaved. In 1918 it was necessary to use 1,200 pounds of powder to blast about 150 trees off a five-mile section of road. Yosemite ranger Gabriel Sovulewski was in charge of keeping the route open, and by 1922 he considered the road to be in excellent condition However, it was not until the 1930s that portions of the Tioga Pass Road were paved. It remained an exciting adventure for motorists until the California Department of Transportation decided in 1957 that the road should be straightened and improved.

Sierra Club supporters battled to keep the highway in its primitive condition. However, they lost to California's desire for a safe, modern highway across the Sierra Nevada to the eastern communities. Highway 120 as we know it opened on June 24, 1961.

How Mather purchased the road

It was not easy for Mather to make his gift to buy the wagon road. In 1916 giving to the U.S. government was so suspect that Congressman Fitzgerald stated that only a black-hearted briber would want to do such a thing. However, Mather found a way. He raised some of the money from friends, put in the rest himself and then persuaded the distrusting Fitzgerald to allow a provision covering gifts to Yosemite. He arranged for his friend, William E. Colby of the Sierra Club, to buy the right of way of the former Great Sierra Wagon Road with the $15,500 he had raised. Colby then donated the road to the United States. Finally, on April 10, 1915, the gift was accepted, and soon after work began to upgrade the western portion of the route. A year later 578 autos checked in at Tioga Pass on their way west.

HWY. 120 E

HISTORY OF HIGHWAYS 120 EAST AND 395

Long before California was discovered and settled by the Spanish, the region along the edge of the mountains east of the Sierra Nevada was home to Native Americans known to us as Northern Paiute. Related in language and culture to the Shoshoni and Bannock tribes of the Great Basin, the Paiute had lived in the area for thousands of years. For hundreds of years before Europeans arrived, these tribes generally lived peacefully with one another.

The Paiute lived in a harsh climate with extreme temperatures and little rain. They made tools of stone and bone, gathered seeds and harvested wildflowers and insects. The staple of their diet was pine nut meal ground from the nuts of piñon pines. They hunted animals for skins and meat, caught fish with small bone hooks and wove various fibers into nets that were used to trap rabbits and other small mammals. The women made willow baskets of all kinds which they used for cooking, storing or carrying items collected during forages into the mountains or desert. They scraped salt from the shores of saline lakes. The Kuzedika Paiute, who lived by the shores of Mono Lake, harvested the larvae and pupae of brine flies which, when dried, were like a yellow grain. The volcanic terrain yielded obsidian for sharp arrowheads and other tools.

Piñon pine cones.

HISTORY OF HIGHWAYS 120 EAST AND 395

The Paiute traded their salt, obsidian and brine flies with the Miwok from the foothills of the Sierra and the Ahwahneeche of Yosemite Valley. Trading was accomplished every summer when they walked up to the high country. Like modern travelers, they enjoyed relief from valley heat as well as good hunting and fishing. The routes that took them over the passes still exist as trails for us today.

When the gold rush was well developed in the western foothills of the Sierra Nevada, Leroy Vining became the first Californian to traverse the range and start digging for gold near Mono Lake in 1852. He did not become rich. Instead he settled on a ranch along the banks of Lee Vining Creek. The word of his find, however, reached others who came to the area in search of wealth.

© *Ellie Huggins*

One of Bodie's abandoned buildings.

North of Lee Vining at the town of Bodie, a real bonanza of $30 million in gold and silver was mined and milled. But the Bodie mines could not support the high level of activity and the mines closed one by one. By 1888 the town's population of ten thousand had dwindled to four or five hundred who continued living in the harsh climate until the 1940s. At that time everyone deserted Bodie leaving the ghost town we can see today.

HISTORY OF HIGHWAYS 120 EAST AND 395

The Mono Lake Story

The Mono Basin was formed by a combination of volcanic activity and faulting, producing subsidence on the north and south sides of the basin. About ten thousand years ago, when the glacial ages came to an end, melting ice produced great rivers that cascaded down the eastern slope into a lake that rose to a level 700 feet higher than today. The ice age lake was approximately 900 feet deep. After the glaciers receded, evaporation took over and the lake level gradually lowered. In 1857, the first time the lake was surveyed, the level was at 6,407 feet above sea level.

At 900,000 years Mono Lake is North America's oldest. This 60-square-mile expanse of water is a kaleidoscope of color and shape often reflecting surrounding peaks or gathering clouds in the sky. Like many other Great Basin bodies of water, Mono is a terminal lake, meaning it has no outlet. Under natural conditions, water leaves the basin only through evaporation, which has caused the salinity of the lake to increase gradually over time. However, this saline environment supports a rich ecosystem of plankton, brine flies and brine shrimp, important food for the many bird species that nest here.

Ranches and Lumber Mills

The mining camps in the eastern Sierra needed food and lumber. Entrepreneurs came over the mountains to raise cattle and sheep, start dairies and build lumber mills. Nourished by abundant runoff from the Sierra, the beautiful flat valleys supported a growing agriculture industry. Cattle ranchers and other farmers from the dry San Joaquin Valley found good soil, ample summer water and ready markets at the mines, especially in Bodie. They even collected gulls' eggs from the shores of Mono Lake. A thriving shipping business in Lee Vining hauled lumber and other supplies across Mono Lake to the north shore and up the road to Bodie.

The mines required lumber to support the tunnels and for miners' homes. The mills were able to supply these needs from the virgin forests of the eastern slope. When the mines closed, much of the forest was gone. The valleys did not change a great deal, for the ranchers were able to find markets feeding the growing population of California.

HISTORY OF HIGHWAYS 120 EAST AND 395

The lake is best known for the strange towers of tufa (pronounced *toofa*) lining its shores. They are formed by fresh water springs that combine with the carbonates of the lake's saline water and precipitate into odd-shaped forms. Submerged and growing for many years, these tufa formations now rise above the lowered water level. However, they are no longer actively forming.

You can get close to the lake at two locations: Mono Lake Tufa State Reserve on the south shore and at the Mono Lake County Park on the north shore. The descriptions are on pages 267 and 268 in "Hiking."

HWY. 120 E

© Ellie Huggins

Looking south from Black Point, the dark form of Negit Island fills the horizon. Every year thousands of California gulls nest here and raise their young.

HISTORY OF HIGHWAYS 120 EAST AND 395

The Water Wars of the Eastern Sierra

For thousands of years the rich runoff of water from the eastern slopes of the Sierra Nevada supported Native American tribes, filled the flumes to run the machinery of the mines and, later, provided water to ranchers in the Owens Valley.

In the early 1900s, certain leaders in the city of Los Angeles realized that they lacked only water to turn their desert into a paradise. They looked at the Owens Valley, 200 miles away, and saw that its rich agriculture was nourished by prolific amounts of water flowing from the mountains. They enlisted the aid of the federal government to win the confidence of valley farmers with promises of a local reclamation project. However, the federal government delayed action until Los Angeles could preempt plans for the reclamation project and purchase the water rights for the city instead.

Hard times for ranchers

Hard times in the 1920s forced Owens Valley farmers to sell their property and water rights when mortgages came due. Few would have a chance against Los Angeles water bosses. The 1930s were sad years for

Acquiring water rights from farmers

The historical water rights of Owens Valley ranchers were ignored by federal and Los Angeles city officials and business tycoons who would profit when water was delivered to their landholdings in the San Fernando Valley. In 1907 even President Teddy Roosevelt became involved, closing off tracts of the Owens Valley floor from homesteaders in order to create the Inyo National Forest and use the water runoff of the eastern slope of the Sierra Nevada for the national forest. That was the catalyst for Los Angeles city managers to conspire with some Bishop bankers to acquire water rights and build an aqueduct to bring water south to a thirsty and growing city. The first Sierra water arrived in Los Angeles in 1913.

HISTORY OF HIGHWAYS 120 EAST AND 395

Owens Valley and its residents. Los Angeles continued to buy land and water rights and even began looking north to the Mono Basin. In 1940 engineers built a delivery system to divert freshwater creeks that flowed into Mono Lake. During dry years, Los Angeles drained all surface water from the Mono Basin and Owens Valley into the aqueduct and pumped groundwater from land it owned. Ranchers who leased land back from Los Angeles could not get any water during the drought. Forlorn houses and barns, dead trees, weed-clogged fields and empty ditches were poignant reminders of shattered dreams. Owens Lake slowly receded until it was nothing but an alkali flat. Storms of alkali dust often blew across the land, covering buildings and people with a fine, white film.

By 1972, a second aqueduct had been built, greatly increasing the city's ability to transport water. The level of Mono Lake dropped dramatically, endangering the entire ecosystem. The dramatically lowered level of Mono Lake emboldened citizens to take action in 1978. Some concerned University of California Davis and Stanford University graduate students were especially disturbed by the increasing salinity of the water. They formed the Mono Lake Committee to fight for the lake's existence.

Mono Lake Committee

The Mono Lake Committee continues its vigilance in order to defend the protective rulings resulting from their 20-year struggle. If you wish to know more, or want to join the Committee, visit the Mono Lake Committee Information Center and Bookstore on Main Street in Lee Vining. Visit their website at www.monolake.org.

To learn more about the Mono Lake ecosystem and take nature walks along its shores, see Mono Lake in "Hiking" on page 267, "Ranger Programs" on page 287 and "Boating" on page 260.

You can also walk along the rewatered and restored Lee Vining Creek. See "Hiking" on page 266 for a description.

HWY. 120 E

Bringing life back to the creeks that feed Mono Lake

In 1998 the State Water Resources Board ruled that LADWP must monitor the rewatering of Rush, Lee Vining, Walker and Parker Creeks. They hired Dr. William Trush to lead the studies to determine the water flow that will ensure restoration of creek habitat for plants, fish and waterfowl. The process requires almost daily observations of water flows during the peak season, and volunteers from the Mono Lake Committee are providing this assistance.

Some members moved to Lee Vining. One man, David Gaines, provided enough scientific evidence of the lake's fragility to take the case to court. It took another five years before the first battle was won. In 1983 the California Supreme Court ruled unanimously that the lake must be protected. They decreed, "Mono Lake is a scenic and ecological treasure of national significance, imperiled by continued diversions of water." The licenses for the Los Angeles Department of Water and Power (LADWP), the court decided, were invalid as originally issued because they failed to consider the protection of the lake.

But this was only the beginning of the struggle. It took until 1991 to get the El Dorado County Superior Court to issue a temporary injunction to stop water diversion and to protect the lake while the California State Water Resources Board prepared new licenses to divert water. In 1994 the board revised the licenses of the LADWP requiring them to release water from four streams that feed the lake until it reaches 6,392 feet, 15 feet above the lowest recorded level after six drought years that ended in 1993.

This was the first car over Tioga Pass in 1919. Your trip will be less adventurous but just as beautiful.

LODGING ALONG HWYS. 395 AND 120 E

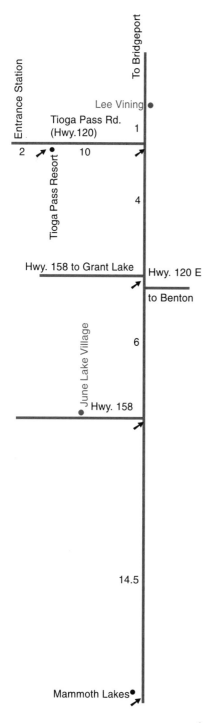

To Bridgeport

Entrance Station

Lee Vining

Tioga Pass Rd.
(Hwy.120)   1

2   10

Tioga Pass Resort

4

Hwy. 158 to Grant Lake   Hwy. 120 E

to Benton

June Lake Village   6

Hwy. 158

14.5

Mammoth Lakes

There are two principle locales for lodging near the Highway 120 East gateway to Yosemite National Park.

Lee Vining provides numerous motels and one unique lodge, all at moderate prices. However, one of the best kept secrets of the region is the June Lake Loop (Highway 158) with a plethora of choices, many of which are very economical. June Lake has many motels, a few resorts with access to the lake, condominiums, chalets and a brand new spa resort that will be open in the summer of 1999. Since the loop is a well known anglers' resort area, if you plan a visit in July or August you should book well ahead.

Tioga Pass Resort, just minutes from the entrance station, has cottages with kitchens and motel rooms. However, you must stay a week in the summer. We recommend this resort if you know that you want to be in the Tuolumne Meadows area for an extended visit, but you must reserve early. The resort is also open for adventurous cross country skiers. See page 290 for a description.

Lodging is listed alphabetically within each community.

Motels and Resorts

Big Rock Resort

The one, two and three-bedroom cabins are located on June Lake with complete lakeside facilities, including boat launch and rentals. There are peddle boats and a lawn stretches down to the water. All units have complete kitchens.

Big Rock Resort
P.O. Box 126
June Lake, CA 93529
760-648-7717 800-769-9831
Fax: 760-648-1067
www.mammothweb.com/
  lodging/bigrock
$85 - $160

Boulder Lodge

The lodge sits on five acres above the lake. There is every kind of accommodation, from motel room to a five-bedroom, three-bath lakefront house. Most units have a deck with lake view, and many have kitchens. The resort has tennis courts and an indoor swimming pool. The main lobby has a pool table, fireplace and large screen television.

Boulder Lodge
P.O. Box 68
June Lake, CA 93529
760-648-7533 800-458-6355
Fax: 760-648-7330
$60 - $300

Courtesy of Double Eagle Resort/Spa

A cabin at Double Eagle Resort and Spa, the newest lodging facility at June Lake. The description is on the next page.

Motels and Resorts

Double Eagle Resort and Spa
Route 3 Box 15B
June Lake, CA 93529
760-648-7004
Fax: 760-648-7017
www.10kvacationrentals.com/
    doubleeagle
$149 - $189

Directions:
Drive approximately eight miles west
on Highway 158 South.

Special Features:
The resort is perfectly situated for all
kinds of June Lake activities,
although you might just want to stay
put and partake of all that the spa
has to offer, from aroma therapy and
massages to a pool and gym.

Double Eagle Resort and Spa

You will want to try this brand new
resort for a few days relaxing in the
lap of luxury. Several modern two-
bedroom cabins nestle in the forest
near Reverse Creek less than a mile
from June Mountain under the
imposing escarpment of Carson Peak.
Each cabin is equipped with a full
kitchen, comfortably furnished livingroom with fireplace or stove, TV and
VCR, phones and an outside patio
with a barbeque. The full-service spa
and fitness center opens in the summer of 1999. There are two catch and
release ponds on their property and
guides to lead you fishing. The spa will
have a director to plan your program,
and the Eagle's Landing (formerly the
Fern Creek Grill) will have outdoor
dining in summer.
See page 251 in "Dining" for a
description. Winter or summer, the
location and amenities make this a
winner.

Fern Creek Lodge
Route 3, Box 7
June Lake, CA 93529
760-648-7722 800-621-9146
www.junelake.com/lodging/fern
$47 - $220 depending on season
    and number of persons.

Fern Creek Lodge

The lodge features a group of very
economical old-style cabins with
kitchens. Some sleep as many as eight
and a few are two-story buildings.
There are fireplaces in some units,
but no maid service is provided.

Motels and Resorts

Four Seasons

Close to June Mountain, these
A-Frames have a rear sun deck,
fireplaces or stove, TV and queen beds.
There are full kitchens and bath with
tub showers. The secluded woods
setting make them an ideal summer
location.

Four Seasons
Star Route 3, Box 8-B
June Lake, CA 93529
760-648-7476
www.junelake.com/lodging/
   foursns
$79 - $199 depending on the
   number of persons.

Gull Lake Lodge

Fourteen 600-square-foot suites, each
with living room, kitchen, bedroom
and bath, are located next to Gull Lake
Park. There are barbeques and the TV
in each suite has a free movie channel.
The lodge is ideally located next to the
Gull Lake marina and only two blocks
from June Lake Village.

Gull Lake Lodge
P.O. Box 25
June Lake, CA 93529
760-648-7516 800-631-9081
www.junelake.com/lodging/gull
$55 - $155

Heidelberg Inn Resort

Step back in time into the original
lobby of June Lake Lodge that
welcomed the rich and famous
movie stars in the 1930s and 40s. The
rooms on the second floor have been
remodelled into suites with living
room, bedroom, kitchenette and bath
with jacuzzi tub. Although now an
RCI timeshare, all units are available
for rent to the general public. The
resort has nightly activities in high
season, and several nights a week in
other months.

Heidelberg Inn Resort
Drawer L
June Lake, CA 93529
760-648-7718 800-438-6493
$80 - $119

Special Features:
For movie buffs the lobby is
decorated with photos of the many
Hollywood nobility who were
regulars at June Lake Lodge.

Motels and Resorts

June Lake Motel
P.O. Box 98
June Lake, CA 93529
760-648-7547 800-648-6835
Fax: 760-648-7147
www.junelake.com/lodging/
  jlmwntr
$90 - $130

June Lake Motel and Cabins

This motel has room configurations
for any group, from housekeeping
units with one bedroom to a lakeview
condominium with three bedrooms
that can sleep up to nine persons.
Located in the center of town, they
have an indoor jacuzzi and sauna and
all rooms have microwaves, TV with
free HBO and direct dial phones.

June Lake Pines
P.O. Box 97
June Lake, CA 93529
760-648-7522 800-481-3637
Fax: 760-648-7282
www.junelake.com/lodging/
  junepines
$50 - $125

June Lake Pines

One, two and three-bedroom cottages
are charmingly arranged on a hill in
the center of town. All have kitchens
and TVs with free HBO, and some
have fireplaces or stoves. Pets are
allowed, but not in winter and they
may not be left unattended.

June Lake Villager
P.O. Box 127
June Lake, CA 93529
760-648-7712 800-655-6545
www.junelake.com/lodging/
  villager
$35 - $120

June Lake Villager

The Villager offers everything from
regular motel rooms to housekeeping
suites and large cabins that can sleep
up to ten people. The rooms are
comfortable and quite spacious. Some
suites and cabins have fireplaces, and
rooms come with coffee makers and
color TV with free HBO and Disney
channel. There is a patio with barbeques and a spa, a fish cleaning
station and even fish freezing so that
you can save your catch for home.

Motels and Resorts

Lake Front Cabins

New owners are redecorating these charming 1960s cabins surrounding a lovely yard with large barbeque pit, tables with awnings and chairs that allow ample opportunity to share your fish tales with new friends. Large groups love these units because of the privacy of the location and the place to gather and socialize. The studios, one and two-bedroom cottages all have large kitchens.

Lake Front Cabins
P.O. Box 696
June Lake, CA 93529
760-648-7527
www.junelake.com/lodging/
lakefront
$65 - $100

Reverse Creek Lodge

David and Denise Naaden and their eleven children care for the duplex A-frames situated in a secluded, woodsy setting near Reverse Creek and close to the ski slopes.

Reverse Creek Lodge
Route 3, Box 2
June Lake, CA 93529
760-648-7535 800-762-6440
www.reversecreeklodge.com
$45 - $140 for a chalet

Special features:
The A-frames are designed so that you can rent both the front and back or just one section. The front of each unit is a simple motel room. The back has a kitchen, fireplace and features a porch looking out on the forest and a barbeque for those whoppers you caught in June Lake.

Courtesy of Reverse Creek Lodge

The Naaden family of Reverse Creek Lodge.

Motels and Resorts

Still Meadow Cabins
P.O. Box 694
June Lake, CA 93529
760-648-7794 800-648-2211
$45 - $150

Still Meadow Cabins

A group of motel units, cabins and A-frames plus a three bedroom cottage with two baths is located in the heart of June Lake Village. You can walk to either Gull Lake or June Lake marinas. All units have TVs with a free movie channel.

The Haven
P.O. Box 157
June Lake, CA 93529
760-648-7524 800-648-7524
www.junelake.com/lodging/
  haven/default.htm
$45 - $75

The Haven

Located adjacent to June Lake in the heart of the village, the motel has two-story cottages with two bedrooms, living room and full kitchen or spacious studios with kitchens for two people. They also have an economy motel room with small kitchenette which is ideal for a short stay. The cottages and studios are attractively furnished and situated around a central patio that has an indoor spa at one end.

Whispering Pines
Route 3, Box 14-B
June Lake, CA 93529
760-648-7762 800-648-7762
www.junelake.com/lodging/
  whisper
$55 - $155

Whispering Pines

Whispering Pines has motel units, cabins and A-frames with kitchens that are on a hill near Fern Creek. They serve continental breakfast and have an indoor spa and daily maid service.

Motels

Best Western Lake View Lodge

This is the largest motel in Lee Vining with 45 units, many with two queen beds. Most upstairs units have a Mono Lake view. With lovely gardens, coffee makers in each room and TVs with a movie channel, this Best Western has a AAA three-star rating.

Open all year.
Best Western Lake View Lodge
30 Main St. - Hwy. 395
Lee Vining, CA 93541
760-647-6543 800-528-1234
$49 - $88

Blue Sky Motel

Eleven economical units, one of which has two-bedrooms, are located next to the barbeque and deli. Coffee, tea and hot chocolate are in the rooms, and the deli-bakery has scrumptious baked goods for breakfast. You won't need to go far for dinner as they put on a barbeque each night in front of the deli.

May to October.
Blue Sky Motel
Hwy. 395
Lee Vining, CA 93541
760-647-6440
$68 - $78

El Mono Motel

Located in back of the Caffé Latte Da are eleven rooms and four cottages that sleep six to eight people and have kitchens. Some rooms share a bath outside the rooms. This is an inexpensive possibility for families with young children. Latte and espresso in the morning can be added to your bagels and other baked goods for a fine breakfast.

May to October.
El Mono Motel
51 Hwy. 395
Lee Vining, CA 93541
760-647-6310
$49 - $80, cottages $110

Motels

May to mid-November.
Gateway Motel
Hwy. 395
Lee Vining, CA 93541
760-647-6467 800-282-3929
$39 - $99

Gateway Motel

From the street it is not apparent but all the units look out on Mono Lake and have sun decks. There is a spa with a lake view. All rooms are air conditioned and have coffee machines, cable TV and phones.

May to October.
King's Inn at Lee Vining
P.O. Box 458
Lee Vining, CA 93541
760-647-6300
Fax: 760-647-6050
$75 - $95

King's Inn at Lee Vining

Located off the main street at 2nd and Mono Ave., the motel offers quiet, nonsmoking rooms in newly renovated units with ceiling fans but no air conditioning. Coffee, tea and pastries come with the room and all have outside seating. Two units were brought from Bodie and although the ceilings are low, there is an upper level separate bedroom. The manager is a longtime local who knows about the area.

May to October.
Murpheys
P.O. Box 57
Lee Vining, CA 93541
706-647-6316 800-334-6316
$38 - $88

Murpheys

Forty-four units are in two-story buildings with rustic exteriors and outside walkways. The motel has a two-star AAA rating. There is a meeting room, large spa and sauna but no air conditioning. Two rooms have kitchens. For anglers there is a fish cleaning and quick freezing facility.

Lodges

Tioga Lodge at Mono Lake

This charming inn is the newest
addition to the overnight possibilities
in Lee Vining. For years it sat vacant
until the present owners moved from
Los Angeles and began the long
job of renovation. You will have a
magnificent view of Mono Lake from
the nine individual rooms in cottages
that have been totally remodelled,
each with a different theme. A favorite
room is the Joseph Walker Mountain
Man Room, complete with handmade
pine bed, wall-mounted long rifle
and elk head. A gazebo on the creek
running through the property
beckons you to relax and take in the
changing scene of Mono Lake and
the surrounding mountains.

Open year-round.
Tioga Lodge at Mono Lake
P.O. Box 850
Lee Vining, CA 93541
760-647-6423 888-647-6423
www.thesierraweb.com/lodging/
   tiogalodge
$50 - $95

Directions:
Drive 2.5 miles north of Lee Vining
on Highway 395.

Special Features:
The excellent restaurant/gift shop
was transported from Bodie. It has a
1900s ambience. See page 249 for
a description of the restaurant.
Breakfast is served May through
October.

Tioga Pass Resort

Eighty-year-old Tioga Pass Resort,
with its housekeeping cabins and four
motel rooms, is just two miles from
the park entrance. At 9,600 feet it
is probably the highest resort in
California. The cabins sleep from
two to six people, have kitchens and
are located next to the creek that runs
through the property. The cabins are
rented by the week in summer and
motel rooms nightly. The resort is
open for adventurous skiers in the
winter. See page 290.

Tioga Pass Resort
Highway 120 (Tioga Pass Road)
P.O. Box 307
Lee Vining, CA 93541
209-372-4471

Special Features:
Breakfast, lunch and dinner are
served daily in the restaurant.
Espresso and sandwiches are
served outside in the summer. The
lodge great room has a store full of
T-shirts, jewelry, books and maps,
and the owners will answer your
questions about all the activities in
the area. This is a popular place with
anglers, so you must reserve early
to get the summer week you want.

Dining

How we rate restaurants:

$ Inexpensive, including soup or salad—under $15.
$$ Moderate, including soup or salad—under $20.
$$$ Moderately expensive, a la carte—entrées $16 to $22.
$$$$ Expensive, a la carte—entrées over $22.
Tips, wine and tax are not included in our estimates of cost.

Restaurants in Lee Vining run the gamut from inexpensive barbeque hamburgers to full service fine dining on the shore of Mono Lake just outside town. In June Lake you will find several eateries in town and two longtime favorites with locals near the western curve of the highway. We have not covered everything but rather have chosen some restaurants that offer something different.

$
Summer only.
Hwy. 395
Lee Vining
760-647-6432

Bodie Mikes

You'll find great hamburgers and other fare that you would expect in a western barbeque restaurant. There is outside seating in warm weather.

$
Year-round, 6:00 a.m. to
**   10:00 p.m., daily.**
Hwy. 395
Lee Vining
760-647-6477

Nicely's

This long established full service restaurant features a menu with most people's favorites. Don't miss the homemade pies.

$$$$
Reservations required.
Dinner, Wednesday thru Sunday.
Closed May and November.
760-647-6581

Directions:
The Mono Inn is 6.3 miles north of Lee Vining on Highway 395.

The Mono Inn

This historic landmark has been totally renovated by the Ansel Adams family. The dining room has the best view in town. Be sure to stop into the gallery before dining here. The menu features Angus beef prime rib on Fridays and Saturdays. The specialties

Dining

of the house are roast duck and lamb shanks. With an excellent wine list to choose from, a full bar in back of the dining room and the superb view of Mono Lake at sunset, you would be hard put to find a finer spot for a special dinner.

Tioga Lodge Restaurant

You'll find fine dining in the charming main building of the lodge. Head chef Rebecca Deakin and her three associates cook up quite a storm with special treats in store. The menu changes weekly, often featuring unusual entrées like chicken Wellington. The appetizers are special and the breads are all baked on the premises. There are only seats for 24 inside. In the summer there are a few outside tables on the porch with a fine view of the lake. Wines and champagne can be ordered by the glass or from a fine wine list featuring wines from the San Bernadino area.

$$$
Reservations required in season.
Breakfast, dinner, daily, May thru October.
Hwy. 395, just north of Lee Vining.
760-647-6423

Dining

$
**Breakfast, lunch and dinner,
daily, year-round.**
Hwy. 120 and Hwy. 395
Lee Vining

$$
**Dinner, Tuesday thru Sunday,
year-round.**
760-932-7780

Directions:
Drive 25 minutes north of Lee Vining
on Highway 395.

$
**Breakfast, lunch and dinner,
year-round.**
Hwy. 395
Lee Vining
760-647-6312

Tioga Gas Mart

This is more than a gas mart. They
offer excellent breakfasts including
espresso coffee, a full array of deli
sandwiches and barbeque entreés and
pizza for dinner. The gift shop has
books, maps and T-shirts, and don't
miss the great view from the lookout
above the station.

Virginia Creek Settlement

This unique old motel and dining
room offers a complete menu of meat,
chicken and burgers as well as pasta
dishes and interesting pizzas. This is a
great place for a family, as the portions
are large and the offerings simple.

Yosemite Trails

This longtime fixture of Lee Vining is
considered by many to have the best
food in town, with a large selection of
good American offerings. It is a great
place for breakfast and dinners are
tasty and economical.

Dining

Carson Peak Inn

The Carson Peak Inn has been serving dinner daily since 1966. They are much beloved by locals and return visitors, especially those who want the "hearty" portions of their combination plates of prime rib or steaks with Alaskan king crab legs or lobster. But you better have a hefty appetite for these servings. They also have "regular appetite" dinners.

$$$
Reservations recommended in high season.
Dinner, daily.
June Lake
760-648-7575

Special Features:
All dinners come with soup and salad, a baked potato with butter, sour cream and chives and their own garlic bread.

Eagle's Landing

The former Fern Creek Grill, a favorite with locals, has moved to spacious new quarters at Eagle's Landing. The menu will feature special selections for clients of the fitness center and spa, as well as a salad bar and rotisserie grilled meats. If the chef brings over the barbeque ribs from Fern Creek, these are a must. Just ski or hike more the next day and you won't feel guilty.

$$
Breakfast, lunch and dinner, daily, year-round.
Double Eagle Spa Resort
June Lake
760-648-7897

Sierra Inn

Located in the center of June Lake Village, they serve a full menu of steak, ribs, chicken and seafood with a salad bar. The special children's menu has everything from cheeseburgers to fried chicken.

$$
Breakfast, lunch and dinner, daily.
June Lake
760-648-7774

Special Features:
For anglers they offer "You catch em, we cook em" served with soup, salad bar and potato or pilaf plus vegetables.

© Ellie Huggins

The Lyell Fork of the Tuolumne is one of the many easy hikes from Tuolumne Meadows. From Lee Vining it is less that an hour of driving with some the Sierra's most spectacular scenery to make the trip enjoyable.

Highway 120 East Activities

You can experience the best of the Muir's High Sierra and the "Range of Light" at our Lee Vining and June Lake gateway. Not only is the mysterious and beautiful Mono Lake there to explore, but all your activities will take place with the backdrop of the eastern escarpment of the Sierra Nevada, the mountains that rise 6,000 to 7,000 feet out of the high desert plain along Highway 395.

Some of the best fishing in California is found at June Lake and the high country lakes are easy to reach from Tuolumne Meadows. You will be able to explore alpine flower gardens, see old mining camps above 10,000 feet, and wander close to Mono Lake's strange tufa formations. In fact there is so much to do that you may wish to extend your stay in the area.

Every kind of winter activity is available at June Lake. For the adventurous there is ice climbing with a guide up Lee Vining Creek or a guided cross country ski trip over Tioga Pass all the way to Yosemite Valley.

© Ellie Huggins

Mt. Gibbs across a glacial tarn on the Tioga Pass Road just west of the entrance station.

Excursions

Summer, open daily, 8:00 a.m. to 7:00 p.m.
The rest of the year, 9:00 a.m. to 4:00 p.m.
Fee to enter park.

Directions:
From Lee Vining drive 20 miles north on Highway 395 to Highway 270 to Bodie State Park. It is 13 miles east to the park with ten miles paved. The last three miles are on a good dirt road. From Bridgeport Highway 270 is 6.4 miles south. The park is open in winter. If there is too much snow, the road is closed and you will need skis or snowshoes to visit. Check at the Mono County Sheriff's office in Bridgeport for snow conditions.

The parking area has restrooms and interpretive signs about the town. There is a nice picnic area down the hill beyond the parking lot.

Bodie State Historic Park

If you want to see an 1890s gold mining town that is frozen in time, take a day to visit Bodie State Historic Park. Bodie became a park in 1962. Over 100 of its buildings are still standing, making it the largest unrestored ghost town in the American West. The park covers 450 acres in the Aurora Canyon.

Gold was discovered here in 1859, triggering the Eastern Sierra's greatest mining stampede. At its peak Bodie claimed ten thousand residents. Ramble through the streets of Bodie where you may look into windows of the buildings and imagine the life led by their inhabitants.

© Ellie Huggins

A view of one of the mines above the town of Bodie.

Excursions

During its heyday, Bodie personified the rowdy spirit of the West. It was notorious as the home of the most wicked men in the West. It was a rough and tumble town where gun fights were frequent and life was tough. Stage holdups, street fights and robberies were said to be a regular feature of daily life. Sixty-five saloons that helped the miners relax after digging gold and rock from the nearby hills probably inspired rivalries and disagreements.

A visit to the town cemetery gives clues to the true character of Bodie. The surprising number of graves of children under three and young men in their teens and twenties demonstrates the effects of harsh living conditions on young people and perhaps how easy it was to get into a deadly fight. People said the town "had its man for breakfast" almost every day.

© Ellie Huggins

You can walk into the church and think of those parents who mourned here before burying their young children in the cemetery above town. During its heyday, not many of the young men who worked the mines would have visited this building. They were more likely to be found in one of the many saloons.

Over the years, as the gold in the ground was mined out, a gradual exodus from Bodie began. Without the shiny metal to lure and hold residents, the rugged environment and isolation took its toll. Fires twice destroyed large parts of Bodie, and the standing buildings today are only a fraction of the original town.

Swimming

Two great swimming locations with views to please beckon those who don't mind the cold, and a beach at Mono Lake lets you experience the buoyancy of very salty water. Gull and Silver Lakes on the June Lake Loop also have locations for a dip, but without the view.

Directions:
From Lee Vining drive five miles south on Highway 395 to Highway 120 E toward Benton. Drive east five miles to a dirt road on your left marked for the South Tufa Reserve. Take the first right fork and continue to Navy Beach.

Mono Lake Navy Beach

If you've always thought you'd never float on water, here's your chance. The salinity of Mono Lake is such that you can turn on your back and read a newspaper as if lying on a couch. Try it! However, you will be salty when you come out and should take a shower as soon as possible, or you'll begin to itch.

Directions:
From Lee Vining drive 10.5 miles south on Highway 395 to Highway 158 South to June Lake. Drive east to Oh! Ridge and turn right on June Lake Road to Pine Cliff Rd. Turn left to the campground following the road down to the beach. The best swimming beach is at the last parking lot. There are picnic tables and restrooms.

June Lake

When the weather turns hot, June Lake offers the best swimming in the area. Since the lake is fed by snowmelt from the peaks above, the water is chilly. However, you can enjoy a good swim as long as you keep moving. If you have come from a hike or bike ride, this lake will provide a welcome cooling off. Picnic facilities along the beach make this an ideal place for a family outing.

Swimming

Tenaya Lake

There is no more beautiful place than this beach to spend a sunny day. The sand is white and makes super castles, the gulls' antics will amuse you and the scenery is spectacular. Swimming and a picnic here after climbing Pothole Dome is the perfect outing for families with small children. See page 278 in "Hiking" for a description. The kids will love the accomplishment of climbing up the dome, adults will enjoy the view from the top and what child doesn't like going to the beach. Tenaya Lake can be windy by mid-afternoon, so plan your trip to reach the beach by noon. The water is shallow and safe, if cold.

Directions:
The lake is 22 miles from the Tioga Pass Entrance Station to Yosemite National Park on Tioga Pass Rd. The swimming beach is a short walk from the parking lot and restroom facilities at the eastern end of the lake.

© Ellie Huggins

A family gets ready to enjoy a day at the June Lake beach at Oh! Ridge.

Boating

The string of lakes on the June Lake Loop (Highway 158) offers some of the best water fun in the High Sierra. The loop road is 15.6 miles long and passes June, Gull, Silver and Grant Lakes in that order. Water skiing is allowed only on Grant Lake where there is a boat launch but no rentals. The boat rentals at each lake are listed below.

June Lake

A launch ramp and beach are located near the Oh! Ridge campground. There is no fee for day use.

June Lake Marina
June Lake
760-648-7726

June Lake Marina

You can bring your own boat and launch it here or rent a slip by the day, week or month. Their rental rates include parking.

Boats, 14-foot with 6 hp motor.
Boats, 16-foot with 15 hp motor.
Float Tubes.

Big Rock Resort
June Lake
760-648-7717

Big Rock Resort

Big Rock Resort has a marina that rents dock or shore space as well as boats.

Aluminum boats with motors.
Barges with motors.
Paddle Boats.

Boating

Gull Lake Boat Landing

The boat landing is located next to
Gull Lake Park with a playground for
the kids and a tennis court. The
landing has a large deck on the lake
with picnic tables. There is a concrete
launch ramp, and you can rent a slip.

Boats with or without motors.
Barges with or without motors.
Paddle Boats.

Gull Lake Boat Landing
760-648-7539

Silver Lake Rentals

Paddle Boats.
Canoes.

Silver Lake Rentals
760-648-7525

Saddlebag Lake Resort

Saddlebag Lake, the largest lake in the
Tioga Pass area, lies at 10,087 feet.
It is the highest lake in California
reached by a public road. Saddlebag
Lake Resort on the south shore has
a store and cafe open July 1 to
October 1. You can rent boats with or
without motors. The resort operates a
sight-seeing trip around the lake and
a water taxi that will drop you off for
easy hikes to the Twenty-Lakes Basin,
a mecca for anglers, photographers
and lovers of alpine scenery. The water
taxi will pick you up at a prearranged
time.

Saddlebag Lake Resort
P.O. Box 303
Lee Vining, CA 95341

Directions:
Drive west ten miles on Tioga Pass
Rd. to Saddlebag Lake Rd. Turn
north and drive 2.5 miles on a dirt
road to the lake.

Boating

Mono Lake Committee Tours
760-647-6595
Fee per person.
Reservations required.
Summer, Saturday and Sunday
  morning.
Tours start from Navy Beach.

Directions:
Drive five miles south of Lee Vining on Highway 395 to Highway 120 E toward Benton. Drive five miles to the sign for South Tufa Reserve. Turn left on the gravel road which immediately forks. The right fork goes to Navy Beach. There is very limited parking here and the Committee suggests that you park at the South Tufa lot and walk the third of a mile to Navy Beach.

Mono Lake Committee Canoe Tours

The perspective from a tour on this lake is like no other. You can glide though groves of tufa and float near diving birds. Experts explain the ecology of this fascinating lake and you will learn about the abundant life in the water and birds that depend on it. Only morning tours are given because fierce winds often come up in the afternoon. Life jackets are provided and required. There are only 12 slots for each tour, so reserve early.

© Ralph Mendershausen

Your canoe trip will come close to these strange tufa formations.

Fishing

The Eastern Sierra boasts some of the best fishing anywhere in the Sierra. However, we are only listing information about lakes and streams close to Lee Vining and June Lake or along Highway 120 on the way to Tuolumne Meadows.

Fishing season starts on the last weekend in April and ends the last day of October. All anglers sixteen and older must display a license, which can be bought at local hardware and fishing supply stores. Be aware of regulations where you wish to fish. At some locations you must use barbless hooks and all locations have limits on size and number of fish per day. Some streams are catch and release only. To obtain information about the regulations check with local stores, or call Fish and Game at 760-872-1171 or use their web site www.dfg.ca.gov.

Alpers Ranch

Cabins and a small store are on the site. Several miles of private river are available to guests for catch-and-release fishing. Catch-and-keep fishing is allowed in a pond on nearby Alpers Creek. Tim Alpers raises his own stock in earthen ponds using special diets. Alpers trout are renowned for their size and fighting spirit and are now planted all over Mono County, in the June Lakes, Mammoth Lakes area and other places along the Eastern Sierra. The best are kept for guests of the ranch, so if you are an avid angler wanting a great experience landing a five to 20-pound trout, book early in the year.

Alpers Ranch
760-648-7334
April to October: 760-647-6652

Directions:
From Lee Vining drive south 15 miles on Highway 395 to Owens River Road, turn east three miles to the ranch.

Fishing

June Lakes

Directions:
Drive south ten miles on Highway 395 to Highway 158 South. Drive west on the June Lakes Loop road to June, Gull, Silver and Grant Lakes.

Ernie's Tackle Shop
June Lake
760-648-7756

John Logue at the tackle shop will gladly fill your fishing needs.

Rush and Reverse Creeks are planted in the following locations:

Reverse Creek
Just east of Carson Peak Inn to Dream Mountain Resort. There are access roads to the creek.

Rush Creek
From the Southern California Edison power plant bridge north to the lake and in the Silver Lake Campground.

June Lakes

The four lakes located around the June Lake Loop are stocked with some of the largest trout in the region.

Steve Kennedy of The Trout Fitter in Mammoth Lakes gives the following suggestions for fishing the Loop. In order to catch the really big ones that like to stay deep in colder water, trolling from a boat is your best bet. However, shore fishing is good at the following locations.

June Lake: Along the highway side which can be reached by parking at the beach and working your way along the shore.

Gull Lake: Along the shore from the west end near the campground.

Silver Lake: Near the south end and western shoreline.

Grant Lake: Hot spots are often near the entrance of Rush Creek.

Double Eagle Resort

The resort has stocked the catch and release Black's Pond with three to ten-pound Alpers rainbow trout. They rent float tubes or you can bring your own. You can also hire a guide to take you to the area's best fishing spots.

Fishing

Lee Vining Creek

Lee Vining Creek is a favorite place to fly-fish. If you drive along the campground access road, you can find many places to cast for trout. Families will find this a great place to picnic, explore or relax. In autumn the canyon is ablaze with golden and orange aspen.

Lee Vining Creek

Directions:
From Lee Vining drive west on Highway 120 for approximately three miles to the turnoff to the Lee Vining Creek campgrounds.

Tioga and Ellery Lakes

Lee Vining Creek between Tioga and Ellery Lakes is planted and provides good fishing. At Tioga Lake park at the campground and walk around the western shore of the lake. You can catch brook and rainbow trout right from the shore. If you have access to a float tube and a fly-fishing rod, you'll probably catch your limit in no time at all.

Tioga and Ellery Lakes

Directions:
Drive west on Highway 120 nine miles to Ellery Lake or eleven miles to Tioga Lake. At the northern end of Ellery Lake a small campground has access to the shoreline.

Saddlebag Lake

You can rent a boat at Saddlebag Lake Resort and try your hand at fishing near the dam for golden, brook or rainbow trout. You can hire the water taxi to take you to the trails to Twenty-Lakes Basin where these fish can be found on a loop trip to any one or all of five lakes.

Saddlebag Lake

Directions:
From Lee Vining drive west ten miles on Tioga Pass Rd. to Saddlebag Lake Rd. Drive north 2.5 miles on a dirt road to the lake.

Special Features:
Saddlebag Lake Resort has a cafe and store to supply all your fishing needs. The proprietor can give you some tips about which lakes from the taxi would make the easiest day.

The Eastern Sierra Nevada is rich in trails with scenic vistas, abundant wildflowers and geologic wonders. We have chosen a group of day hikes and some longer hikes for the ambitious. The hikes in the Lee Vining area are listed first. These are more walks than hikes and get you close to Mono Lake and its streams. The June Lake hikes are listed next followed by those on the way to or near Tuolumne Meadows inside the park. There is a fee to enter the park that is good for seven days.

Remember that all hikes will take you to elevations above 7,000 feet. If you live at sea level, it is wise to plan an easy hike your first day. The weather in the high mountains can be changeable, even in summer. You will need good hiking boots, an extra jacket and plenty of water. In early summer mosquitos abound, so pack repellant. Anglers will want to bring a fishing rod, and photographers will find memorable vistas around every corner. A flower guide is also helpful. See the list in the Bibliography on page 298.

You can get close to the rising lake on the South Tufa hike. See page 268.

© Ellie Huggins

Hiking

The permit system for overnight camping

During heavy use periods, from July 1 to September 15, many trails within Inyo National Forest and Yosemite National Park are subject to daily overnight quotas. You may obtain a wilderness permit from the pertinent ranger district. No permit is necessary for day hikers.

Approximately one-half of the daily quota is available on the day of entry. These permits can be applied for on a first-come, first-served basis at the ranger station closest to the trailhead. Permits for Inyo National Forest can be obtained at the Mono Basin Scenic Area Visitor Center one mile north of Lee Vining, or in Tuolumne Meadows at the Wilderness Permit parking area on the road to Tuolumne Meadows Lodge. If your trailhead is outside the park, your permit is issued from the Visitor Center. If you start your hike inside the park, you must get your permit at Tuolumne Meadows.

Inyo National Forest
873 North Main St.
Bishop, CA 93514
760-873-2400

Mono Lake Ranger District
P.O. Box 10
Lee Vining, CA 93541
760-647-6525.

Yosemite National Park
** Wilderness Permits**
P.O. Box 577
Yosemite , CA 95389
209-372-0265 or 209-372-0200
** for a 24-hour taped message.**

Demand for permits for overnight use is highest Fridays, Saturdays and Sundays. You can obtain a permit by mail before May 31. A fee of $3 per person is charged for a confirmed wilderness permit reservation. Since bears are a problem in all the wilderness areas, you need to rent or purchase a bear-resistant cannister for your food.

Hiking

Lee Vining Hikes

Lee Vining Creek Trail.

Directions:
In Lee Vining the clearly marked south trailhead is east of the highway across from the Best Western Motel. The north trailhead is at the Mono Basin Scenic Area Visitor Center.

Visit the Mono Lake Committee Information Center and Bookstore in Lee Vining to pick up the nature guide that describes the one-mile walk to the Mono Basin Scenic Area Visitor Center. (The nature guide costs 50 cents.)

Lee Vining Creek Trail

This is an easy two-mile round trip on a trail that was dedicated in 1993. It is a product of cooperation between local businesses, the Mono Lake Committee, the U.S. Forest Service and the Los Angeles Department of Water and Power. It was built entirely with volunteer labor. The Mono Lake Committee has developed an interpretive pamphlet for the trail, which follows the course of Lee Vining Creek on its journey toward Mono Lake. Water now flows year-round in this reborn stream because of court decisions in recent years. This is a unique opportunity to walk along the creek and learn from the nature guide about a freshwater stream ecosystem. Willows and other shrubs that like to be near water are close at hand and provide a colorful border in autumn.

After viewing the excellent exhibits at the Visitor Center, you can retrace your steps along the cool stream, or take Mattly Ave. back to town. If the old Schoolhouse Museum is open, stop in and see collections of nineteenth century Lee Vining and Bodie memorabilia. See the description on page 294.

HWY. 120 E ACTIVITIES

Hiking

Mono County Park North Tufa Reserve

The park has a picnic area, restrooms, a broad lawn lined by trees and ramadas with tables near children's play equipment and swings. A trail leads to a half-mile walk on a boardwalk out over the lake's rising waters. The water has risen over once dry land, testament to the success of the Mono Lake Committee to bring the lake's level back and keep the correct salinity for the thriving aquatic life.

The walk passes several tufa towers on its way to the water's edge. In summer watch the busy brine shrimp and swarming brine flies. (The flies are harmless.) Before the arrival of Europeans the Kuzedika Paiutes collected the larvae and pupae of the flies and dried them. They were considered to be a delicacy.

Panum Crater

A one-mile hike offers a unique opportunity to walk up and into one of the most recent volcanic eruptions in the Eastern Sierra. A short, easy walk leads to the top of Panum Crater's pumice ring, formed when this volcano exploded about 640 years ago. Once the ring was formed, thick

Mono County Park North Tufa Reserve

Directions:
From Lee Vining drive five miles north on Highway 395 to the signed road to the county park. Turn east and drive 0.4 mile to the park, clearly visible on the right at the bottom of the hill.

Special Features:
The brine shrimp eat the microscopic algae in the water thus keeping it clear. Birds thrive on the shrimp, and because fish cannot live in the salty water, birds have the shrimp feast for themselves. And there are hundreds of thousands of birds. You will see some of the thousands of California Gulls that nest here. In the fall and winter, it is estimated that more than one million avian travelers stop here on their way from the north to points as far away as the southern tip of Chile.

Panum Crater

Directions:
From Lee Vining, drive five miles south on Highway 395 to the intersection of Highway 120 E toward Benton. Drive east three miles to a dirt road, then north to the Panum Crater parking lot.

HWY. 120 E ACTIVITIES

The volcanic eruption that formed Panum Crater is one of a series of eruptions over the last hundred thousand years that have moved northward from the Long Valley caldera south of Mammoth Lakes. As recently as 1890 a volcano erupted from the depths of Mono Lake.

South Tufa Nature Trail
Fee to use the trail.

Directions:
Drive east on Highway 120 E toward Benton until a dirt road signed for South Tufa Reserve. Turn north and take the left hand fork to the parking lot.

There are interpretive hikes each evening in the summer. See "Ranger Programs" on page 287 for a description. The hike times are also posted on a board in front of the Mono Lake Committee Center.

lava rose slowly out of the volcano's throat like toothpaste from a tube, plugging its vent. This jagged plug dome is largely composed of obsidian, a volcanic glass that forms when lava cools rapidly. Local Native American tribes used obsidian to fashion arrowheads. Pick up a piece and notice the sharp edges.

The view from Panum Crater is expansive. To the west rises the Sierra Nevada escarpment, uplifted by three and one-half million years of faulting. Mono Lake with its two islands fills the northern horizon, while the Mono Craters form a long line to the south.

South Tufa Nature Trail

This is an easy half-mile loop with closeup views of tufa. Interpretive signs teach about its formation. Recent court decisions and wet winters in 1997 and 1998 have resulted in a rapid rise of the lake level, forcing an ever changing route for the trail at the water's edge. Past lake levels are clearly marked along the trail and interpretive panels describe the unique ecosystem of Mono Lake. The visible tufa towers are surrounded by dying grasses and shrubs, dramatic evidence of the lake's previous low level.

Hiking

June Lake Hikes

Fern Lake

This is a very strenuous 3.4 mile hike with 1,300 feet elevation gain in 1.7 miles. It is not recommended for small children or those unaccustomed to the altitude and steep climbing. The trail proceeds steadily uphill for one mile through aspens and a fir forest to the junction with the Yost Meadow and Lake trail. The Fern Lake trail leaves to the right ascending very steeply from this point for 0.7 miles to a lake nestled under jagged metamorphic peaks. The setting is beautiful and well worth the effort.

Fern Lake

Directions:
Drive west on Highway 158 about a mile beyond the ski area to the trailhead. The turnoff to the parking area is marked for the Fern Lake trail.

Special Features:
One can swim in late season and there are fine picnic spots around the lake. The U.S. Forest Service has removed campsites near the lake, so respect the signs and don't picnic in restricted areas.

Yost Meadow and Lake

The trail to Yost Meadow and Lake is strenuous. It is 4.8 miles round trip with 1,000 feet elevation gain. It follows the Fern Lake Trail for the first mile. After crossing Fern Creek you climb gently across a ridge with excellent views of Gull and Silver Lakes. This is an easier ascent than to Fern Lake, but Yost Lake and its meadow are not as pretty a place for a picnic. However, there are spots along the way where you can stop by the creek.

Yost Meadow and Lake

Directions:
See the directions to Fern Lake trail above.

Rush Creek and Agnew Lake

Directions:
The trailhead is near the Frontier Stables east of Silver Lake.

Special Features:
The trail to Agnew Lake along Rush Creek takes you to one of the dams built by Los Angeles Department of Water and Power to trap water from the eastern Sierra spring runoff. The water in Agnew Lake falls to Silver Lake and on to Grant Lake where it is stored. Below Grant Lake, Rush Creek used to be a dry bed until 1994 when the California Supreme Court declared that Rush Creek must flow freely into Mono Lake. For a full description of the controversy, see page 234.

Summit Safaris
P.O. Box 656
June Lake, CA 93529
760-648-1129
Reservations necessary one day in advance for all trips.

Rush Creek and Agnew Lake

This is a strenuous hike of 4.4 miles round trip with 1,200 feet elevation gain. After crossing Alger Creek, which in high water years may be difficult, the trail traverses an exposed east-facing ridge. For this reason the hike is best done in the afternoon as the sun is setting behind the mountains. Gentle switchbacks lead along a ridge above Silver Lake. After about 1.5 miles, you will climb steeply up along the cable way to the dam and Agnew Lake. If you are a strong hiker, you can extend the trip another two miles and another 800 feet elevation gain to the shores of Gem Lake. If you elect to go this far, you should start early in the morning to avoid the heat on the first section of trail. Carry plenty of water.

Summit Safaris

Jenny Robins' leaders will take you on visits to high glacial lakes and flower-filled meadows. They will provide the lunch and the expertise. You won't need to worry about maps or parking. Once a week they offer a two-hour childrens' hike.

Hiking

Off Tioga Pass Road

Bennettville

This is an easy hike of two miles round trip with little elevation gain. The walk starts on a section of the old Tioga Pass Road that began its life as the Great Sierra Wagon Road, built to haul machinery to the Great Sierra Consolidated Silver Company in Bennettville. Begun in 1883 with great fanfare and a large crew of workers, many of whom were Chinese, it was completed before snowfall that year. The Great Sierra Consolidated Silver Mine might better be called the Great Sierra Mining Bust, for the mine ceased operation in 1884 leaving only the road and a few buildings in Bennettville.

The first section of trail leads past a series of glacial tarns, then slightly uphill for about a quarter of a mile. In late summer the last few hundred yards of road is lined with beautiful lupine and Indian paint brush. In one mile tailings from a mine tunnel come into view. To your right two reconstructed buildings on a hill are the only reminders of the mine and its founders' dream of riches. An ore cart, some twisted track and the opening to a mining tunnel are all easy to spot.

Bennettville

Directions:
Drive west eleven miles on Tioga Pass Rd. to Tioga Lake. The trailhead is on the north side of the road just before the Tioga Lake overlook. It is signed.

As you return to your car along this pleasant stretch of old road after viewing the ghosts of Bennettville, think on the harsh life of miners living at 9,300 feet where snow lay more than ten feet on the ground for up to six months. The town was big enough for a post office, and a local old timer from Lee Vining told us that his grandfather delivered the mail here in winter. He skied on his 12-foot Norwegian snow shoes (skis), climbing up from Lee Vining to the May Lundy Mine above Lundy Lake then over the crest to Bennettville.

The Mono Ranger District conducts interpretive hikes to Bennettville from Junction Campground near Tioga Pass Resort. More information on this hike is on page 287.

Hiking

Hikes near Tuolumne Meadows

Gaylor Lakes.

Gaylor Lakes

Directions:
Park in a parking lot on the north side of Tioga Pass Rd. a few yards west of the Tioga Pass Entrance Station.

The hike is moderately strenuous. It is three miles round trip to Middle Gaylor Lake with 600 feet elevation gain followed by a 200-foot descent to the lake. The Gaylor Lakes lie in a high alpine meadow where you will feel that you can touch the sky. The trail makes a steep, rocky and sometimes dusty ascent from the parking lot in less than a mile. You may huff and puff to the saddle, but once there you will be treated with 360-degree views. Across the saddle the Gaylor Lakes will come into view. Take the trail that bears right and scramble down 200 feet to Middle Gaylor Lake with its fringe of white and red heather. The meadows around the lake are another paradise for flower lovers. The lake is not for swimming or fishing, just a lovely spot for a picnic.

Hiking

Dog Lake and Lembert Dome

From the Lembert Dome parking lot take the trail north toward Ragged Peak and Young Lakes. In 0.8 miles you will come to the trail from the Dog Lake parking area. Here you can scramble up Lembert Dome or continue on to Dog Lake.

From the Dog Lake parking lot, cross Tioga Pass Rd. and take the trail uphill through the forest to the back of Lembert Dome. Continue to the junction with the trail from Lembert Dome. Turn east and walk about 0.8 miles to Dog Lake.

Dog Lake and Lembert Dome Loop

Directions:
Drive to just east of the Tuolumne Meadows Campground. The loop leaves from either the Lembert Dome parking area on the north side of the road or from the Dog Lake parking lot near Tuolumne Meadows Lodge. To reach the latter turn south on the road to the lodge. Drive less than a mile. The parking lot is on the left up a hill. Do not leave food in your car. Use the bear proof containers.

Lembert Dome is named for a hermit, John Lembert, who lived in a cabin here in the 1880s.

Courtesy of Yosemite Concession Services

Lembert Dome as seen from the parking area on Tioga Pass Road.

Mono Pass

Directions:
Drive a mile and a quarter west from Tioga Pass on Highway 120. The trailhead parking is on the south side of the road.

Look for the lovely Shooting Star in wet places in the early summer.

Mono Pass

The trail to Mono Pass is one of the author's favorites, for it offers an easy route to one of the Sierra's most historic passes and affords a chance to experience the high alpine grandeur of the Sierra with moderate effort. The four miles to the pass with about 700 feet elevation gain traverse a few lateral moraines through a lodgepole forest interspersed with meadows and streams.

For the first quarter mile the trail descends to the Dana Fork of the Tuolumne River, which in high water may require reconnoitering to find a dry crossing. Soon the trail crosses moraines until the first of many meadows appears on your right. In all seasons wildflowers line the trail and fill the meadows. Those traveling this way at the end of summer will encounter clumps of blue gentian everywhere. For the second mile Parker Creek rushes down meadows to the west to meet the Dana Fork.

The first fork in the trail comes at about two miles from the trailhead. Take the trail marked for Mono Pass and Parker Pass. Here the only serious climb occurs but is soon over and the last mile of trail is an easy ascent, where you will encounter remains of sheepherder cabins. Finally the trail

Hiking

crosses a ridge overlooking the high meadows under Mono Pass. Sooner than you think the pass is reached and Summit Lake is below you, with many places to rest or picnic. Those wishing to go another 20 minutes or so down the trail toward Walker Lake will be rewarded with views of Mono Lake.

Across the lake on a bluff you will notice a few remains of cabins of miners seeking silver for the Golden Crown and Ella Boss mines.

© Ellie Huggins

The view across the summit meadows as you approach Mono Pass.

Lyell Canyon and the Lyell Fork of the Tuolumne River.

Directions:
Park at the Dog Lake parking lot near Tuolumne Meadows Lodge (see directions on page 273). Be sure to lock any food in the bear proof lockers provided at these trailheads. Bears are smart. They know that coolers contain food and can smell any left in your car. No car is strong enough to resist a hungry bear.

You see many pink Indian paintbrush in the meadows on hikes in this area. The flowers can be pink to red or even purple.

Along the Lyell Fork of the Tuolumne River

This hike is as long as you wish to make it and has little elevation gain. Start your hike along the marked John Muir Trail that begins across the road from the parking lot. You will soon come to a bridge that crosses the Lyell Fork. Continue for as many miles as you desire and then stop by the river for a fine picnic. Ambitious hikers can go as far as Rafferty Creek, another fine picnic location. This hike is particularly good for families with small children because you can stop where needed and they can play near the shallow portions of the river. However, the river is usually very cold, not inviting for a swim.

The trail up Rafferty Creek leads to Vogelsang High Sierra Camp, seven miles from Tuolumne Meadows. If you want to know more about going on a High Sierra Loop Trip, see page 280 for a description of the High Sierra Loop and page 5 for information about reserving a spot.

Hiking

Soda Springs

A trip to Tuolumne Meadows would not be complete without this stroll across the meadow in the height of summer. On this easy, half-mile walk you will be surrounded by a colorful array of flowers. Close inspection will reveal the immense variety of species that inhabit this high alpine meadow—penstemon, lupine, elephants head, Indian paintbrush and many more. Take your flower guide with you and you'll find you can identify many of them.

Eventually you cross the Tuolumne River on a bridge that is famous as the spot where John Muir and Robert Underwood Johnston, editor of Century Magazine, talked about creating Yosemite National Park. Stop to take in the view across the meadow. To the southwest are the distinctive forms of Cathedral Peak and Unicorn. To the east the rounded, brown metamorphic peaks of Mt. Dana and Mt. Gibbs stand guard over this meadow in the sky.

Continue walking to the springs. The stone cabin on the knoll above is known as Parson's Lodge. See the sidebar for information about ranger programs here.

Soda Springs

Directions:
Drive one mile west of the Tuolumne Meadows store and gas station. Look for a trail marker on the right and park off the road.

During summer months the Parson's Lodge has interpretive programs once a week. Check at the Tuolumne Meadows Visitor Center for times and days of these talks.

Another way to reach Soda Springs is from the road to the stable. Take the dirt road past the Lembert Dome parking lot and drive until the road turns north. Park here where permitted. The trail starts here and follows an old road to Soda Springs and the lodge. This is the preferred route for those attending the ranger programs.

HWY. 120 E ACTIVITIES

Pothole Dome

Directions:
Drive 2.2 miles west from the Tuolumne Meadows Campground. On the right is a pullout for Pothole Dome. This is an excellent climb for families with children who will love the accomplishment of achieving the high point.

Pothole Dome

This interesting formation is left from the glaciers that covered Tuolumne Meadows more than 15,000 years ago. Signs at the parking area ask that you do not cross the meadow to the dome in order to protect the fragile land, especially when it is wet. Instead take the easy trail that goes west along the edge of the meadow and over to the trees at the base of the dome. Find a place to climb the smooth rise of granite to the top. As you make this easy ascent, look east toward Mt. Dana and Mt. Gibbs, the peaks that dominate the horizon. Lembert Dome is in the near distance. The meandering path of the Tuolumne River on its way to Hetch Hetchy Reservoir traverses the grassy space before you.

© Ellie Huggins

Pothole Dome from the start of the trail.

Hiking

May Lake

Here is your chance to see a High Sierra Camp and also be in the very center of Yosemite National Park under Mount Hoffman. The moderate hike is two miles round trip with 500 feet elevation gain. Start hiking around the tarn and follow the trail through a forest of fir and lodgepole. Presently your route brings you to granite slabs where the trail is bordered by a series of rocks. Be sure to turn around while you rest to take in the views to the east. You can easily identify Cathedral Peak and you may catch a glimpse of the Cathedral Lake outlet that cascades down to Tenaya Lake. You will also be able to see Half Dome to the south. A few switchbacks will bring you to the saddle above the white tents of the High Sierra Camp and its lovely round lake. As you descend, stay straight on the trail to the lake shore. Follow along on the south shore until you find the perfect picnic spot.

May Lake

Directions:
Drive 19.5 miles west from the entrance station on Tioga Pass Rd. Turn right on the one-lane road and drive 1.8 miles to the May Lake trailhead. Park near a dark pond called a glacial tarn.

Climbing Mt. Hoffman

Never fear, the white cliffs of Mt. Hoffman to the north of May Lake are not what you climb to ascend this 10,850-foot peak. Walk west along the south shore. A trail circles around the south shoulder of the mountain and you can easily find a route up to a crest below the thumb. You do not need to go farther than the rocks below the thumb for the spectacular views in every direction. The author's 80-year-old father-in-law and 10-year-old grandchildren made it this far, so you can too. Just take it easy with plenty of stops.

The High Sierra Loop Trip

Six hikes totalling 46.3 miles to five High Sierra Camps in seven days traverse some of the park's, and indeed the Sierra Nevada's, most beautiful high country. The official trip is seven days with one layover day at Merced Lake Camp. The elevations range from 7,250 feet to as high as 10,300 feet. The most miles traveled in one day is 10 miles, mostly downhill between Sunrise and Merced Lake. It is possible to plan your own combination of camps, or even just go to one camp and stay a few days. See page 5 for an explanation of the lottery for the High Sierra Camps.

Tents may be assigned by gender, although the camp managers try to keep family groups together.

The High Sierra Loop Trip

For those who love to hike this can be the trip of a lifetime, and for families with children over seven who are good hikers, this trip will provide many wonderful memories. Steel-framed beds with mattresses, pillows, fresh linens, wool blankets and comforters are provided in canvas tents. All camps have central bath facilities and hot showers, although environmental conditions at each camp may limit availability. Breakfast and dinner is served and picnic lunches are provided for the trail.

You may choose to take a seven-day naturalist-led trip, a six-day saddle trip, a four-day saddle trip, or plan your own itinerary.

The Camps

Glen Aulin is at the foot of the White Cascades of the Tuolumne River at 7,800 feet. Famous and spectacular Waterwheel Falls is four miles downstream. Many trips spend the first night here.

May Lake is underneath the eastern wall of Mt. Hoffman on the shore of May Lake at 9,270 feet.

Hiking

Sunrise Camp is on a granite shelf above Long Meadow, with its beautiful meadows of wildflowers. Nearby ponds and lakes offer fishing, sunbathing and swimming.

Merced Lake is at the lowest elevation and offers dependable fishing at Merced and Washburn Lakes. This is the layover spot on the seven-day guided hikes.

Vogelsang is the highest and to many the most dramatic of all. It is above timberline under craggy Vogelsang Peak (11,516 feet) and near good fishing at Boothe, Fletcher, Vogelsang, Evelyn, Hanging Basket and Townsley Lakes.

Tuolumne Meadows Lodge is where most trips begin and end. It is on the banks of the Dana Fork of the Tuolumne River and is large enough to provide tent accommodations for visitors who come by car and stay for a few days. You may reserve a seat for dinner here without staying at the camp.

Courtesy of YCS

Vogelsang, the highest camp on the trip.

Courtesy of YCS

Looking across the meadow from Sunrise Camp with Cathedral Peak in the distance.

Horseback Riding

Frontier Pack Train
Reservations required 24 hours
in advance.
Summer:
Star RT 3, Box 18
June Lake, CA 93529
760-648-7701
Winter:
1012 East Line St.
Bishop, CA 93514
760-873-7971

Directions;
Drive west on Highway 158 to Silver Lake. The pack station is on the north side of the road.

Frontier Pack Train

Frontier Pack Train offers all-day, half-day and one-hour rides starting May 15 and running all summer. They have a base camp where professionals teach fly-fishing. Throughout the summer they offer five-day family adventures, Tuolumne Meadows trail rides via Donohue Pass and fishing for golden trout from their high country base camps. You can arrange spot trips to anywhere. Special four-day trips in June and September let you lead the life of a real cowboy driving the horses between June Lake and their winter pasture. Riders of all ages and experience can do this exciting trip. Frontier will match you to a horse, give you three gourmet meals a day, provide all camp gear and transport your clothes and sleeping bag to the night camp.

Courtesy of Yosemite Concessions Services

Riding out of Tuolumne Meadows Stables.

Horseback Riding

Virginia Lakes Pack Outfit

For 17 years Tom and Martha Roberts have been taking riders out for wilderness adventures. They operate from four trailheads (Virginia Lakes, Green Lakes, Mono Village and Buckeye) to access some of the most spectacular country in the west in northern Yosemite National Park and the Hoover Wilderness. You can choose a base camp trip, or you can plan your own to a special corner of the Sierra and let them take you there. They will bring along and cook gourmet food, and supply fishing gear if you don't have your own. They also offer spot trips and two-hour, four-hour or all-day guided rides into the Virginia Lakes wilderness.

Virginia Lakes Pack Outfit
Reservations required.
Summer:
HC route 1 Box 1070
Bridgeport, CA 93517
760-937-0326
Winter:
4300 Cox Road
Fallon, NV 89406
775-867-259

Directions:
Take Highway 395 north to Virginia Lakes Rd. at Conway Summit. Drive west 4.6 miles to the pack station.

Special Features:
For those who want to hike to their camps, but not carry gear, they will pack everything in, bring along the cook and all the food and meet you each night with a campfire burning and tents all set up. And, if you don't want to hike, you could always elect to take a horse each day, but you have to decide at the beginning of the trip.

Tuolumne Meadows Stables

The stables are run by Yosemite Concession Services. You can take a two-hour scenic ride, half-day or all-day ride to the famous Waterwheel Falls or Young Lakes. These rides do not go every day. Riders must be at least seven years old or 44 inches and weigh less that 225 pounds. The stables will also provide spot packing to a site of your choice, or all expense guided trips. Believe it or not, you can board your own horse here.

Tuolumne Meadows Stables
Summer only.
Make reservations at the stables
or call 209-372-1327.

Directions:
At the Lembert Dome parking lot head east on the dirt road to the stables.

You can also arrange a High Sierra Camp Loop with the stables. However, you must have entered the lottery and secured dates to arrange to ride instead of hike. See page 5 for information about the lottery.

The Eastern Sierra is laced with hundreds of U.S. Forest Service dirt roads that lend themselves to short loops or extended technical rides for cyclists of all abilities. This guide could not begin to cover even a fraction of the possibilities, nor is it necessary. In the Bibliography on page 300 we have listed the best guides and maps that contain detailed descriptions with elevation gain, terrain and whether on road or single track.

For visitors coming to Yosemite with bicycles, we have chosen a short ride in the June Lake area, and rides on paved and dirt roads to the South Tufa Reserve and to Black Point on the north side of Mono Lake, plus a ride off Tioga Pass Road up Lee Vining Creek to the power station. So pack bikes onto your car and head for the trailheads for a glorious day in the saddle. Be advised that most rides do not have water available along the route, so fill those water bottles full, and always take one more that you think you need.

Spring and autumn are truly the best times for bicycling here. Views are spectacular when snow still caps the peaks and fall color can be found around every corner in the June Lakes area and the Lee Vining Creek drainage.

June Lake Loop

Directions:
The June Lake Loop begins from the June Mountain parking lot, or from Oh! Ridge campground. A perfect end to your summer day of cycling could be a dip in June Lake from the beach below Oh! Ridge.

June Lake Loop

An easy five mile loop starts from Oh! Ridge campground. Head out to June Lake Drive and ride up the hill south toward Gull Lake and eventually reach Highway 158 at the June Mountain Ski Area. You can stop at the Gull Lake Park for a picnic before returning to Oh! Ridge. If you want to try some dirt roads, there is one that leaves near June Lake Drive and heads northeast out to the power pole line near Highway 395. You can try this on your return trip.

Bicycling

South Tufa State Reserve and Navy Beach

The first five miles of riding is on paved Highway 120 toward Benton. Turn north on a dirt road signed for the South Tufa Reserve. Continue straight to its parking area. The Nature Trail here is described in "Hiking" on page 268. There is a fee.

If you wish to swim at Navy Beach, take the right hand fork immediately to the beach. A description is in "Swimming" on page 256.

Black Point Ride

Black Point is the high volcanic cliff on Mono Lake's north shore. Start riding on the road north from the county park past the cemetery. The road crosses Mill Creek where the pavement ends and turns into an up and down ride on a dirt road.

After crossing a second creek (Wilson Creek) bear right. Stay left at the next junction and right at the second one. Keep right around the north side of Black Point until the lake and Negit Island come into view. The road will curve southwest along the edge of the lake to a parking lot.

South Tufa State Reserve and Navy Beach

Directions:
Park your car and start your ride at the intersection of Highway 120 to Benton and Highway 395. This is an easy ride of eleven miles round trip to the South Tufa Reserve, a little farther to Navy Beach.

Black Point Ride

Directions:
Drive five miles north of Lee Vining on Highway 395, then about a half mile east to the Mono County Park. Park here and start your moderate ride of eleven miles with a number of hills. No water or facilities are along the way, so fill your water bottles and use the county park restrooms.

When you reach the Black Point parking lot, you will have a closeup view of Negit Island, nesting site for the lake's thousands of California gulls.

HWY. 120 E ACTIVITIES

Lee Vining Creek

Directions:
Drive west two miles on Highway 120 (Tioga Pass Road) to the entrance to the Lower Lee Vining Creek Campground. Park here. Or you can ride from the Tioga Gas Mart at the corner of Highways 395 and 120.

Ernie's Tackle and Ski Shop
June Lake
760-648-7756

Ernie's tackle and ski shop rents mountain bikes as well as providing fishing and other advice.

Lee Vining Creek to Poole Power Plant

This is a particularly good family outing, as there is little or no traffic on the road. Your ride will take you three miles up a dirt road along Lee Vining Creek which started its life at 12,000 feet, above Saddlebag Lake. The road passes numerous campgrounds along the way with many places to stop to play in the creek or picnic. Even on the hottest days it is cool in the aspen forest that lines the creek. These trees create a colorful autumn adventure, a chance to be surrounded by a golden wonderland.

The road ends at Poole Power Plant. The steep cliffs on the south side of the road are a favorite place for ice climbers in the winter. If you start your ride from the gas mart, it is ten miles round trip.

Ranger Programs

Mono Lake Ranger District

The Mono Lake Ranger District interpretive programs are held at June Lake and at Mono Lake. Patio talks occur daily in the summer. Schedules are posted in front of the Visitor Center and at the South Tufa Reserve.

Mono Lake Ranger District
760-647-3044

Directions:
The Mono Basin Scenic Area Visitor Center is one mile north of Lee Vining on Highway 395. Check here to sign up for a nature walk to the South Tufa Reserve.

South Tufa State Reserve Walks

The Mono Lake Committee and the Mono Lake Tufa State Reserve provide interpretive walks and talks about Mono Lake. Talks given by the state park continue throughout the year, while the Committee's walks are on weekends during the summer. The Committee publishes a list of their various week-long courses given by experts.

South Tufa State Reserve Walks

Walk times are posted at the Mono Lake Committee Information Center in Lee Vining. See Mono Lake Committee in "Boating" on page 260 for information about canoe tours on Mono Lake.

Bennettville

On this moderately strenuous hike with 300 feet elevation gain, you can mix a little botany with the history of an old ghost town as your naturalist leads you up to Bennettville. It is now just a few weathered buildings and a mine shaft that yielded little for the investors. The ranger will tell you the stories of the Great Sierra Mine and its short, ill-fated life.

Bennettville

Directions:
Meet at the Junction Campground at the intersection of Tioga Pass Rd. and the road to Saddlebag Lake, ten miles west of the entrance station.

If you want to explore Bennettville on your own see page 271 in "Hiking" for a description of an easy-to-find route that leaves near Tioga Lake along the trace of the Great Sierra Wagon Road.

HWY. 120 E ACTIVITIES

June Mountain and Carson Peak reflected in June Lake.

A broad run at June Mountain with Mono Lake in the background.

Winter Activities

In winter, you can approach the east side of the Sierra only on Highway 395. Visitors from Los Angeles have been coming north for 60 years to enjoy the bountiful snow, the miles of cross country ski and snowmobile trails, and the skiing at Mammoth Mountain. However, June Mountain and the surrounding area offer a full menu of winter adventures in a more relaxed atmosphere. And those in search of a challenge can find certified guides to climb the famous ice falls in Lee Vining canyon. See below.

Highway 120 is closed at the snow line and remains that way until the snow melts in late spring or early summer. However, visitors from the north or south can use Highway 395 to reach Lee Vining or June Lake.

Ice Climbing Seminars

Led by AMGA certified guides, you can take two-day seminars to learn protection, anchoring, belaying and overall safety.

Nidever Mountain Guides
760-648-1122
Fax: 760-648-7221
www.themountainguide.com

Doug Nidever also leads spring ski tours for experienced skiers. You can take the Mammoth/June Traverse, the classic Trans Sierra Yosemite Haute Route or the Kuna Crest Tour.

Courtesy of Yosemite Concession Services

You will find solitude like this if you ski from the Tioga Pass Resort or take the Trans Sierra Trip.

Cross Country Skiing

Neither Lee Vining nor June Lake has any official groomed trails for nordic skiers. Most of those are on Highway 395 South of June Lake or in the Mammoth Lakes area. However, with miles of forest roads in the area, you can take off anywhere and ski across the countryside. There are two adventures above the road closure on Tioga Pass Road. We list them below.

Tioga Pass Resort
P.O. Box 307
Lee Vining, CA 93541
209-372-4471

Special Features:
One and two-bedroom cabins are electrically heated. Centrally located hot showers and flush toilets and the main lodge with two wood burning stoves, couches, video library and books and games supply all the comforts of home. Your rate includes all meals. No smoking is allowed in any buildings.

The Tioga Pass Resort

The resort opens in winter to offer some of the best skiing anywhere. There are easy tours into Yosemite National Park at Tioga Pass as well as ski mountaineering in the Twenty Lakes Basin or on Mt. Dana. Your hosts will pick you up at the gate on Tioga Pass Road and transport you to the snowline where you begin the 6.3-mile ski to the resort, with 2,600 feet elevation gain. They take your pack to the resort. You will need to bring your own sleeping bag.

Trans Sierra Expedition
Yosemite Nordic Ski School
209-372-8444

Special Features:
Tours depart weather conditions permitting. All tours include three meals a day, lodging, your guide and instruction. You must be able to carry a pack and ski more than 20 miles in a day. At least three persons must sign up for a trip to go.

Trans Sierra Ski Tour

The Yosemite Nordic Ski School conducts two six-day, trans-Sierra ski tours in the spring. If you are coming from the west, you will be flown to Lee Vining. Skiers are brought to the snowline to ski up Tioga Pass Road about 2,600 feet to Tioga Pass Resort. After two nights at the lodge you are off to Tuolumne Meadows for two nights in the ranger's cabin. The

Cross Country Skiing

longest day of skiing is more than 20 miles to Snow Creek cabin above Yosemite Valley. The last day is spent descending to the Valley. Depending on snow conditions you may have to walk the last few miles.

The Obsidian Dome Trail System

The first loop, the best for beginners, heads 45 degrees south into the trees from the major junction. Pass to the right of an orange Forest Service sign marked with a green circle high up in tree. Follow the blue diamonds for the remainder of a 2 km counterclockwise loop that circles back toward the highway and ends slightly west of the parking lot.

Another loop heads north toward Wilson Butte from the major junction in a clockwise route. After about 200 meters, the trail turns left 45 degrees northwest, contouring into the forest along the west side of the meadow. Look for an orange Forest Service sign in the trees marked with a blue square, and contour slightly uphill, following the blue diamonds usually posted on your left. Just before you are due west of Wilson Butte, the trail drops down and out of the trees. Cross the north end of the meadow, then turn south and follow a small rise back to the trail junction.

Obsidian Dome Trails

Directions:
Drive 3.5 miles south of Highway 158, the June Lake Loop, on Highway 395. The parking lot is on the west side of the road.

From the parking lot head west over a small rise to the main trail junction.

This description is from *What Shall We Do Tomorrow in the Mammoth Lakes Sierra* by Don Douglass and Ellie Huggins. Don supplied the cross country ski descriptions.

June Lake Cross Country Skiing

Highway 158 is unplowed between the Edison Plant near Silver Lake all the way to Highway 395. All you need to do is find a place to park and take off on the highway.

Downhill Skiing and Boarding

June Mountain
Hwy. 158
June Lake
760-648-7733 Fax: 760-648-7367
www.junemountain.com

Directions:
Drive 4.5 miles west from Highway 395 to the base parking area.

June Mountain was one of the first ski areas to open all its terrain to snowboarders. With a special half-pipe and the snowboard park Boardertown in a separate area, June Mountain is a great choice for families with both skiers and boarders. The runs are broad and the ski patrol applies a "No Reckless Skiing" policy to everyone.

June Mountain

What you see when you drive into the parking lot is not what you get. Up the steep slope via the chair lift lies a family ski area with superb beginner and intermediate terrain above the mid-mountain June Meadows Chalet. All the wide-open runs end at the Chalet making it perfect for families.

Intermediate skiers will be able to ski all of the mountain from its 10,135-foot peak. However, before skiing down, be sure to take in the view. From the vantage point at the top Mammoth Mountain lies to the south where on a clear day you can see the lifts. The peaks of the eastern edge of Yosemite National Park seem close enough to touch. To the northeast all 60 square miles of Mono Lake and its distinctive islands are before you. Novice skiers can ride the J6 chair to Rainbow Summit at 10,050 feet and ski two miles down Silverado to the Chalet. June Mountain often has fewer clouds and less wind than Mammoth Mountain, so you can head here when storms are brewing.

The runs from mid-mountain down the face are for advanced skiers. There is an easy road if you want to ski down without negotiating the bumps or you can take the chair lift.

Snowmobiling and Ice Skating at June Lake

Miles of snow-covered, forest roads become snowmobile trails in winter. Approximately 75,000 acres of land east of Highway 395 are open to smowmobilers. If you have your own snowmobiles, you can get a map from the U. S. Forest Information center in Mammoth Lakes that will tell you all about the miles of marked trails in the area. Please respect the skier only trails.

June Lake Junction

Experienced drivers can reserve a snowmobile by calling Bob Hudson in Mammoth Lakes, then drive to June Lake Junction. The attendant will provide a map. Your vehicle is right there; no need to trailer it anywhere. You simply climb on and take off across the miles and miles of trails located east of Highway 395.

Bob Hudson Snowmobiles
760-934-6888

Directions:
Bob Hudson snowmobile rentals is located at the June Lake Junction gas station at the intersection of Highways 158 and 395.

Ice Skating

A pond at the Double Eagle Resort is open for skating after it has frozen. Call the resort to check on where to park and enjoy their skating pond.

Double Eagle Resort
760-648-7004

Directions:
Drive approximately eight miles west of Highway 395 on Highway 158 South.

**Mono Basin Historical Museum
Lee Vining
May to October, Thursday thru
  Sunday, 12 noon to 8:00 p.m.
760-647-3003**

Directions:
The museum is one block east of
Highway 395 in Lee Vining at Hess
Park.

**Mono Lake Scenic Area Visitor
  Center
Fee to see the exhibits.
Daily, 9:00 a.m. to 5:00 p.m.
760-647-3044
Bookstore: 760-747-3042**

Directions:
Located about one mile north of Lee
Vining.

Golden Age Passes for entrance into
Yosemite and other federal lands are
sold here as well as Wilderness
Permits for back country camping
from nearby trailheads.

Old School House—Mono Basin Historical Museum

Lee Vining's early school, built in 1925, houses a diverse assortment of artifacts of the region's history. The displays feature both commonplace and delightfully odd artifacts. You can look at photographs and equipment chronicling the cultural history of the Mono Basin. The volunteer staff is happy to answer your questions about the pioneer settlers of Lee Vining and Bodie. Outside exhibits feature farming and mining equipment used in the region.

Mono Lake Scenic Area Visitor Center

The Visitor Center is a marvel, filled with beautiful dioramas that explain the unique habitats that make up the Mono Lake ecosystem. You will be able to see all the animals and birds that depend on the lake for sustenance. Regular showings of the Ice and Fire film introduces you to the formation of Mono Lake.

The gift shop and bookstore are open without charge. You can buy maps of the region and helpful Forest Service personnel can answer any questions you may have.

Museums

Mono Lake Committee Information Center and Bookstore

The center has interpretive displays that tell the story of Mono Lake and the committee's efforts to save the oldest lake in North America. You can learn about the Committee's legal battles to protect what the California Supreme Court declared as a "scenic and ecological treasure of national significance." See page 234 for more of this story.

The exhibits and numerous books and pamphlets help you understand the special qualities of Mono Lake. If you are looking for mementos of your trip, this store not only sells books and calendars but beautiful jewelry and other art connected to the region. The knowledgable staff can answer questions about the area and you can sign up for their canoe trips on the lake or hikes at the South Tufa State Reserve.

**Mono Lake Committee
  Information Center/Bookstore**
Daily, 9:00 a.m. to 7:00 p.m.
760-647-6595

Directions:
The visitor center is in the center of town on the west side of Highway 395.

Art Galleries

Tree Wizard Gallery
June Lake Village
Daily, 8:00 a.m. to 5:00 p.m.
760-648-7642

Tree Wizard Gallery

You may watch Gary "Wiz" Burns working on his special wood carvings in his shop. He sells hand-thrown pottery as well, and everything in the gallery is one of a kind.

Mono Inn
Lee Vining
Wednesday thru Sunday.
Closed May and November.
760-647-6581

Directions:
Mono Inn is 6.3 miles north of Lee Vining on Highway 395. Call about times they are open.

Mono Inn Gallery

The gallery features photo collections and books of Ansel Adams and others. They hang special shows of other artists at times throughout the year. Handmade ceramics and beautiful jewelry are also for sale.

Yosemite Outfitters
Lee Vining
**Summer only, daily, 9:00 a.m. to
  6:00 p.m.**
760-647-6464

Yosemite Outfitters

The store is full of rugs, authentic Native American jewelry, leather goods and Stetson hats as well as those amazing Bev Doolittle originals.

Yosemite Trading Company
Lee Vining
Daily, 9:00 a.m. to 5:00 p.m.
760-647-6369

Yosemite Trading Company

Owner Briscoe Sanderson has been collecting Native American art and jewelry for many years. His shop is also a museum featuring his own collection of artifacts. Briscoe's grandmother lived in Bodie and married a Paiute chief. Besides the old jewelry, you'll also find modern silver, pottery, rugs and of course T-shirts.

Special Events

There are lots of events run by the Mono Lake Committee in Lee Vining. June Lake has a Frontier Days celebration at the foot of June Mountain during the summer. Craft fairs and art shows also come to town. Check with your lodging about specific dates.

Courtesy of Double Eagle Resort

June Lake is famous for its fishing, so you might want to be in town for Opening Day of fishing season on the last Saturday in April.

Bibliography

Note: Books followed by *(YA)* are available from the Yosemite Association directly by calling 209-379-2648. Most books are also sold at retail outlets in and near the park.

History

Discovery of the Yosemite and the Indian War of 1851 which Led to the Event (YA)
    Lafayette H. Bunnell
Galen Clark
    Shirley Sargent
Indian Life of the Yosemite Region: Miwok Material Culture (YA)
    W. A. Barrett and E. W. Gifford
Legends of the Yosemite Miwok (YA)
    LaPena, Bates and Medley
One Hundred Years in Yosemite - Omnibus Edition (YA)
    Hank Johnston
Railroads of the Yosemite Valley (YA)
    Hank Johnston
Short Line to Paradise: The Story of the Yosemite Valley Railroad
    Hank Johnston
The Wild Muir: 22 of John Muir's Greatest Adventures (YA)
    Selected and introduced by Lee Stetson, illustrated by Fiona King
The Yosemite Grant, 1864-1906: A Pictorial History (YA)
    Hank Johnston
Yosemite and its Innkeepers
    Shirley Sargent
Yosemite Indians (YA)
    Elizabeth Godfrey, revisions by James Snyder and Craig Bates
Yosemite: Its Discovery, Its Wonders, and its People (YA)
    Margaret Sanborn
Yosemite Yesterdays Volume I
    Hank Johnston
Yosemite Yesterdays Volume II
    Hank Johnston

Bibliography

Natural History and Geology

Domes, Cliffs and Waterfalls: A brief Geology of Yosemite Valley (YA)
    William R. Jones
The Geologic Story of Yosemite National Park (YA)
    N. King Huber
A Field Guide to Pacific States Wildflowers — A Peterson Field Guide
    Theodore F. Niehaus, Charles L. Ripper
Birds of North America — A Golden Guide
    Chandler S. Robbins, Bertel Bruun, Herbert S. Zim
    Illustrated by Arthur Singer
Discovering Sierra Reptiles and Amphibians (YA)
    Harold E. Basey
Discovering Sierra Trees (YA)
    Stephen F. Arno, illustrated by Jane Gyer
The Sequoias of Yosemite National Park (YA)
    H. Thomas Harvey
Sierra Nevada Tree Identifier (YA)
    Jim Paruk
Sierra Nevada Field Cards of Mammals, Wildflowers and Trees (YA)
    Elizabeth Morales
Wildflower Walks and Roads of the Sierra Gold Country
    Toni Fauver
Yosemite Wildflower Trails (YA)
    Dana C. Morgenson
*A Wildflower by any other Name — Sketches of Pioneer Naturalists
    who Named our Western Plants (YA)*
    Karen Nilsson

Bibliography

Fishing, Hiking, Biking and Cross Country Skiing

Eastern Sierra Fishing Guide for Day Hikers
    John Barbier
Hiking between Groveland and Yosemite
    Hap Barhydt
Hot Showers, Soft Beds, and Dayhikes in the Sierra
    Kathy Morey
Mountain Biking The Eastern Sierra's Best 100 Trails
    Réanne Hemingway-Douglass, Mark Davis, Don Douglass
Ski Tours in the Sierra Nevada Vol. 3 — Yosemite and South
    Marcus Libkind
Ski Tours in the Sierra Nevada Vol. 4 — East of the Sierra Crest
    Marcus Libkind
Yosemite Trout Fishing Guide Including the Eastern Sierra
    Steve Beck

Campgrounds

*California Camping: The Complete Guide to More Than 50,000 Campsites
    for RVers, Car Campers and Tenters*
    Tom Stienstra
This is the best detailed review of all camping possibilities in the
Yosemite region and throughout the state.

Each National Forest has free campground listings at U.S. Forest Service
offices. However, these do not tell you about the ambience of the sites.

Index

Index

Index

Index

Index

Index

Index

Index

Index

Index

Other Books By Coldstream Press

What Shall We Do Tomorrow at Lake Tahoe
by Ellie Huggins

> This 320-page guide is packed full of activities, lodging and dining suggestions for Lake Tahoe, Truckee and Carson Pass. $12.95

Northwest Passages from the Pen of John Muir in California, Oregon, Washington and Alaska Designed and Illustrated by Andrea Hendrick

> The perfect gift, this beautiful 64-page book has selections of Muir's most inspirational and perceptive insights, revealing the man who signed his name "John Muir — Earth-planet, Universe," each illustrated with original blockprints. $15.00

Mountain Dreamers: Visionaries of Sierra Nevada Skiing
by Robert Frohlich. Photographs by Carolyn Caddes and Tom Lippert

> Meet 28 pioneers of Sierra Nevada skiing. Present-day portraits plus aerials and more than 80 historic photos make this a very special book. Dave McCoy (Mammoth), Alex Cushing (Squaw Valley), Bill Klein (Sugar Bowl), Nic Fiore (Yosemite) and many, many more. Softcover: $29.95, Hardcover: $50.00

Due in October 1999

Magic Yosemite Winters: Celebrating a Century of Winter Sports in the Park
by Eugene Rose

> This first comprehensive history of the park in winter is filled with stories of pioneers on skis and the development of winter sports activities in the park and illustrated with fine historical photographs from 1890 to the present. $40.00

Skiing with Style: Sugar Bowl 60 Years
by S. E. Humphries

> A celebration of of the last 60 years of skiing at this pioneer ski resort on Donner Summit. Illustrated with hundreds of never before published historical photographs. $40.00

You may order through our website www.coldstreampress.com or call us directly at 1-800-916-7450.

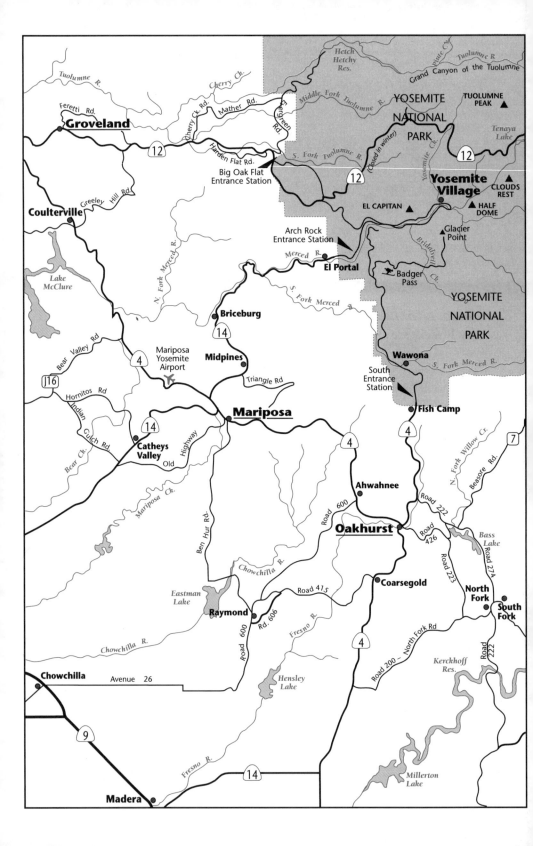